THE AA GUIDE TO
Wales

D0452829

About the author

Gwyneth Rees spent all of her childhood in Wales. She grew up in north Cardiff, filling any time she wasn't at school with exploring the hills surrounding the city. Each holiday, she spent at the family caravan on Poppit Beach, Cardigan, where she still regularly visits. In her early twenties, she learnt of the joys of mountain biking and climbing, and this passion has taken her all around Wales, but particularly up to north Wales. She is now a mum of one, and works as a freelance writer from over the bridge in Bristol, most often writing fun talking-point features for *The Daily Mail*. She also writes travel and food articles for various publications.

Published by AA Publishing (a trading name of AA Media Limited, whose registered office is Fanum House, Basing View, Basingstoke, Hampshire RG21 4EA; registered number 06112600)

© AA Media Limited 2016
First published 2014
Second edition 2016

Maps contain data from openstreetmap.org
© OpenStreetMap contributors Ordnance Survey data © Crown copyright and database right 2015.

A CIP catalogue record for this book is available from the British Library.

ISBN: 978-0-7495-7765-0

Cartography provided by the Mapping Services Department of AA Publishing.

Printed and bound in Italy by Printer Trento Srl.

A05342

Visit AA Publishing at theAA.com/shop

THE AA GUIDE TO
Wales

CONTENTS

USING THIS GUIDE

Introduction – has plenty of fascinating background reading, including articles on the landscape and local mythology.

Top attractions – pick out the very best places to visit in the area. You'll spot these later in the A–Z by the flashes of yellow.

Before you go – tells you the things to read, watch, know and pack to get the most from your trip.

Campsites – recommends a number of caravan sites and campsites, which carry the AA's Pennant rating, with the very best receiving the coveted gold Pennant award. Visit theAA.com/self-catering-and-campsites and theAA.com/bed-and-breakfast-and-hotel for more places to stay.

A–Z of Wales – lists all the best of the country, with recommended attractions, activities and places to eat or drink. Places Nearby lists more to see and do.

Eat and drink – contains restaurants that carry an AA Rosette rating, which acknowledges the very best in cooking. Pubs have been selected for their great atmosphere and good food. Visit theAA.com/restaurant-and-pub for more food and drink suggestions.

Index – gives you the option to search by theme, grouping the same type of place together, or alphabetically.

Atlas – will help you find your way around, as every main location has a map reference, as will the town plans throughout the book.

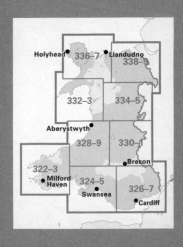

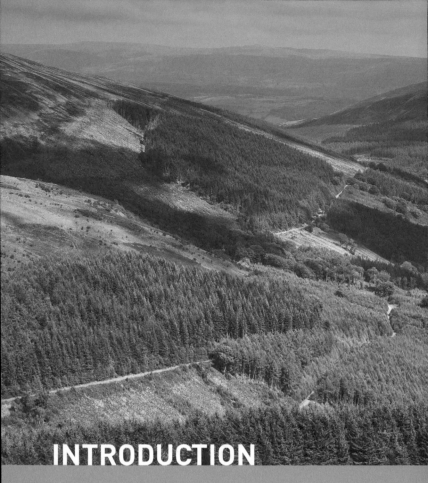

INTRODUCTION

At around a sixth the size of England, with just three million people, Wales is the *cwtch* of Britain. This evocative Welsh word – pronounced 'cutsh' – refers to a snug, cosy place of warmth and comfort. It's a place where people still know each other, and the name of the local vicar and pub landlord. But don't be mistaken, this is no sleepy backwater. It is a nation of bravado and fire, a nation where – as they boast at the Principality Stadium come match day – *y ddraig goch* (the red dragon) roars. At the moment, Wales – or *Cymru*, rather – is definitely breathing fire.

You'll probably have heard that it rains – and yes, it does. That's what makes the grass so very green and lush and the air so fresh. But Wales, particularly the coastal regions, also has some serious micro-climates, where the sun beats down on you. What is more, short of a truly tropical climate, this nation has every conceivable holiday attraction you could wish for.

Just take its history and culture, for instance. Even if you spent a year trying, you wouldn't see half of its castles or dolmens – ancient neolithic tombs with enormous capstones.

Now mostly under the care of Cadw, the Welsh government's historical environment arm, these ancient monuments are around every corner, perched on cliffs overlooking tidal estuaries or acting as lookouts on flat-topped hills. Clearly those who constructed these fortresses and sacred sites capitalised on the natural beauty of the land.

Fortunately, this beauty still exists today – from the craggy mountains of the north to the central verdant valleys and crumpled coasts. There's also no better place to try outdoor pursuits, and even if you're planning a tour of the main cities – say, Cardiff, Swansea and Aberystwyth – you'll never be more than 20 minutes from remote landscapes where you can walk, cycle or meditate to your heart's content. It's this heady mix of culture and nature that makes Wales so appealing. Take this hearty brew and add a friendly, humorous, self-deprecating psyche – prone to singing, taking the mickey, drinking beer and chattering away in its own mother tongue – and you've got a killer destination. There are no pretensions here – a spade is a spade and a leek a leek. Rain is rain, so put your coat on.

There's more though, like the sense of space, good food and sandy beaches galore, where seagulls will mug you for your fish and chips and the waves will tempt you in on your bodyboard. Again, due to Wales' status as a *cwtch*, all these gems are often found close together. It is one of the reasons why Wales is so popular with film crews in need of an array of different backgrounds without the hassle of long-distance travel. The Welsh, of course, know this, though they're not a nation to boast. They spent 700 years fighting the English and fending off arrogant unfounded appraisals of their culture and intellect, but now they've got a Welsh Assembly, language and, most important, their own spirit and identity. The Welsh do still, of course, retain a good-natured antipathy to their neighbours. Some of the identities of Wales are perhaps slightly clichéd – the male voice choirs, the coal town brass bands, the sheep-shearing farmers – but there's also so much that's new and refreshing. The nation is leading the environmental and safe-cycling movements across Britain. Restaurants and B&Bs have shaken off their tired, fusty images to become stylish and boutique. Old industrially scarred hillsides are being turned into world-class mountain-biking venues and the Eisteddfod,an ancient literary competition, is growing mightier year on year. And did we mention that 2016 is the year of adventure, be that surfing in Snowdonia, trampolining in Cardiff or zip lining across a mining town?

The television, film and music industries have done much to revive the image of the Welsh, while big names on the acting scene – think Rob Brydon and Ruth Jones from the popular sitcom *Gavin & Stacey* – have helped people associate Wales with big belly laughs. Importantly, Wales remains real, alive and gritty. It's not a Celtic pastiche. In stark contrast to Devon and Cornwall – its two main coastal rivals – Wales is not overrun with second-home owners and Jack Wills-wearing yachters. Here, at the height of summer, you can still find low-key campsites next to glorious blue-flag beaches (Wales has upwards of 40), usually with a relaxed seaside cafe just a stroll away. The westbound M4 comes to an end in Carmarthen, an hour from the coast, and much of the northern terrain is only accessible by winding country roads used regularly by tractors, and so Wales has managed to keep its original charm. Traditional communities do still exist, work and function here.

Wales is a nation with a vision, too, and one that's embraced reinvention. It's got heaps of independent businesses, from the super-cool Howies alternative clothing store to children's

◀ Talybont Reservoir, Brecon Beacons National Park (previous page)
▶ Dolbadarn Castle, Llanberis

clothing retailer JoJo Maman. It's got sporting prowess – not just rugby but also two premier league football teams, Cardiff and Swansea. It's gaining more and more powers from Westminster, and has an abundant history to fall back on. The iconic oval ball is being kicked high over the goalposts and it's going to land somewhere good.

TOP ATTRACTIONS

▲ Climb a mountain in Snowdonia National Park
No trip to Wales is complete without a visit to the country's oldest and largest national park (see page 299). An ascent up Snowdon (Yr Wyddfa) is the obvious attraction. Several tracks lead up to the summit, though be warned – even the easy ones, such as the Pyg track, can take you near steep edges and loose scree. The mountain railway (see page 196) chugs up to the warm, stylish Hafod Eryri visitor centre on the summit.

▼ Be the Doctor's companion
One of Wales' latest attractions is the Doctor Who Experience (see page 136), where kids and big kids can become the Doctor's companion, helping to fight off Daleks and Cybermen through time and space. If you survive, there's an exhibition to go round as well.

◀ Take a tour of the four great castles of North Wales

Of the many castles in Wales, Beaumaris (see page 87), Caernarfon (see page 114), Conwy (see page 151) and Harlech (see page 177) are among the finest and most fearsome. Built by Edward I in the 13th century, the Fab Four represent medieval architecture of international importance.

▶ Catch a game at Wales' Principality Stadium in Cardiff

There's no better way to inhale a large dose of Welshness than watching a game of rugby at the iconic stadium (formally the Millennium Stadium, see page 129). It's not just the sport, it's the singing, the atmosphere, the brass bands and even the goat.

◀ Return to medieval times at St Fagans

St Fagans (see page 294) is Europe's largest open-air museum – and one that kids are welcome to run around. Explore Celtic roundhouses and workmen's institutes and feed the native livestock. It's a whistle-stop tour of Wales' heritage and culture.

▲ Watch wildlife on Skomer and Skokholm

Bring your binoculars for this one. Whether you want to see bottlenose dolphins, seals, the odd whale or even a leatherback turtle, these coastal islands are the place to head to (see page 297). They're teeming with birdlife, from thousands of nesting puffins to rare choughs. Back on the mainland there are also otters in the Bosherston lily ponds. If you've had your fill of nature and need some culture go inland to St Davids, named after Wales' patron saint and the smallest city in the UK.

▼ Visit Italy at Portmeirion

Privately owned Portmeirion (see page 271) is a fantasy; a classical Italianate village transplanted in northwest Wales. The project of architect Sir Clough Williams-Ellis, it's a world of Mediterranean piazzas and pastel-painted buildings. Wander through the village and its gardens filled with exotic plants.

▲ Star gaze in the Brecon Beacons

Inspire your children to be astronauts and scientists with a night out under the stars. This national park (see page 105) is now the world's fifth and Wales' first destination to be awarded the prestigious International Dark Sky Reserve status. Check out the Milky Way and remind yourself how light from distant stars and galaxies can take millions of years to reach us. By the way, daytime in the Beacons isn't bad either.

▼ Get lost in Bodnant Garden

The plants at this spectacular 80-acre, National Trust site come from all over the world, grown from seeds and cuttings collected over a century ago. Bodnant (see page 100) includes terraces, woodland, formal gardens and herbaceous borders in an ever-changing landscape that's a sharp contrast to the wild backdrop of nearby Snowdonia.

◂ Explore Cardiff Castle

Vast Cardiff Castle (see page 126), in the heart of the city, has stood – bits of it at least – for 2,000 years. From Roman fort to Norman castle to Victorian Gothic fantasy, it's far less traditional than the castles you'll encounter in north Wales, but no less interesting.

▸ Go deep, deep, deep underground

So much of the making of Wales is down to its geology. At Blaenavon and the Big Pit National Coal Museum in the south Wales valleys (see page 96) you can descend 300 feet down an old colliery, where a former coalminer will take you on a fascinating tour. See life at the coalface before resurfacing to explore the rest of this Heritage Site.

◂ Go up Great Orme

Take the tram or cable car – or, if you feel entirely up to it, walk – up Great Orme (see page 204) from Llandudno for wide-ranging views across this stretch of the Welsh coastline, and plenty of historical bits to catch your interest – notably the Bronze Age Mines (see page 205). If ancient remains and nature reserves get old, there's always the crazy golf.

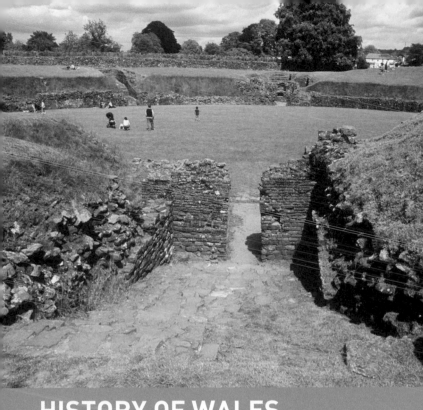

HISTORY OF WALES

You only need to glance at the castles, ancient hill forts and derelict mines to understand that Welsh history is not something to be sniffed at. It's a history of great characters and dramatic events, riots and revolts. Most importantly, it tells of Wales' 700-year roller-coaster struggle to free itself from the grip of the English.

Ancient Wales

Admittedly we don't know much about very early Welsh history. The earliest evidence of inhabitation dates from around 225,000 BC, in the shape of some teeth found in Pontnewydd Cave in Denbighshire's Elwy Valley. We also have a skeleton from around 24,000 BC, found in Paviland Cave on the Gower. It initially became known as the Red Lady of Paviland as the bones had been coloured with red ochre. Technological advancements, however, show it is actually the remains of a young man, and is Britain's earliest known example of a ritual burial. Between 9,000 and 5,000 BC melting ice caps led to Britain becoming an island, leaving Wales

▲ Roman amphitheatre, Caerleon

covered by a thick canopy of trees. Mesolithic communities lived by hunting and gathering, then gradually were sustained by agriculture. The most striking tomb or cromlech from this era is Barclodiad y Gawres (Welsh for 'apronful of the giantess') in Anglesey. Inside are stones decorated with spirals and chevrons, thought to be the earliest examples of art in Wales. By around 2000 BC Wales had received most of its original stock of peoples. It was around this time that 80 blue stones, each weighing an astonishing four tonnes, were quarried from the Preseli Hills and somehow transported to Wiltshire to form Stonehenge.

It was the arrival of the Celts from across Europe in AD 600 that really changed things. They brought with them the Druids, poets and priests, and then busied themselves constructing hill forts, making great technical advances and creating a social structure, with a new language, morals and oral traditions. The Druids, a priestly class who practised human sacrifice, were very important. According to the Roman historian Tacitus, when the Druids of Anglesey were attacked by the Romans in AD 61, their altars were 'drenched with the blood of prisoners'.

The Romans

This gruesome sacrifice didn't hold back the Romans, though. They conquered the nation and built a large fort at Caerleon. They also built the first proper town in neighbouring Caerwent. For the next 300 years they ruled Wales but, in many ways, their impact was minimal as the Welsh were able to live alongside them, keeping their language and traditions. Following the demise of the Roman Empire in the 5th century, visiting missionaries began spreading Christianity, with *Dewi Sant* (St David) becoming a key figure, and establishing his Pembrokeshire town as a centre of religion and learning. The first forms of Welsh literature date from this period – poems, written by Aneirin and Taliesin.

A new Wales

Although *Cymru* and its distinct identity was developing, it didn't stop territorial scuffles, a reminder of which is the 8th-century fortification of Offa's Dyke, marking the boundary between the Welsh and the Saxons. It wasn't just the Saxons who were after Wales, though. During the 9th and 10th centuries, Wales came under savage coastal attacks by Norse and Danish pirates. Rhodri Mawr (Rhodri the Great) managed to unite most of the kingdoms, but his careless sons then lost them again. His hugely popular grandson – Hywel Da (Hywel the Good) – reunified the country and made progressive changes to help women, children and the poor. For centuries to come, life under the Law of Hywel would be one of the defining times for the Welsh people.

The Princes of Wales

Alas, the good times didn't last long. Come 1066 the Welsh were being pushed back as William the Conqueror sought to secure his position. It was in the 12th and 13th centuries, though, that the real fights occurred. Llywelyn ap Gruffydd (Llewellyn the Last) adopted the title Prince of Wales and forced England – then ruled by Henry III – to recognise him as such. But when Edward III came to power all hell broke loose. Edward resented these feisty Welsh leaders and eventually killed both Llywelyn and his brother Dafydd. He then set up his Iron Ring of castles to prevent further revolt. Needless to say, this didn't go down too well with the Welsh. By 1400 they were ready for another fight, this time led by Owain Glyndwr, who declared himself the new Prince of Wales. He captured Harlech and Aberystwyth, and even held a parliament at Machynlleth, but then he too started suffering too many defeats and his army began to desert him.

Come the 16th century big changes were afoot with Henry VIII's Acts of Union, giving England sovereignty over Wales and making the English language and law official. He also dissolved the many Cistercian abbeys, which had been centres of learning for so long.

Industrial times

The Victorians may have put the Welsh coast on the map, but there was also a bigger factor – the Industrial Revolution. Initially it was iron, not coal, that transformed the face of the valleys of south Wales and the maritime ports around the country. These huge exports, however, didn't make the workers happy. People began to demand the universal right to vote, better working conditions and pay. The year 1839 saw the Chartist Riots break out in Newport, while the Rebecca Riots took hold in the rural west. Farmers, angry at having to pay road tax, dressed in women's clothes and tore down the turnpike tollgates. They used the term 'Rebecca' in reference to a passage from Genesis in the Bible. Today a race across the Preseli Hills commemorates these riots – the winner smashes down a fence at the end of the race.

This fire in the bellies of the Welsh was stirred further by the publication of the *Blue Books* in 1847. An educational review found the Welsh education system to be inferior and low in moral structure, thus a ban was imposed on speaking Welsh in school, creating outrage and a renewed sense of nationalism. By the second half of the 19th century coal grew as the mineral of choice. Workers were given the vote and, over ensuing decades, reforms helped reduce some of the hardships faced by the industrial masses. During World War I living standards rose further and it was the boom time for many towns such as Blaenavon, now a World Heritage Site. Political fervour was also stirring at this time.

David Lloyd George, a Liberal MP in the Caernarfon Borough, led the country and a wartime coalition between 1916 and 1922. He was initially deemed the champion of Welsh democracy, however, his popularity faltered at the end of the war and he eventually resigned.

The year of 1925 saw the launch of *Plaid Cenedlaetol Cymru*, later shortened to Plaid Cymru, the first political Welsh party focused entirely on nationalism. Two decades later, in 1948, Aneurin Bevan – a Labour MP from Tredegar, then serving as health minister in the post-war Attlee government – founded the National Health Service.

Depression to nationalism

After the end of World War II Wales sunk into a depression, with former mining towns left ghostly and empty on the hills. The 1960s saw something of a revival, with a vibrant pop scene and the growth of publishing houses. Support for Plaid Cymru grew, as did a vague notion of self-governance. In 1976 the Welsh Development Agency was created to establish new business ideas and an interest in the Welsh language was kick-started, helped by the launch in 1982 of S4C, the Welsh-language television channel. Still, these were shaky years, and the collapse of the miners' strike

▼ Preseli Hills

in the mid-1980s brought morale crashing down again. By 1997 Tony Blair's New Labour finally brought the issue of devolution to the table. Following a referendum, the National Welsh Assembly was created. Although it didn't have the powers of the Scottish parliament, it forged a new path for Wales. Redevelopment, particularly in Cardiff, took off with the Principality (Millennium) Stadium stealing the rugby scene from England, and new bands putting a cool, trendy Wales on the map. Pride began to soar again.

Modern Wales

This pride has surged ahead. Further developments at Cardiff Bay saw the opening of the *Senedd*, or National Assembly building, and also the Wales Millennium Centre, where the Welsh National Opera is housed. The Assembly pursues powers from England on matters that are close to its heart, such as the environment. Following the Scottish referendum on independence in September 2014, Wales was promised more powers. Proposals have been drawn up to give the nation more control over energy – including fracking and onshore windfarms – and clearing the way for 16-year-olds to vote. Whether it diverges further from England or not over the coming decades and centuries, it has reached a place, solid and inspiring, from which it can move forward positively.

▼ National Assembly for Wales

BACK TO NATURE

You won't need to search hard in Wales to find stunning natural landscapes. It seems that around almost every corner there are mountains, lakes, forests, rocky outcrops and – due to the enormous tidal range – simply ridiculous amounts of sandy beach to explore.

Geology

Much of the gritty beauty of the Welsh landscape is down to what lies below the surface. Whether you are skimming stones by a lake, caving in the Brecon Beacons or eyeballing Llanberis' slate quarries, it's impossible to escape Wales' geology. The nation has one of richest geological heritages in the world. North Wales – once underwater – consists of a whole hotchpotch of rock, from sandstone to slate, granite to rhyolite. In fact, the rocks here are so important that scientists have used them to help date the Earth. The terms Cambrian, Silurian and Ordovician – all epochs used throughout the world – were named after Welsh tribes. Broadly speaking, these mountains were formed around 450 million years ago. Sitting on a border between two grumbling tectonic plates, the region was frequently subject to massive volcanic eruptions, which, in turn, created mountains that would have been the size of today's Himalayas. Millions of years of

◀ Llanberis and Llyn Padarn
▲ Sgwd-y-Pannwr waterfall, Brecon Beacons

erosion and glacial periods – the last one around 20,000 years ago – have worn them down to today's level. Massive sheets of ice, collecting high in the mountains, worked their way down the slopes, carving out the steep ridges and towering cliffs that climbers so enjoy today.

Further west, around St Davids in Pembrokeshire, some of the oldest rocks in the world can be found, while the Brecon Beacons have an equally distinct geology. Towards the eastern parts near Pen-y-Fan, it's mostly sandstone, graduating into limestone in the east towards the Usk Valley. The dissolution of this limestone by acidic rainwater has created astonishing waterfalls, cave systems and sink holes. Wales has two geoparks. For more information, visit fforestfawrgeopark.org.uk or geomon.co.uk.

Wildlife

Top tip – if you are looking for specific wildlife in Wales, you need to come at the right time of year. From April to August it's all about seabirds. The island of Grassholm has one of the world's largest gannet colonies, with 34,000 pairs nesting there during breeding season. Skomer and the lesser-known Skokholm islands are chock-full with puffins, guillemots and razorbills, while nearby Ramsey Island hosts around 30 per cent of the world's shearwater population and some rare choughs. Come late summer and autumn, and eyes switch from the skies to the seas. At this time of year bottlenose dolphins and porpoises swarm into Cardigan Bay. In September and early October Atlantic grey seals also deliver around 1,000 fluffy white pups on Pembrokeshire's shores. Salmon can also be seen leaping upriver, mainly at the cascading Cenarth Falls in Ceredigion – the first obstacle the migratory fish face in their return to the River Teifi. They can also be spotted at Gilfach Nature Reserve in Radnorshire. There are, however, year-round treats, namely the red kites. Wales' largest bird of prey is also its biggest success story. After being seen as a pest and nearly driven to extinction in the 16th century, 300 pairs are now thriving in mid-Wales. Machynlleth's ospreys also attract around 40,000 visitors a year. Pine martens and polecats are seen almost everywhere, while otters are re-establishing themselves along the River Teifi and in the Bosherston Pools in Pembrokeshire Coast National Park. For more information, see wtwales.org.

▼ Ramsey Island

Flora

Thanks to its industrialised past, only 12 per cent of the Welsh countryside is still covered by woodland. However, what remains is wonderful. The country has around 234,750 acres of ancient woodland consisting of native oak, ash and birch, the largest example being at Wentwood, near Newport. Variations in landscape and rock type support a diverse plant life. Orchids can be found in certain spots along the Gower Peninsula and Alpine-Arctic plants breed in the mountainous regions. Marram grass, sea bindweed and evening primrose may be spotted on the coast between dunes, while the butterwort, one of Britain's few insectivorous plants, devours insects in the grasslands of Cwm Cadlan, near Penderyn in southwest Wales.

Stunning wild flowers can be seen in the Monmouthshire Hills at the Gwent Nature Reserve, and also at the Ystradfawr Nature Reserve near Ystradgynlais in Powys. Some rare species, such as the Ley's whitebeam or the Black Mountain hawkweed are endemic and found only in Wales. Others are found elsewhere globally, but only in Wales will you find plants such as the Snowdon lily or yellow whitlow grass. Others are rare on an international basis, such as perennial centaury or wild asparagus.

Environmental protection

Wales is pretty militant about protecting these natural wonders – largely due to them being the main draw for so many tourists. It boasts one marine nature reserve (Skomer Island), more than 60 on-land nature reserves, 216 Wildlife Trust reserves, 1,019 SSSIs (Sites of Special Scientific Interest), 11 RSPB sanctuaries, three national parks and at least six categories of protected land. Important environmental protection work, which used to be undertaken by the Countryside Council for Wales, Environment Agency Wales and Forestry Commission Wales, has now been taken over by one body, Natural Resources Wales. Its role is to advise the Welsh government on policy, as well as managing and promoting the environment.

The Welsh Assembly – now with independence from the rest of Britain to implement its own environmental legislation – has stated a commitment to sustainable development. By 2025, Wales aims to reduce the use of carbon-based energy by 80–90 per cent and for all new buildings to be carbon-neutral. In October 2011, it also imposed a five-pence levy on plastic bags. This levy now raises in excess of £800,000 annually, which goes to charities such as the RSBP and Keep Wales Tidy. Ministers also claim the policy has resulted in far less litter on the streets. By 2014, their usage had fallen by 79 per cent. For more information, visit naturalresourceswales.gov.uk.

LORE OF THE LAND

Legends of the land of the red dragon begin, naturally enough, with the beast itself. Long ago, a battle ensued between the red dragon of the Welsh and the white dragon of the Saxons. When their fearsome shrieks caused women to miscarry, crops to fail and animals to die, Ludd, King of Britain, drugged the pair with mead and imprisoned them for hundreds of years at Dinas Emrys in Snowdonia. However, when King Vortigern tried to build a castle here, the castle kept crumbling and no walls would stay standing. To solve the problem, a boy with no natural father was sought as a sacrifice. The boy, on hearing of his fate, told Vortigern about the dragons, which were then set free to resume hostilities. Finally, so the *Mabinogion* – a collection of medieval tales – tells it, the red dragon was the victor and so destined to become a symbol of the people whom Saxon invaders failed to conquer. The Welsh flag finally became official in 1959 and the dragon is now emblazoned on the flags and rugby shirts of millions.

◀ Llyn Llydaw, Snowdonia National Park

Arthurian connections

In Wales, King Arthur imposes his character in no uncertain terms. Scattered around the country are caves, each reputed to be the place where he awaits the call to rescue the country from invasion or disaster. A stone on the banks of Llyn Barfog near Betws-y-Coed is said to bear the hoof mark of Arthur's horse Llamrai when the hero and his mount successfully dragged a monster from the deep waters of the lake. The pebble he removed from his boot and threw over his shoulder on his way to the Battle of Camlann now forms the massive Arthur's Stone on the Gower Peninsula. While on Snowdon Arthur is said to have killed the giant Rhitta – notorious for making a cape from the beards of his enemies – and covered the corpse with the stones that now stand on the mountaintop. Just below the summit is Llyn Llydaw, the lake into which Arthur's magical sword Excalibur was thrown, following the hero's final battle at Bwlch y Saethau (the Pass of the Arrows).

Claimed as a candidate for the fabled land of Avalon, Bardsey Island – off the coast of the Llyn Peninsula – is said to be where the body of Merlin lies in a glass coffin, surrounded by nine bardic companions and the 13 treasures of Britain, one of which is Arthur's mantle.

Dog of legend

Of all the animals in Welsh folklore, most famous is Gelert, whose grave can be found at Beddgelert. Gelert was presented as a gift to Llywelyn the Great by England's King John. One day, on his return from the hunt, Llywelyn discovered his dog with blood around his mouth, and his baby's cradle empty and overturned. Consumed with anger, Llywelyn immediately drew his sword and slew the dog. Then he heard the baby's cries and found him beneath the cradle alongside the body of a wolf that had attacked him, and been killed by Gelert. After this, it is said that Llywelyn never smiled again.

Spirit forms

Known as the Mother's Blessing (Bendith y Mamau) or the Fair Family or Folk (Y Tylwyth Teg), the fairies of Wales were once thought to be the souls of Druids who, although not Christian, were considered too good to suffer the fires of hell. Wales is also home to elves, goblins and bogeys that dress in garments of green or white. Many of these spirit forms were seen as lake-dwellers, inhabiting waters such as Llyn Irddyn and Llyn Barfog in north Wales, from where fairies would emerge on moonlit nights and dance holding hands in a circle. Any young man seeing these beautiful creatures was in danger of falling instantly in love, with dire consequences. Fairies could also be malign, stealing unguarded babies from their cradles.

Legend also tells of spirit marriages, sometimes with prenuptial arrangements that even movie stars might find hard to fulfil, as in the tale of the Lady of the Lake. The story goes that a young man fell in love with a woman who emerged from Llyn y Fan Fach, above Myddfai in Carmarthenshire. On condition that he was faithful, did not hit her or touch her with iron, marriage was allowed. After the wedding three sons were born, but the husband broke his vows (albeit in jest) and his wife returned to her watery home. The three sons were frequent visitors to the lake, and the lady told the eldest, Rhiwallon, that he must take up medicine. He duly did so, as did his sons. The fortuitous result was a treatise on herbal medicine called *The Red Book of Hergest*, packed with prescriptions for treating all kinds of ills.

The remote heights of Cadair Idris in Snowdonia are home to the giant astronomer and philosopher Idris, endowed with the power to bestow madness or poetic inspiration to anyone who spent a night at the summit – or to ensure that they never wake. The mountain was also the hunting ground of the warrior Gwyn ap Nudd and his canine companions. When his wild hounds howled, they presaged the demise of anyone witnessing their voices. As death ensued the dogs would sweep up their victim's soul and herd it directly to the Underworld.

The power of superstition

In a land where coal has been mined for centuries, strongly held superstitions – which could reduce the strongest man to a quivering wreck – reflect the dangers of the dark depths. If a miner, on his way to the mine, was unlucky enough to meet a rabbit, a bird or even someone with a squint, the encounter would force him to return home for the day. If any item should be forgotten, going home for it would also mean a day's lost labour. At the pithead, a robin, dove or pigeon seen flying around were omens of disaster, and the sight of them would make men refuse to enter the mine. Friday, associated with the death of Christ, was always an unlucky day – whether or not it was the 13th. Only the hardest hearted or impecunious miner would work on Good Friday. No miner wishing to live to an old age would ever whistle while underground, or let the word 'cat' pass his lips. Even outside the mines, whistling was frowned on, as it was considered a way of summoning up the Devil.

On 10 March 1890, an explosion hit the Marfa Colliery near Port Talbot, killing 87 miners. Some say that the disaster could have been foreseen, since the pit was filled with the scent of invisible 'death flowers' and lit by the flickering of ghostly lights, believed to be the ghosts of dead miners and phantom horses pulling coal trams.

In Wales, even the trees evoke superstition. The yew tree was once regarded as a sacred guardian of the dead and so should never be cut down or burned. In the churchyard at Nevern grows a mysterious bleeding oak from which blood-red resin drips. Here an innocent monk was once hanged, and it is said that the bleeding will continue until a Prince of Wales is installed in the town. All over the land groves of oak trees – places where Druids' spirits assemble – were never entered at the midnight hour for fear of invoking misfortune.

Folk hero

Wales' most famous everyday hero is Jack o' Kent, renowned for making deals with – and getting the better of – the Devil. When Jack promised the Devil the tops of his crops in return for good growing weather, he planted turnips, leaving the Devil with only the leaves. The following year the Devil was promised the bottoms or 'butts', so Jack planted wheat. In another tale Jack persuaded the Devil to build him a bridge, offering him the first soul to cross it. When the bridge was finished Jack threw over a bone, which was chased by a hungry dog. At Trellech in Monmouthshire it is alleged that Jack hurled the standing stones into place in a competition with the Devil.

Jack's effigy at Grosmont Church commemorates his final promise to bequeath his corpse to the Devil, whether he was laid inside or outside the church. But clever Jack fooled him one last time by being buried neither in nor out of the building, but beneath its walls.

▼ Craig Cau on Cadair Idris, Snowdonia National Park

LAND OF SONG

Rumour has it that when the Welsh are born, their first cry is a rendition of that old favourite hymn, *Calon Lan*. Indeed, an old Welsh proverb goes, 'To be born Welsh is to be born with music in your blood and poetry in your soul.' No nation on earth, it seems, can rival their honey baritones and nonconformist choral harmonies. If truth be told, if Wales had a solo entry to the Eurovision Song Contest, it would win hands down – fact.

It's the might of this talent that's produced some of the nation's most famous exports. It's got Tom Jones and Katherine Jenkins, Charlotte Church and Cerys Matthews. It's even got Goldie Lookin Chain, Newport's famous rap group – look them up if you haven't heard of them. More than this, though, come match day in the Principality Stadium, it's got the combined efforts of 70,000 fans throwing their heads back to thunder out the anthem *Hen Wlad Fy Nhadau (Land of My Fathers)*. Even if most of them are dressed as giant leeks and daffodils, it's a formidable spectacle. New Zealand may have the *Haka*, but Wales has singing en masse.

As early as the first century there are references to the Welsh being a musical race, with scholars writing of bards – professional poets who wrote and sang songs of eulogy. From the early 19th century there are records of traditional Welsh songs and also a growing movement of folk music, accompanied by the national instrument, the harp. These were performed in folk dancing sessions, at festivals or traditional parties similar to Scottish ceilidhs. The *eisteddfod* (festival) also grew in popularity from the mid-1850s when a brutal English attack on the Welsh education system sparked public anger, leading to a renewed national pride. Its resurgence brought together musical tradition with poetry, the influence of chapel and the joy of choral music.

During the industrial boom there was also the rise of the male voice choirs, such as the Morriston Orpheus Choir and Treorchy Male Voice Choir. Although they dwindled in prominence with the collapse of the coal-mining communities, lately they've seen something of a resurgence, helped by television shows such as the BBC's *Last Choir Standing*. These choirs have helped keep national songs alive too. Favourite hymns include the 19th-century *Calon Lan (A Pure Heart)*, sung in Welsh before almost every test match, and *Men of Harlech*, a military song and march about the seven-year siege of the castle (1461–68). It gained international recognition when it featured in the 1964 film *Zulu*. *Myfanwy*, composed by Dr Joseph Parry, is another favourite of the choirs, as too is *Cwm Rhondda*, commonly known as *Bread of Heaven* and usually sung in English. As for the national anthem, it was written and composed by son and father Evan and James James, of Pontypridd, Glamorgan, in 1856. Although first performed in the vestry of the original Capel Tabor, Maesteg, it only really became a hit when it was sung at the Llangollen Eisteddfod of 1858. As it gained popularity at patriotic gatherings, its original six-eight, quick-waltz tempo slowed to accommodate large crowds. In 1905, it became the first national anthem to be sung before a game was played – Wales were playing host to the first touring New Zealand team, and went on to win in a match that was dubbed the 'game of the century'.

Since then the Welsh music scene has continued to flourish, and change. During World War I singer-songwriter Ivor Novello became an international star – his name is still connected to one of the biggest annual British singing awards. Come the 1960s, and musicians such as Tom Jones, Shirley Bassey and John Cale – of Velvet Underground fame who went on to have a massive solo career – took the world by storm, closely followed by the likes of Bonnie Tyler in the 1970s and 1980s. They, together with such musical legends as Sir Harry Secombe, helped defined the Welsh vocal style for several generations. Later, in the 1990s, Welsh bands such as the Manic Street Preachers and Stereophonics didn't sing in Welsh, but helped towards creating a strong Welsh identity through their lyrics and accents.

The growth of the Welsh National Opera, established in 1946, and stars such as Bryn Terfyl, helped draw global attention to the giant lungs of this small nation. Further support came from Radio 1 DJ John Peel, who championed Welsh-language punk bands Anhrefn and Datblygu. Today, although not as prolific as the Cool Cymru 1990s, there's a vivid music scene. Popstar Duffy released her album *Rockferry* to global acclaim, winning a Grammy in 2009. Alternative rock band Feeder, from Newport, have carved out a name for themselves, as have Caerphilly's Attack! Attack! Other names to watch are Blackout and Funeral For A Friend. The popularity of music festivals – particularly The Green Man, held in August each year in the Brecon Beacons – has boosted interest in alternative Welsh music. The 160-piece Welsh choir Côr Glanaethwy even came close to winning Britain's Got Talent in 2015. Wales is still the land of song, and has much to sing about.

▼ The Green Man ▶ BikePark Wales

MOUNTAIN BIKE WALES

Wales may be the land of song. It's also the land of dirt, downhilling and varying degrees of danger, as the nation's love of two wheels is second to none and the array of its modern bike parks, the envy of the world.

Today, if you cross paths with anyone wearing heavy boots, a thick jacket and with muddy fingernails, chances are they'll be a 'trail builder'. It is these single-track trails of varying technicality that have become the backbone of the sport. The country now boasts 375 miles of them, criss-crossing the land from north to south, attracting hundreds of thousands of mud-splattered, adrenalin-seeking visitors each year and bringing new cash to deprived areas. The first one was Coed-y-Brenin in Snowdonia, built in the mid-1990s by forestry ranger Dafydd Davis. Initially, his concept of managed, waymarked trails for bikers was mocked. So he began building them himself unofficially with help from volunteers. Eventually, when he could prove his small trails were boosting numbers to the area, he was given a few thousand pounds to put up a visitor centre and cafe, and employ some labourers – locals from the RAF – to help lug rocks. It took just a few years for visitor numbers to skyrocket (the figure now is around 150,000 a year). South Wales' Afan Forest Park and Cwmcarn soon followed, as did

▲ BikePark Wales

Nant yr Arian in mid-Wales, and Gwydyr Forest and Coed Llandegla in the north. Nowadays the new tracks are much more technical than of old, largely because there's more money, so materials can be shipped in and experts used to build them. The breadth and depth of routes has also evolved, with many centres boasting runs of varying technicality (green to black) and length (5km–10km–30km-plus). With the increased demand, these trail centres have grown to include upmarket cafes, bunkhouses and tourist centres. Some even offer bike spares, bike hire and bike-washing facilities to keep you rolling. The fact that many are so accessible, such as Afan, located just off the M4 by Port Talbot, means they attract people from all over Britain and, increasingly, further afield.

The Welsh mountain bike scene is far more than just trail riding, though. It also boasts downhill tracks, freeride hotspots and skills parks. In terms of downhilling there's plenty for the full-face gravity fans. Cwmcarn has both a fantastic new freeride area, while the legendary Y Mynydd has a permanent course, with huge wall rides, corkscrew bridge sections, rock gardens and jump fields. It's

also got a dedicated uplift service via a van, so fans needn't push once. Other downhill sites can be found at Afan, Coed Llandegla and Brechfa.

Since August 2013 the nation has also welcomed BikePark Wales, Britain's first designated bike park where people pay to ride. Located in the heart of the south Wales valleys where, as one trail builder put it, 'there's an abundance of steep slopes no one really cares about,' the park aims to rival those around the world. It took five years to build, but promised to offer an 'incredible biking experience unlike anything you've experienced in the UK before.' If you're struggling to imagine it, picture a ski resort, remove the snow, replace the pistes with an array of bike trails meandering to the bottom of the mountain and you are close. Oh, and don't forget to replace the ski lifts with a fleet of mini-buses ready to transport you 1,610 feet (491m) to the top of Mynydd Gethin. Day passes without the lift are relatively inexpensive, but the price rises fairly steeply if you wish to use the lift. It might seem expensive, especially when you can ride for free in so many other places, but the money goes into improving the trails and creating new sections.

It's not all about extreme cycling though. There are family-friendly routes at the centre. Starter routes with no steep hills or traffic can also be found at Coed Llandegla and Coed y Brenin in north Wales. At Brechfa in Carmarthenshire there's the easy Derwen Route, and a great selection in the Brecon Beacons.

Trails are one thing, but there is also the great outdoors to explore too. From iconic routes in the Black Mountains to big rocky descents off Snowdon – where bikers are now allowed on some major bridleways – it's hard to beat Wales' natural mountain bike terrain. If you really fancy a challenge make for Sarn Helen, an epic route across the country through Snowdonia and the Brecon Beacons, roughly following an old Roman route. At 270 miles long and running from Conwy to Gower it's thought to be the most ambitious off-road ride in Britain and is estimated to take over a week to complete.

For more information check wmbwales.com, a site about the main bike parks, or wmtbwales.co.uk, which has articles on routes and where you can hook up with other riders. Information about BikePark Wales can be found at bikeparkwales.com. Local bookshops and bike stores stock relevant guides, but some of the best trails in the country are covered by *Bikefax: The Best Mountain Bike Trails in Snowdonia* and *The Good Mountain Biking Guide*.

▼ BikePark Wales ▶ Welsh-language version of Scrabble

THE WELSH LANGUAGE

It may feature the words *popty ping* for a microwave, *moron* for carrot and *pili pala* for a butterfly, but that doesn't mean the Welsh language should be taken anything but seriously. Welsh – *Cymraeg*, in fact – is the most ancient and, dare we say it, poetic language of Britain, dating back possibly 4,000 years. It evolved all those years ago from a language now known as Proto-Indo-European, a theoretical language, which developed into nine sub-languages, one of which was Celtic. This Celtic tongue again branched into different forms, and was spoken pre-Roman Empire across much of Europe.

The Celtic languages that survived were those that migrated from mainland Europe over to the western islands of Britain and Ireland. Closely related to Cornish and Breton, it's by far the strongest Celtic language in terms of numbers and relevance in society. This stake was drilled down in the sixth century when the written word migrated from the Bible to literature. The poems of early Welsh poets Taliesin and Aneirin, from the 6th and 7th centuries, are the earliest surviving examples of Welsh literature. Today, according to the 2011 census, roughly 19 per cent of the population (around half a million people) are able to speak the language. Looking at it the other way, 73 per cent have no Welsh language skills at all. However, as the Minister for Heritage Alun Ffred Jones pointed out in 2010, the Welsh language is a source of great pride for the people of Wales 'whether they speak it or not.'

Measures are now in place across the country to ensure Welsh speakers can access a range of facilities, from tribunals to train times – which, of course, can at times be slightly frustrating when you're late for a train, need to know what platform it's on and the helpful announcement is in Welsh. Really, it's just more incentive to learn it – and people are, especially the young. More and more children are attending Welsh-language schools. And even in English-speaking schools in Wales, children must learn it between the ages of five and sixteen. Helping promote it are the Welsh-language radio station Radio Cymru, the television channel S4C and a weekly news magazine *Golwg*.

While travelling around Wales you will find Welsh is spoken freely, particularly in the west and north, though Cardiff has a vibrant Welsh-language community too, as many young people have migrated here to work in the media, National Assembly and other large organisations. Even if you don't know any words, a friendly *diolch* (thank you) can go a long way. Take note on how to pronounce the 'ch' though – it gets the back of your throat. Admittedly, to an outsider, the language can look daunting, especially if you arrive at *Llanfairpwllgwyngyllgogerychwyrn-drobwllllantysiliogogogoch* – a train station in Anglesey and also the longest place name in Europe. It actually translates somewhat

▼ Millennium Centre, Cardiff

ridiculously as 'Saint Mary's Church in the hollow of the white hazel near a rapid whirlpool and the Church of Saint Tysilio of the red cave'. Other baffling words include *ddiddordebau* for 'hobbies', *llongyfarchiadau* for 'congratulations' and *cyfrifiadur* for 'computer'. By the time you've said 'pleased to meet you' – *braf eich cyfarfod chi* – the person will have probably disappeared around the corner *(rownd i gornel)*. Even the simple word for 'please' is *os gwelwch yn dda* – probably the reason some Welsh speakers say *plis*. Perhaps one of the simplest to learn is *bendigedig* for 'excellent' – one of the few that sounds as it is written, ben-di-ged-ig.

Really, there's no let up with the language. It's famously renowned for its mutations and complicated word endings. 'Earthquake' for instance is *daeargryn*; the plural, however, is *daeargrynfeydd* – a far cry from the English trick of adding a simple 's'. Don't be confused either by English-sounding words, as they are likely to have an entirely different meaning, such as *dim* (which means 'nothing'), *hen* (which means 'old'), *crows* ('brain') and *plant* ('children'). The only words that a listener might be expected to recognise are anglicised words, such as iPad. It might be prudent to try and get a grasp of words used frequently, though. Place-names are often linked to geographical features – *aber* is 'river', *llan* is 'church', *cwm* is 'valley' and *coed* is 'forest'. Do remember, if it all seems a bit much, even the Welsh struggle with it sometimes. Recently a town in Torfaen called 'Varteg' proposed to change its anglicised name to a Welsh version, as so many towns have in recent decades. The problem? There is no 'v' in Welsh, meaning it would be replaced by a 'f', rendering the town Y Farteg. If stressed out by it all, just remember that and laugh.

▼ Welcome sign at Llangua, Monmouthshire

LOCAL SPECIALITIES

Wales is full of specialities, from food to whisky, beer to art. These also range from the ancient, such as cheesy rarebit and cawl soup, to the cool and modern, like Penderyn whisky.

FOOD

You're lucky. Wales has had a food revolution of late, with a distinct move towards organic and locally sourced produce, preferably sold at local farmers' markets. If you're into meat, then try Welsh Black beef, an ancient breed descended from pre-Roman cattle, or salt-marsh lamb, which is reared in coastal locations such as Harlech in Snowdonia. The lamb's saline-rich diet imparts a sweet, delicate – though not salty – flavour. Other delights include oysters from the Conwy Estuary and Menai Strait, crab and lobster from Pembroke or Penclawdd cockles from The Mumbles, harvested on the Gower and sold at Swansea's farmers' market. Laver bread, despite its misleading name, is also a product of the water. It's a nutritious seaweed, cooked until it becomes like jelly, and then often mixed with oats and served in a traditional Welsh breakfast. Cawl is another favourite, a hearty soup of lamb, leeks and potatoes.

Cheeses are big business, too. The best known is Caerphilly, a crumbly white variety from south Wales. Other types include Y Fenni and Tintern, Black Bomber from Snowdonia and Collier's Powerful Welsh Cheddar. Recently, artisan cheese-makers, such as Carmarthenshire's Caws Cenarth and Pembrokeshire's Pant Mawr, have become increasingly popular. Both have visitor centres and offer tastings. Cheese is also linked to a favourite Welsh export – rarebit, effectively a tasty mix of ale, cheese and mustard that's grilled on toast. Historians say its original name was Welsh rabbit – the idea being that the Welsh were too poor to buy meat, so referred to cheese as if it were meat as a joke – but rarebit has unfortunately stuck.

For pudding, the Welsh love nothing more than a slab of Bara brith, their old-fashioned fruited tea bread, or a Welsh cake, a type of flat scone cooked on a griddle and sprinkled liberally with caster sugar. Finally, if it's a little seasoning you're after, nothing beats Snowdonia's Halen Môn Sea Salt, now used by top chefs throughout the world. The company offers a 'behind the scenes' tour (see halenmon. com). To sample these delights head to the Bodnant Welsh Food Centre in the Conwy Valley (bodnant-welshfood.co.uk), the Rhug Estate Farm Shop (rhug. co.uk) or the Trealy Farm charcuterie (trealy.co.uk).

DRINK

Beer is the national drink of Wales, with SA Brain and Felinfoel breweries existing since the late 19th century. In 1854 it was noted that Welsh beer had its own distinct style, being made from pale malt and hops. Even though pubs are closing across the nation, microbreweries are booming – there are currently 52 breweries from which to choose. There are also more than 20 vineyards in Wales, a leading one being Penarth vineyard (penarthwines.co.uk), which makes fruity wines. If spirits are more your thing, then try Wales' leading whisky – Penderyn – which was launched in 2000. It's not just alcohol though. The Welsh have a lot of water, and they bottle it. Leading brands include Brecon Carreg, Cerist Natural Mineral Water and Ty Nant.

ART

Wales has spawned a number of great artists, both ancient and modern. Anglesey has – or had rather – Sir Kyffin Williams, who died in 2006 and is highly regarded as one of the defining artists of the 20th century. West Wales has the brilliant John Knapp-Fisher (johnknapp-fisher.com), whose work defines moody Welsh landscapes like no other. Helen Elliot creates the most endearing and cheerful works of art (helenelliott.net), while a leading light is Eloise Govier, a contemporary fine artist who paints in neon colours (eloisegovier.com).

THINGS TO READ

From top poetry – Dylan Thomas' *Do Not Go Gentle Into That Good Night* – to cutting-edge screenplays – think *'Oh, what's occurin?'* from *Gavin & Stacey* – Wales has got every conceivable genre of literature covered. Perhaps that's why it's home to one of the world's leading literary festivals at Hay-on-Wye, where this work is showcased annually.

In terms of Welsh-language literature, the national Eisteddfod is still the breeding ground for this. Inspiring poets and writers Menna Elfyn, Ifor ap Glyn and Iwan Llwyd have all helped popularise the medium in recent years.

There is plenty of English-language literature too. Key writers include R S (Ronald Stuart) Thomas, whose late 20th-century works concerned the Welsh landscape and people, and Dylan Thomas, acclaimed for writing a handful of the greatest poems in our language, including *And Death Shall Have No Dominion* and *Fern Hill*. *Under Milk Wood* was considered highly innovative at the time, as Dylan Thomas wrote it for radio; it is also hugely popular and entertaining, describing Wales' insular, gossipy community. The nation has also helped shape the writing of classic children's author Roald Dahl, great contemporary writer Martin Amis and fantasy author Philip Pullman, who spent his youth in north Wales. In 2016, Wales will celebrate the centenary of Roald Dahl's birth with a host of events throughout the year.

If you wish to learn about Wales, a great place to start is *The Story of Wales* by Jon Gower (2012), with an introduction by veteran Welsh broadcaster Huw Edwards. Similarly, there's also *A History of Wales* by renowned historian John Davies (2007). He's also the co-author of *Wales: 100 Places to See Before You Die* (2010).

A brilliant modern travelogue is *Bred of Heaven* by Jasper Rees (2011). A charming book about one man's quest to reclaim his Welsh roots, it saw the author join a male voice choir, play rugby and learn the language. Older travelogues include Dannie Abse's *Journals from the Ant Heap* (1988) and Anthony Bailey's *A Walk Through Wales* (1992), an engaging account of a three-week cross-country ramble. There's also *Know Another Way* (2002), a compilation of stories by six of Wales' leading writers, reflecting upon the ancient pilgrimage route from Tintern Abbey to St Davids.

More historic travelogues from the 19th century include *A Tour in Wales* (1773) by Thomas Pennant – which popularised Wales during the Romantic Movement – and George Borrow's *Wild Wales: Its People, Language and Scenery* (1862). Both books can be picked up in second-hand books shops. If you are looking for more information on things to do and see in Wales, Daniel Start's *Wild Swimming* (2008) has a chapter on Wales. So too does *Tiny Islands: 60 Remarkable Little Worlds Around Britain* by Dixe Wills (2013).

For relatively recent novels from Wales try *Work, Sex and Rugby* (1999) by Lewis Davies. His critically acclaimed debut novel chronicles life on the dole in the south Wales valleys. *Grits* (2001) and *Sheepshagger* (2002), two books by Niall Griffiths, both chronicle gritty Welsh life. If you are interested in learning the lingo try *Spreading the Word: the Welsh Language* by Harold Carter (2001) and *Welsh Roots and Branches* (2005) by Gareth Jones. And if you are interested in Welsh food, try *The Very Best Flavours of Wales* (1997) by Gilli Davies – a celebration of Welsh cookery by a Cordon Bleu chef.

THINGS TO WATCH

Wales, and especially Cardiff, is a major centre for television and film, and is used as a film location for some of Britain's most popular programmes. The BBC Wales studios in Cardiff Bay were used for the filming of BAFTA-winning *Doctor Who*, *Casualty*, *Wizards vs Aliens* and the Welsh-language series *Pobol y Cwm*. Other programmes such as *Sherlock*, *Being Human* and the drama series *Merlin* are all filmed on location in and around the city. The latter drew on the legend of King Arthur and Merlin. Critically acclaimed comedy *Gavin & Stacey*, written by James Corden and Ruth Jones, was also filmed nearby in Barry, in the Vale of Glamorgan. Its offbeat humour is very true to life. The 1960s TV classic *The Prisoner* was filmed in the Italianate village of Portmeirion and fans from around the world still visit in droves.

Many movies have also been filmed in Wales, including *Mr Nice* (2010) starring Rhys Ifans and *Outlaw* (2007) with Sean Bean and Bob Hoskins. Snowdonia has provided the backdrop for an array of classic films, including *The Inn of the Sixth Happiness* (1958) and *Tomb Raider II* (2003).

The Wales Screen Commission markets Wales as a location for all types of productions, assisting them on a practical basis and ensuring that their spend within the Welsh economy is maximised. Older films about Wales include Karl Francis' *Above Us the Earth* (1977), set in the valleys and based on the true story of a colliery closure, and John Ford's *How Green Was My Valley* (1941). A more recent blockbuster was *The Edge of Love* (2008), about the life of Dylan Thomas, starring Matthew Rhys and Keira Knightley.

Media creations are not always positive about Wales, though. There have been numerous documentaries, in particular focusing on Cardiff as the binge-drinking capital of Britain. Recently BBC3 aired *Call Centre*, a fly-on-the-wall documentary based on a Swansea call centre and the characters who work in it – and there are a great many characters.

THINGS TO KNOW ABOUT WALES

It's only small but Wales has produced an awful lot of famous people in its time, and not just singers. Famous actors and actresses include Timothy Dalton and Catherine Zeta-Jones, while the industrial town of Port Talbot alone has produced actor and comedian Rob Brydon, Richard Burton, Sir Anthony Hopkins and Michael Sheen. Others include the geographer George Everest, after whom Mount Everest was

▼ Portmeirion

named, the designer Laura Ashley and explorer Henry Morton Stanley, famous for his line 'Dr Livingstone, I presume?' Mary Quant was born in London but both her parents were Welsh. There are also plenty of famous Americans who think they are Welsh, or have legitimately descended from there.

Notable Americans with at least partial Welsh heritage include presidents Thomas Jefferson, John Quincy Adams, James Monroe and Abraham Lincoln, as well as architect Frank Lloyd Wright, aviator and film producer Howard Hughes, US Secretary of State Hillary Rodham Clinton and Hollywood actor Tom Cruise. Perhaps it's not surprising to see such an illustrious list, given that according to the 2000 census, 1.7 million Americans claim Welsh ancestry. The true figure is actually thought to be even higher due to the large number of Welsh surnames in the country. Such surnames include lots of given names but ending with an 's' – such as Williams, Davies, Edwards, Roberts, Hughes and Evans. Other traditional names include Owen, Lloyd, Morgan, Vaughan, Jenkins, Meredith and Griffith or Griffiths.

Wales is also home to quirky and record-breaking inventions. In 1873, it – or rather, a certain Major Walter Clopton Winfield – invented lawn tennis to entertain his guests at Nantclwyd House in Llanelidan, Denbighshire. The 16th-century Welsh mathematician Robert

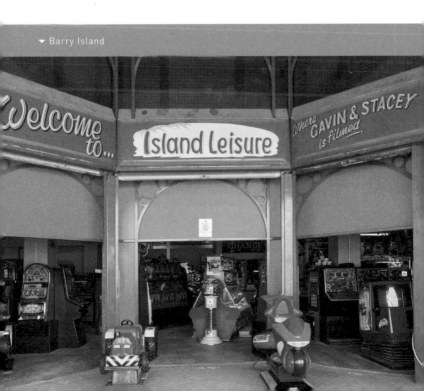

▼ Barry Island

▲ Bring sturdy walking boots

Recorde invented the equal sign (=) and introduced the plus (+) and minus (-) signs as well as algebra to Britain. The nation also had the most successful pirate of the golden age of piracy, Pembrokeshire-born Bartholemew Roberts. It is also thought that he named the pirate's iconic flag 'Jolly Roger' in 1721.

In terms of breaking records Wales is also a success, and is home to Britain's oldest tombstone, that of *Cadfan ap Iago*, King of Gwynedd from AD 616 to AD 625. Cardiff has been home to Spillers record shop – the longest running in the world – since 1894. Wales also wins a record – somewhat unsurprisingly – for sheep. The Smithfield Livestock Market in Welshpool, Montgomeryshire, is the largest one-day sheep market in Europe.

THINGS TO PACK

Come to Wales and the chances are that you'll be doing something outdoorsy, be it canoeing, walking or cycling. For that you'll need proper outdoor equipment and clothing. This basically breaks down to waterproofs (top and bottom), fleecy layers, insulated bottom layers, proper walking socks and shoes, such as sturdy walking boots. If you are going up the high mountains of Snowdonia or visiting in winter you'll also need a thick hat and gloves, and a survival kit. For summer days on the beach you'll need the usual – swimming costume or wetsuit (the water never gets that warm), a towel, some flip-flops, high-factor sun cream and a hat. If you want to spot wildlife, then bring your binoculars and perhaps a notebook to record your sightings. A camera with a large lens might also be useful for catching shots of seal pups on rocky outcrops or soaring red kites. For those with kids, it's probably best to bring – or buy when here – some buckets and spades and maybe some crabbing or fishing lines.

Obviously you'll need to get around so a satnav is always handy. Be warned, though, in rural locations, they often aren't that accurate, so a good map is essential. Equally, if you plan on travelling by public transport, an iPod and earphones might be some comfort along the long and winding roads.

There are plenty of upmarket restaurants, so a 'tidy' outfit would be sure to get an outing. Clearly it does rain, so an umbrella or hood might come in useful but, unlike Scotland, midges aren't a problem here, so you won't need to pack insect repellent.

Remember that many attractions and national parks have smart phone apps you can access for free. A tide timetable might be helpful too. After that, all you need to pack is a smile and a good pair of lungs to join in the revelries.

USEFUL TIPS FOR TRAVELLING

Tourist information

Luckily, Wales is blessed with an array of government-funded tourist offices with a branch in nearly every town, all run by local, knowledgeable staff. The provision can be a bit patchy, though, in mid-Wales, and some other offices may be extremely busy during peak periods. Staff can provide you with maps, ideas of where to go and what to see, and books on the local area. They can also suggest and book accommodation or events.

Shopping

Shops are open every day, with shorter trading hours on Sundays. Many – particularly in tourist hotspots – are open on bank holidays. Be warned, though, many towns are quite seasonal with cafes, bars and beach shacks shut in the winter, so it's a good idea to call or check before travelling to a particular restaurant or pub. Take cash as many of the more rural outlets and visitor centres may not take credit cards.

Keeping the kids happy

Wales is a paradise for kids – it has rocks to climb, crabs to catch, waves to bodyboard and the amazing old-fashioned sweetshop called Yum Yums on Cardigan High Street, if they're in need of spoiling. The nation is well geared towards children. Even the high-end restaurants make them feel welcome and have modified their menus to cater for them. Facilities are uniformly good and many attractions have discounted tickets. Under-fives often go for free, as they do on trains. Public transport is quite easy to navigate with buggies, although if you plan on getting the bus into town from Cardiff Airport, be warned – it's not a terribly slick service, particularly with young, tired children.

If the weather is truly terrible during your visit, there are plenty of things to keep kids occupied. One option is Greenwood Forest Park – an all-day centre with rides, activities and a very cool roller coaster (see page 173). A similar experience can be found further south in Oakwood (see page 256). The Centre for Alternative Technology (see page 222) is another sure-fire winner – and educational too. If they are into sci-fi, then a *Dr Who* close-up in Cardiff Bay is an obvious choice (see page 136). Snowdonia, meanwhile, now has a cool surfing centre (see page 150), while Cardiff has an indoor trampoline hub (see page 127). Pick up a copy of *Wales: View*, available from all tourist information offices, which gives plenty of tips for family-orientated holidays.

Gay and lesbian travellers

In general, Wales is tolerant of sexual preferences, especially in the cities. Cardiff and Swansea have active gay and lesbian scenes, as have Aberystwyth, Bangor and Newport, to a degree. Wales' biggest gay and lesbian festival is the Cardiff Mardi Gras, held in late summer.

Travellers with disabilities

Sadly, the provision for travellers with disabilities can be a case of 'sometimes good, sometimes bad', which isn't terribly helpful. New buildings and public transport have excellent facilities, but the older B&Bs and public buildings, due to their construction, don't allow easy access. It's best to ask in a tourist office for ideas of where to go, or call ahead to check what facilities might be available.

Internet access

If you are travelling with a portable laptop, tablet or smart phone, getting access to WiFi should prove to be very easy in Wales. Increasingly, it's offered for free in cafes and trendy bars, while most hotels and B&Bs will also have it – although sometimes password protected. If you don't have a laptop and need to get access to the web or print off a boarding pass, the best place to head for is a public library. Most towns will have a library with two or more computers that are free to use and have access to a printer. In some cases, though, they can be busy, so you may have to come back at another time or book a slot. Internet cafes can be found in the main towns and generally charge per hour. Do remember to check there isn't a minimum charge for usage before you sit down.

▶ Centre for Alternative Technology, Machynlleth

FESTIVALS & EVENTS

From the insane to the quirky, Wales has a festival for everyone. Top of the list is the National Eisteddfod, an age-old competition of poetry and music that still forms the backbone of Welsh culture. Each year it alternates between north and south Wales, giving communities across the country a chance to welcome up to 160,000 visitors over an eight-day period. In the past, it was occasionally held in Liverpool or London, but this seems to have stopped. The Welsh language is integral to the festival, but the organisers go to great lengths to ensure that non-speakers enjoy themselves too. Many towns also have their own annual arts and food festivals. If you want to find something really obscure, try bog snorkelling in Llanwrtyd Wells, or maybe even coracle racing in Cilgerran. Following is a list of the top events throughout the year.

▶ JANUARY–APRIL

Six Nations Rugby Championship
Feb to Mar
Don't miss it – try to get a ticket, but if not, watch in a pub anywhere in the country.

St David's Day
1 Mar
Wales' national day, with celebrations nationwide, particularly in schools.

Wonderwool Wales
Mid-Apr
wonderwoolwales.co.uk
Enjoy a brilliant range of artisan products in Builth Wells.

▶ MAY

Aberystwyth Cycle Festival
late May
abercyclefest.com
With some of Britain's top cyclists making a rare appearance in mid-Wales, festival visitors can watch all the on- and off-road action, as well as experience the beautiful and undiscovered lanes of Ceredigion on two wheels.

Hay Festival
Late May to early Jun
hayfestival.com
You don't need to be a book fan to enjoy this one.

Snowdonia Slateman Triathlon, Llanberis
Late May
snowdoniaslateman.com
This new triathlon is held over two days. The two race options will be the Full Slateman (1,000m swim, 51km cycle and 11km run) or the Slateman Sprint (400m swim, 20km cycle and 6km run).

Urdd National Eisteddfod
End May to first week Jun
urdd.org
Witness a hugely enjoyable youth eisteddfod.

St Davids Cathedral Festival
End of May to first week Jun
stdavidscathedral.org.uk
Ten days of classical music with excellent acoustics.

Tredegar House Folk Festival
May or Jun
tredegarhousefestival.org.uk
A weekend of international dance, music and song at this grand 17th-century mansion.

▶ JUNE

Great Welsh Beer & Cider Festival
Mid-Jun
gwbcf.org.uk
The best way to sample around 200 brews, many from Wales, plus award-winning local street food, held in Cardiff.

Cardiff Singer of the World Competition
Mid-Jun, alternate years
Check out the star-studded list of competitors from around the world.

Gŵyl Ifan
Mid-Jun
gwylifan.org
Enjoy a weekend of folk-dancing workshops, displays and processions in Cardiff.

Man Versus Horse Marathon
Mid-Jun
green-events.co.uk
Watch this strange 22-mile race between runners and horses at Llanwrtyd Wells, Powys. Also hosts bog snorkelling and the Real Ale Wobble.

Gower Walking Festival
Mid-Jun
gowerwalkingfestival.org
Get fit with 71 walks over 16 days.

Velethon Wales
Mid-Jun
velethon-wales.co.uk
This new event has more of a festival feel, when 15,000 road bikes take to closed roads around south Wales.

▶ JULY

Beyond the Border
Early Jul
beyondtheborder.com
Get creative at this three-day international storytelling festival at St Donats Castle, in the Vale of Glamorgan.

Cardigan Bay Seafood Festival
Early Jul
www.aberaeron.info/seafood
Treat your taste buds with the best of local seafood, fresh fish and delights from the sea.

Cardiff Festival
Jul & Aug
cardiff-festival.com
This large and varied festival encompasses theatre, food and drink, a Mardi Gras and lots more.

Gower Festival
Last half of Jul
gowerfestival.org
Get ready for two weeks of mostly classical music in churches around the Gower.

Llangollen International Eisteddfod

First or second week Jul
international-eisteddfod.co.uk
This competition has more than 12,000 participants from all over the world, including choirs, dancers, folk singers, groups and instrumentalists.

The Big Cheese

Late Jul
your.caerphilly.gov.uk/bigcheese/great-cheese-race
Who can resist such a quirky race?

Royal Welsh Show

Late Jul
www.rwas.co.uk
Europe's largest agricultural show and sales fair at Builth Wells is an absolute Welsh institution and a top day out.

Snowdon Race

Late Jul
snowdonrace.co.uk
Feel for the runners of this one-day race from Llanberis up Snowdon.

▶ AUGUST

Cardiff Mardi Gras

Aug
cardiffmardigras.co.uk
This lesbian and gay festival takes over Coopers Field with live music and lots of partying.

Brecon Jazz Festival

Mid-Aug
breconjazz.co.uk
This is widely regarded as one of the best jazz festivals in Britain; run over three days.

Green Man Festival

Late Aug
greenman.net
This independent music festival in Brecon has evolved into a hugely popular event, with live music across five stages, as well as DJs playing everything from dub-reggae to electro, all through the night. There's also comedy, secret gigs and things for the kids.

Monmouth Show

End Aug
monmouthshow.co.uk
Spend a day learning about the country way of life.

Llandrindod Wells Victorian Festival

Late Aug
victorianfestival.co.uk
A week of family fun, street entertainment and Victorian costumes rounded off with a firework display.

Royal National Eisteddfod

First week Aug
eisteddfod.org.uk
The centrepiece of Welsh culture is Wales' biggest single annual event, with crafts, literature, Welsh-language lessons, theatre and more. Don't forget the poetry competitions. Check for venue.

▶ SEPTEMBER

Abergavenny Food Festival

Mid-Sep
abergavennyfoodfestival.com
This weekend scoff-fest is Wales' premier gastronomic event with a smorgasbord of fresh food showcased by celebrity chefs.

Tenby Arts Festival

Late Sep
tenbyartsfest.co.uk
This is a well-established week-long arts romp in Tenby, with a lively fringe too.

Abersoch Jazz Festival

End Sep
abersochjazzfestival.com
New Orleans comes to Wales' beaches during this jazzy spectacle.

▶ OCTOBER

Artes Mundi
artesmundi.org
Wales' biggest contemporary
visual art show is held biennially
in Cardiff.

**Swansea Festival of Music
and the Arts**
Oct
swanseafestival.org
Three weeks of jazz, opera and
ballet throughout the city.

Sŵn
Mid- to late Oct
swnfest.com
This showcases the best new
music from around Wales at
venues across Cardiff.

▶ NOVEMBER–DECEMBER

**Bonfire Night and Lantern
Parade**
Early Nov
Superb procession in
Machynlleth, culminating in
fireworks and performance.

Dylan Thomas Festival
Early Nov
dylanthomas.com
Held in Swansea with talks,
performances, exhibitions,
readings and music based on
Wales' greatest poet, Dylan
Thomas, whose most celebrated
works include *Do Not Go Gentle
Into that Good Night* and the play
that he wrote for radio, *Under
Milk Wood*.

▼ Dylan Thomas Memorial Statue, Swansea Marina

CAMPSITES

For more information on these and other campsites, visit theaa.com/self-catering-and-campsites

Aeron Coast Caravan Park ▶▶▶
aeroncoast.co.uk
North Road, Aberaeron, SA46 0JF
01545 570349 | Open Mar–Oct
This well-managed family holiday park has direct access to the beach. On-site facilities include an extensive outdoor pool complex, multi-activity and outdoor sports area.

Caerfai Bay Caravan & Tent Park ▶▶▶▶▶
caerfaibay.co.uk
Caerfai Bay, St Davids, SA62 6QT
01437 720274 | Open Mar to mid-Nov
Offers magnificent coastal scenery and an outlook over St Brides Bay, and is close to a bathing beach. The facilities are great, and there is an excellent farm shop just across the road.

Daisy Bank Caravan Park ▶▶▶▶▶
daisy-bank.co.uk
Snead, Churchstoke, SY15 6EB
01588 620471 | Open all year
Located between Craven Arms and Churchstoke, this idyllic park is for adults only. The immaculately maintained amenity blocks provide smart, modern fittings and excellent privacy options. Camping pods, and free Wifi are also available.

Fishguard Bay Resort ▶▶▶
fishguardbay.com
Garn Gelli, Fishguard, SA65 9ET
01348 811415 | Open Mar–9 Jan
A clifftop site with outstanding views of Fishguard Bay, the resort is extremely well kept, with a good toilet block, a common room with TV, a lounge/library, decent laundry and a well-stocked shop.

Home Farm Caravan Park ▶▶▶▶▶
homefarm-anglesey.co.uk
Marian-glas, LL73 8PH
01248 410614 | Open Apr–Oct
A first-class park set in an elevated and secluded position sheltered by trees. The peaceful rural setting has views of farmland, the sea and the mountains of Snowdonia. There are excellent play facilities for

children, a smart reception and shop.

Pencelli Castle Caravan & Camping Park ▶▶▶▶▶

pencelli-castle.com
Pencelli, Brecon, LD3 7LX | 01874 665451 | Open 15 Feb–30 Nov
In the heart of the Brecon Beacons, this charming park is bordered by the Monmouthshire and Brecon Canal. As well as the well-equipped heated toilets with en-suite cubicles, there is a drying room, laundry and shop. Buses to Brecon, Abergavenny and Swansea stop just outside the gate.

Pitton Cross Caravan & Camping Park ▶▶▶

pittoncross.co.uk
Rhossili, SA3 1PT | 01792 390593
Open all year
Surrounded by farmland close to sandy Mewslade Bay, Pitton Cross is a grassy park divided by hedging into paddocks; hard-standings for motorhomes are available. Rhossili Beach is popular with surfers, while walkers can give the nearby Wales Coastal Path a try. Performance kites are sold, and instruction in flying is given. You can have a go at geocaching and paragliding too.

Plassey Holiday Park ▶▶▶▶▶

plassey.com
The Plassey, Eyton, LL13 0SP
01978 780277 | Open Feb–Nov
A lovely park set in several hundred acres of quiet farm and meadowland in the Dee Valley. As well as a campsite, a large complex of Edwardian farm buildings have been converted into a coffee shop, restaurant, beauty studio and craft outlets. There's plenty for the family, from scenic walks and a swimming pool to free fishing and the use of a 9-hole golf course. There's also a sauna, badminton and table tennis.

Trawsdir Touring Caravans & Camping Park ▶▶▶▶▶

barmouthholidays.co.uk
Llanaber, Barmouth, LL42 1RR
01341 280999 | Open Mar–Jan
Well run by friendly owners, this quality park enjoys views to the sea and hills. Tents and caravans have designated areas divided by attractive dry-stone walls, and the site is very convenient for large RVs. There's a great children's play area, plus glorious seasonal floral displays. Don't miss the illuminated dog walk that leads directly to the nearby pub.

Trefalun Park ▶▶▶▶

trefalunpark.co.uk
Devonshire Drive, St Florence, Tenby, SA70 8RD | 01646 651514
Open Easter–Oct
Set within 12 acres of sheltered, well-kept grounds, Trefalun Park offers well-maintained level grass pitches separated by bushes and trees, with plenty of space in which to relax. Children will enjoy feeding the park's pets, and there are plenty of activities available at nearby Heatherton Country Sports Park.

VISIT THE MUSEUMS | GET OUTDOORS | EXPLORE BY BIKE | GO BACK IN TIME | TAKE A TRAIN RIDE | MEET THE WILDLIFE | TAKE IN SOME HISTORY | HIT THE BEACH | EAT AND DRINK | GET INDUSTRIAL | VISIT THE GALLERIES | GO CANOEING | TRY HORSE-RIDING | PLACES NEARBY | CATCH A PERFORMANCE | GO ROUND THE GARDENS | TAKE A BOAT TRIP

A–Z of Wales

▲ Aberaeron harbour

▶ **Aberaeron & New Quay** MAP REF 328 B3

Move over Highway 101 – the coastal road between Cardigan and Aberystwyth through the county of Ceredigion is every bit as alluring. Two of the key delights are the towns of Aberaeron and New Quay, 20 miles and 15 miles northeast of Cardigan respectively.

Aberaeron, meaning 'mouth of the River Aeron' – Aeron being a Welsh god of war– is the jewel of Cardigan Bay. Visit and enjoy its pretty architecture and harbour. It has carved out a reputation for fine local food, based largely but not exclusively on the Harbourmaster Hotel and its restaurant. It's also a town steeped in history. Although long been claimed by the sea, in the 12th century the town was ringed by a wooden fortification known as *Castell Cadwgan*, thought to have been constructed by King Cadwgan around the year 1148. In the 19th century the town became a hub for craftworkers. Records from the 1830s show there was one woollen manufacturer, one bootmaker, one baker, one corn miller, one blacksmith and shovel maker, two shipwrights, one carpenter and one hat maker here. Once the harbour was built, the town became a port regularly visited by steam ships. Unusual architecture grew up around the harbour, namely elegant, flat-fronted, Regency-style buildings, designed by Edward Haycock, a renowned 19th-century architect from Shrewsbury whose work was sufficiently well thought of to feature on British postage stamps. Many of the houses were owned by local sea captains and named after far-flung destinations, such as Gambia and Melbourne. Through the decades the town was transformed from a small fishing village into one of the main trading centres of Cardigan Bay, with shipbuilding, ironworks and 35 pubs, around a quarter of which still operate today. The site of the local woollen mill still stands on the banks of the River Aeron, and the famous Aberaeron shovel was produced in the local ironworks.

Today you can enjoy a small half-tide harbour used for recreational vessels and a town that is a real architectural gem and charmingly unspoilt. Most of the buildings, including The Harbourmaster are on the north side, and a wooden pedestrian bridge crosses the estuary. The shoreline consists of two quite steep pebble beaches that are great for a stroll. Many of the shops are independent. You can get fresh lobster and crab off the pier and buy Aberaeron's renowned honey and honey products, such as ice cream and mustard.

Five miles down the coast is New Quay. As with Aberaeron, the 19th century saw it grow as a hub for shipbuilders, with 300 men employed. Streets of terraced houses crept up the slopes around the hilly bay. Sailing vessels large enough to sail to the Americas and Australia were built here, and the industry supported blacksmiths, sailmakers, rope works and a foundry. It also became a centre for navigation training and New Quay men captained some of the last sailing ships in operation.

Sea-based pursuits are still at the core of this little town's appeal. Big attractions include boat trips along the coast to spot Cardigan Bay's permanent colony of bottlenose dolphins, and courses in kayaking, windsurfing and sailing. Each August the town hosts the Cardigan Bay Regatta as it has done since 1879. You can also go fishing here – off boats or the shore – and the small stall just up from the harbour is simply the best place in the area to buy fresh mackerel.

Dylan Thomas wrote much of *Under Milk Wood* in New Quay, where he lived with his family in a rented bungalow in the last years of World War II. In fact, the town may have partially inspired his fictitious community of Llareggub. Some melodramatic events from his stay are depicted in the 2008 biopic *The Edge of Love*, and a Dylan Thomas trail links New Quay with Aberaeron, which the writer and poet called 'the most precious place in the world'.

TAKE IN SOME HISTORY
Llanerchaeron
nationaltrust.org.uk
Ciliau Aeron, near Aberaeron,
SA48 8DG | 01545 570200
Open daily. Times vary;
call or check website for details
Designed by John Nash (the chap responsible for Buckingham Palace), this is an 18th-century gentry estate with house, walled gardens and home farm. The house is almost unaltered from its heyday, with its own service courtyard of dairy, laundry, brewery and salting house. You can escape for a peaceful walk in the pleasure grounds and parkland. There's also a working organic farm with Welsh Black cattle, Llanwenog sheep and rare Welsh pigs.

ENTERTAIN THE FAMILY
New Quay Honey Farm
thehoneyfarm.co.uk
Cross Inn, SA44 6NN
01545 560822 | Open Easter–Oct daily 10–5, Nov–24 Dec 10–4; closed Sun and Mon, except BHs
A few miles out of New Quay, this delightful and informative honey farm is a treat for all the family. Producing some of the finest honey and mead in Wales from hives dotted around the local area, it has a shop selling natural products, a tea room and an exhibition about the honeybee.

TAKE A BOAT TRIP
New Quay Boats
newquayboattrips.co.uk
The Moorings, Glanmor Terrace,
SA45 9PS | 01545 560800
New Quay Boats offers trips lasting a couple of hours and wildlife and bird sightings are high.

WALK THE CEREDIGION COAST PATH
The popular Ceredigion coast path runs between Aberaeron and New Quay.

VISIT THE FESTIVAL
www.aberaeron.info
In July, Aberaeron holds the Cardigan Bay Seafood Festival, and in August the Aberaeron Festival has a colourful carnival and procession.

EAT AND DRINK
The Crown Inn and Restaurant
the-crown-inn.moonfruit.com
Llwyndafydd, SA44 6BU
01545 560396
Just down the coast from New Quay is this delightful family-friendly pub. The setting is a traditional Welsh longhouse dating from 1799 with award-winning gardens. There's a

carvery every Sunday and a varied menu with a good selection of dishes, bar food and light snacks. There's also an easy walk leading to a cove with caves and cliffs in the care of the National Trust.

The Harbourmaster

harbour-master.com
SA46 0BT | 01545 570755
The three-storey, former harbourmaster's house has pride of place on the quayside close to the mouth of the harbour. It's stylish, modern, friendly and sets the standards in these parts – in fact, it's probably the leading restaurant on the west coast. The kitchen makes the most of the wealth of

surf 'n turf produce available from this favoured locale. The fare is a medley of traditional and contemporary dishes. The bar is well stocked too, with Purple Moose Glaslyn, HM Best and Halletts real cider.

Ty Mawr Mansion ⑳⑳

tymawrmansion.co.uk
Cilcennin, SA48 8DB
01570 470033
This stone-built Georgian mansion in a lofty position above the Aeron Valley is tucked away in 12 acres of gorgeous grounds. Its splendid restaurant uses local organic produce from Cilcennin village's farms and fresh fish and seafood from just up the coast.

▶ Aberdaron & Bardsey Island MAP REF 332 A3

This old whitewashed fishing village with its bustling beach lies at the very tip of the Llŷn Peninsula. Often described as the Land's End of North Wales, it was always the last stop for ancient pilgrims before they ventured across the wild and sometimes treacherous waters to Bardsey Island – known as the island of 20,000 saints. The Y Gegin Fawr cafe, found in the centre of the village by the little stone bridge, dates from the 13th century when it was used as a communal kitchen for those intrepid pilgrims. In the 18th and 19th centuries the village developed as a shipbuilding centre and port while the mining and quarrying industries also became major employers, exporting limestone and lead around the world. There are still the ruins of an old pier running out to sea at Porth Simdde – the local name for the west section of Aberdaron Beach.

Today you'll find a popular seaside holiday resort waiting to entertain you. Take your shoes off and enjoy the wide sand and pebble beach, which is popular for fishing, water sports and bathing. The coastal waters are part of the Pen Llŷn a'r Sarnau Special Area of Conservation, one of the largest designated marine sites in the UK. At high tide check out the waves crashing against the exposed and sea-battered St Hywyn's

Church, found right by the beach. It's in two halves, one dating back to 1137 and the other an extension from around 1400. The poet R S Thomas (1913–2000) – a nominee for the Nobel Prize for Literature – was the local vicar here between 1954 and 1967 and the church contains interpretations of his life and works.

The island of Bardsey, which has been included in the community of Aberdaron since 1974, lies nearly two miles off the mainland. It's been an important site of religious pilgrimage since St Cadfan built a monastery here in AD 516. Even after Henry VIII demolished the monastery in 1537, pilgrims still flocked here; it was said that three visits to Bardsey were the equivalent of one to Rome in religious merit. Pilgrims took a refreshing drink from Aberdaron's St Mary's Well and prayed for a safe crossing before entrusting themselves to the tidal races and whirlpools that gave the island its Welsh name of Ynys Enlli or Isle of Currents. With such a reputation, it's not surprising that many graves have been discovered here, and it is known as the resting place of 20,000 saints. According to local tradition, Merlin, the master magician of the Arthurian legends, retired to the island and was never seen again. Some say it's the burial site of King Arthur, adding to its sense of sacredness.

Today the island is owned by a private trust and is just as famous for its wildlife and rugged scenery. Take your binoculars and enjoy the bird field observatory and holiday accommodation in old farmhouses. Bardsey is of European importance, cited as a nesting place for Manx shearwaters and choughs, while its rare plants and habitats are undisturbed by modern farming practices. Come autumn and chances are you'll spot countless grey seals. You can catch a boat here from Aberdaron or Abersoch.

HIT THE BEACH

Aberdaron beach is popular with both bathers and surfers, while nearby Porth Iago is tiny, rock-bound and reminiscent of the Greek Islands. All you need is a bit of sunshine.

TAKE A BOAT TRIP

Enlli Charter and Bardsey Boat Trips both run boat excursions from Aberdaron to Bardsey Island.

Bardsey Boat Trips
bardseyboattrips.com
07971 769895

Enlli Charter
enllicharter.co.uk
07836 293146

GO WALKING

Head along the Llyn coastal path to Pen y Cil Point and soak up the fabulous views of Bardsey Island.

▲ Bardsey Island (Ynys Enlli)

EAT AND DRINK
Y Gegin Fawr
penllyn.com
Aberdaron, LL53 8BE
01758 760359
This 13th-century building, simply decorated on two floors, once catered for Bardsey pilgrims. Specialities include locally caught crab and lobster, homemade cakes and scones.

▶ **PLACES NEARBY**
Near to Aberdaron is an interesting manor house and Whistling Sands (Porth Oer), a splendid, isolated beach.

Plas-yn-Rhiw
nationaltrust.org.uk
LL53 8AB | 01758 780219
Open daily. Times vary; call or check website for details
This small manor house – part medieval with Tudor and Georgian additions – has delightful gardens to explore with tropical specimens, a waterfall and its own snowdrop wood.

▶ **Aberdulais** MAP REF 325 E3
This village in the Vale of Neath grew up around the Aberdulais Falls – a series of beautiful waterfalls and now the site of a hydroelectric station. It has a great industrial heritage, being the home of two ironworks, a copper smelting plant, a corn watermill and a tinplate factory. From here you can explore the Neath and Tennant Canal and the Cefn Coed Colliery Museum. Former Labour MP Peter Hain has a house in the village, which is also the birthplace of former Welsh champion triathlete, Aled Thomas.

▲ Aberdulais Falls

GET OUTDOORS
Aberdulais Falls
nationaltrust.org.uk
SA10 8EU | 01639 636674 | Open
Jan–Mar Mon–Fri 11–4, Apr–Oct
daily 10–5, Nov–Dec Fri–Sun 11–4
Here water thunders into a
natural amphitheatre of rock
in a wooded setting. Cover your

ears as it's impressively noisy;
it has powered industry for
more than 400 years. Currently,
the hydro plant produces
electricity, with any surplus
sold back to the national grid.

▸ **PLACES NEARBY**
Close to Aberdulais is the town
of Neath (see page 242).
Further north, near the village
of Crynant, you'll find the Cefn
Coed Colliery Museum.

Cefn Coed Colliery Museum
npt.gov.uk
Neath Road, Crynant, SA10 8SN
01639 750556 | Open May–Sep
daily 10.30–5
This museum tells the story of
coal mining at Cefn Coed pit,
once the deepest anthracite
coal mine in the world. It was
also one of the most dangerous
in Wales, gaining the nickname
'The Slaughterhouse'. The
museum is also host to the
Neath Historical Model
Railway Club.

▸ **Aberdyfi** MAP REF 333 E5
This small thriving seaside village nestles within the
Snowdonia National Park on the north side of the Dyfi
Estuary, a nature reserve rich in birdlife. Although most
seaside resorts on the Welsh coast have access to some
beach or other, Aberdyfi (also known in English as Aberdovey)
has come up trumps with four miles of glorious uninterrupted
sands stretching northwards to Tywyn. In 1941, the UK's
first ever outward-bound centre was opened here and you
can see why. If you come here prepare to get wet and try
many of the water sports on offer, such as sailing, yachting,
sailboarding, rowing, canoeing and going on fishing and boat
trips. If you're not really that way inclined try the championship
golf course, stretching along the links, with fantastic views
out to sea.

The town grew up as a port, with its major exports being slate and oak bark. Shipbuilding was also big business and between 1840 and 1880 some 45 ships were built at the seven Penhelig shipyards on the easterly outskirts. A jetty was built in 1887, with railway lines connecting it to the wharf and the main line. This promoted links with Liverpool and Ireland, from where livestock was imported and taken further inland. Many Aberdyfi men sailed on international voyages from the city. Away from the water, the town is surrounded by steep hillsides dotted with sheep farms. Due to its relative proximity to large populated regions of the UK – the West Midlands is just 100 miles to the east – Aberdyfi has become a hotspot for returning visitors and second home owners, which has resulted in higher house prices than some other more remote towns. If you want to explore further, check out the little-walked Tarren Hills, which run from Aberdyfi northeast towards Machynlleth. This compact range of hills provides some excellent walking, particularly along the ridge that extends for several miles in a southwest direction from the Tarrens' highest point, Tarren y Gesail (2,188 feet/667m). Although blighted by coniferous forest in parts, there are many neolithic cairns and on a fine day the views of the mountain coast and estuary are superb.

HIT THE BEACH
The beach at Aberdyfi is big, sandy and ideal for family fun.

GET ON THE WATER
Dovey Yacht Club
doveyyachtclub.org.uk
The Wharf, Aberdyfi, LL35 0EB
01654 767607
You'll receive a warm welcome at this friendly club catering for cruisers, sailboarders and kite surfers.

PLAY A ROUND
Aberdovey Golf Club
aberdoveygolf.co.uk
Aberdyfi, LL35 0RT
01654 767493 | Open daily
A fabulous championship links course, which has hosted many prestigious events. Spectacular views and easy walking.

EAT AND DRINK
Penhelig Arms Hotel and Restaurant
penheligarms.com
Terrace Road, LL35 0LT
01654 767215
This popular waterside inn has been in service since 1870 and offers spectacular views over the mountain-backed tidal Dyfi Estuary. The bar is snug and cosy while the waterfront restaurant offers a brasserie-style experience. In warmer weather you can sit outside on the sea wall terrace.

▶ **PLACES NEARBY**
Visit **Tywyn Beach**, four miles to the north. Although mostly pebbled, good sand appears at low tide.

▶ Abergavenny MAP REF 327 D2

With its annual local produce market, Abergavenny is a buzzing town and is busy creating a name for itself as the foodie capital of the Usk Valley. Shops brim with local produce and it has held a weekly cattle market on the same site since 1863. There are, however, controversial plans led by Monmouthshire County Council to knock down the old market and replace it with a supermarket and library and relocate the site out of town. Whatever the future holds, you'll have plenty to entertain you here. Originally the site of a Roman fort, Gobannium, it became a medieval walled town within the Welsh Marches – the area that historically fluctuated between England and Wales. Indeed, its close proximity to the English border, just six miles away, means it's often described as the 'gateway to Wales'.

Location is a big factor in its appeal. Surrounded by three very distinctly shaped mountains – the cone-shaped Sugar Loaf Mountain and the craggy Ysgyryd Fawr in the north, and the Blorenge in the south – you can easily access the wilderness from here. It's also the perfect base from which to explore slightly further afield into the Black Mountains and Brecon Beacons. Offa's Dyke Path is close by, and the Marches Way, the Beacons Way and the Usk Valley Walk all pass through.

Although it took a pounding after the Civil War, Abergavenny's Norman castle is still worth seeing, as is the museum next door. There's no shortage of castles in the surrounding area too. Raglan lies 10 miles east along the A40, while the lesser known 'three castles' of Grosmont, Skenfrith and White Castle (see page 173) are hidden away in low, rolling hills a few miles to the east. Along some of the narrowest country lanes imaginable in the beautiful Vale of Ewyas lie the romantic ruins of Llanthony Priory, founded by Augustinian canons early in the 12th century.

If you find Abergavenny a little too busy, Crickhowell (see page 155), further west up the Usk Valley, is a picturesque village that is also well sited for visiting the many tourist attractions in the area.

TAKE IN SOME HISTORY
Abergavenny Museum and Castle

abergavennymuseum.co.uk
Castle Street, NP7 5EE
01873 854282 | Open Mar–Oct
Mon–Sat 11–1, 2–5, Sun 2–5,
Nov–Feb Mon–Sat 11–1, 2–4

Set in the grounds of a ruined Norman castle, the museum, formerly a hunting lodge built by the Marquess of Abergavenny, tells the story of this historic market town. You can have a picnic here or stroll the grounds in cooler weather.

There is a regular programme of changing exhibitions and a small gift shop.

Llanthony Priory
cadw.wales.gov.uk
North of Abervagenny, off A465
01443 336000 | Open daily 10–4
This partly ruined Augustinian priory was established in 1103 by the son of a Marcher lord, William de Lacey. After an attack by Owain Glyndwr the priory was left ruinous, but there are still substantial arches, walls and towers to explore that stir the imagination. Located in the beautiful Vale of Ewyas, it basks among hedgerows, woodland and the backdrop of the Black Mountains. You can enjoy the view over a pie and a pint, as there's a pub in the grounds, which is a very pleasant surprise indeed.

VISIT THE GALLERY
Court Cupboard Gallery
courtcupboardgallery.co.uk
New Court Farm, Llantilio Pertholey, NP7 8AU
01873 852011
Open Apr–Dec daily 10.30–5, Jan–Mar 10.30–4
Check out local paintings, pottery, woodturning, jewellery, textiles and ironwork, all for sale in a converted barn. There is a coffee shop here too.

EXPLORE BY BIKE
Hopyard Farm
hopyardcycles.co.uk
Govilon, Abergavenny, NP7 9SE
01873 830219

▲ Abergavenny Castle

What are you waiting for? Hire a bike and start exploring the wonderful Welsh countryside.

TAKE A BOAT TRIP
Beacon Park Boats
beaconparkboats.com
The Boathouse, Llanfoist Wharf, NP7 9NG | 01873 858277
Hire a boat and take a punt on the Monmouthshire and Brecon Canal. Full training is given on arrival, so no prior experience is required.

PLAY A ROUND
Monmouthshire Golf Course
monmouthshiregolfclub.co.uk
Gypsy Lane, Llanfoist, NP7 9HE
01873 852606 | Open daily all year
Set in picturesque parkland, this course has several par 3 holes and a testing par 4 at the 15th.

EAT AND DRINK

Angel Hotel ◉

angelabergavenny.com
15 Cross Street, NP7 5EN
01873 857121

In its heyday, this Georgian hotel was a staging post on the Fishguard to London route. It's still a refuge for travellers, although locals flock here too. Eat in the bar or the more formal restaurant.

Clytha Arms

clytha-arms.com
Clytha, NP7 9BW | 01873 840206

Tucked away off the old Abergavenny to Raglan road, this eye-catching converted dower house, standing on the edge of parkland, offers enchanting views over the Vale of Gwent and Blorenge Mountain. The pub is renowned for its range of real ales and wines, and a good selection of artisan ciders and perrys.

Goose and Cuckoo Inn

gooseandcuckoo.com
Upper Llanover, NP7 9ER
01873 880277

Popular with walkers, this friendly, whitewashed pub in the Brecon Beacons National Park has views of the Malvern Hills, traditional flagstones in the bar area and a wood-burning stove. It's the perfect place to sip a pint of Rhymney Bitter or one of the 85 single malt whiskies. All the food is homemade on the Aga by landlady Carol Dollery. There are two beer festivals – in May and August.

The Hardwick ◉◉

thehardwick.co.uk
Old Raglan Road, NP7 9AA
01873 854220

Owner and chef Stephen Terry has gone for the rustic-chic look in terms of decor, and fresh, locally sourced produce for the menu. Be warned, if you're with a large group, service may be a tad slow.

Kings Arms

kingsarmsabergavenny.co.uk
29 Nevill Street, NP7 5AA
01873 855074

This 300-year-old coaching inn has a plaster relief of Charles II's coat of arms on its frontage, and soldiers stationed here in the early 1800s scratched their names on one of the pub beams. Records show the pub has brewed its own ales for at least 150 years.

Llansantffraed Court Hotel ◉◉

llch.co.uk
Old Raglan Road, Llanvihangel Gobion, Clytha, NP7 9BA
01873 840678

This Georgian mansion set in 20 acres of landscaped grounds, has all the comforts of a country house, friendly staff and fine artisan products. The restaurant, situated in the oldest part of the house, is smartly contemporary.

Restaurant 1861 ◉◉

18-61.co.uk
Cross Ash, NP7 8PB

Under the stewardship of Simon and Kate King, this restaurant has become a force to be reckoned with in Monmouthshire. The building was once a pub, and has been made over with a gently contemporary look involving black beams, stone walls, and Welsh slate place mats on bare wooden tables.

Walnut Tree Inn ☺☺☺

thewalnuttreeinn.com
Llandewi Skirrid, NP7 8AW
01873 852797

This simple white-painted inn, located in a hamlet not far from Abergavenny, has been known for excellent food for more than 50 years. With a hero of modern British cooking, Shaun Hill, now in charge, it looks set to continue that way.

▶ PLACES NEARBY

Close to Abergavenny you'll find two of Wales' best attractions – the Big Pit National Coal Mine (see page 97) and the Blaenavon World Heritage Site (see page 96), plus the towns of Crickhowell (see page 155), Monmouth (see page 233) and Usk (see page 315).

5 top pubs for a pint

▶ **Bunch of Grapes** (Ynysangharad Road, Pontypridd, CF37 4DA; 01443 402934) This pub brews its own beers, bakes its own bread and creates unique seasonal food.

▶ **Goose and Cuckoo Inn** (see page 68) A small pub up the mountains – everything is homemade and there's lashings of great real ale.

▶ **Griffin Inn** (Dale, Haverfordwest, SA62 3RB; 01646 636227; griffininndale.co.uk) A traditional seaside pub in Dale, Pemprokeshire, specialising in local seafood and often hosting some wonderful live music.

▶ **The Inn at Penallt** (see page 235) In the beautiful Wye Valley, this award-winning inn is a traditional country pub with a welcoming atmosphere.

▶ **Tafarn Sinc** (see page 273) Welsh-speaking, old-fashioned, sawdust on the floor; this pub is a one-off.

▶ Abergele MAP REF 338 B2

The views are stunning, the sand white and soft, and Abergele itself is a quaint and ancient market town situated between the well-loved holiday resorts of Colwyn Bay (see page 148) and Rhyl (see page 286). Just down the A55 is St Margaret's, the famous 'white marble' church at Bodelwyddan, with its shining white limestone spire – a prominent landmark visible for miles around. But in the summer Abergele and its northern suburb, Pensarn, can become chockablock with portable homes, which park up close to a five-mile stretch of sand and shingle beaches.

HIT THE BEACH
Abergele Beach
A good beach, albeit of the shingle variety, popular with windsurfers and canoeists, and with car parking. There is also a promenade for a bracing walk along the front.

PLAY A ROUND
Abergele Golf Club
abergelegolfclub.co.uk
Tan-y-Gopa Road, LL22 8DS
01745 824034 | Open daily all year
A stunning course with a testing par 4 16th.

EAT AND DRINK
The Kinmel Arms ◉◉
thekinmelarms.co.uk
The Village, St George, LL22 9BP
01745 832207
This stone-built coaching inn occupies a lovely spot in the secluded hamlet of St George, overlooking the north Wales coast, and is a combination of bar, with a wood-burning stove and real ales, and restaurant with rooms. The pub's coastal location determines much of the menu, which majors on local seafood.

▶ Abergynolwyn   MAP REF 333 F5
Lying in southern Gwynedd at the confluence of the Nant Gwernol and the Afon Dysynni, Abergynolwyn was historically known for its slate quarrying. It was founded in the 1860s to house workers at the nearby Bryn Eglwys quarry, and now relies on farming, forestry and tourism. The local Railway Inn is named after the Talyllyn Railway, which once reached into the heart of the village. It now terminates at Nant Gwernol station above the village.

TAKE A TRAIN RIDE
Talyllyn Railway
talyllyn.co.uk
Wharf Station, LL36 9EY
01654 710472 | Opening times vary; call or check website for details
A product of the Industrial Revolution, the narrow-gauge Talyllyn Railway was created in 1865 to carry tons of slate from the local Bryn Eglwys quarry down to the sea at Tywyn, a journey of around seven miles. Although the line closed in 1946 following a series of rock falls, it was reopened a few years later as the Talyllyn Railway Preservation Society. It now carries thousands of passengers every year on a unique trip through the countryside of the beautiful Fathew Valley, stopping at picturesque Dolgoch Falls on the way.

EAT AND DRINK
The Railway Inn
LL36 9YN | 01654 782279
The Railway Inn is known far and wide in this part of Wales as a great, atmospheric pub serving good food. It can get very busy at the bar in summer time when it is besieged by thirsty customers.

▶ Abersoch & St Tudwal Islands MAP REF 332 B3/C3

Found on the south side of the Llyn Peninsula, Abersoch is a former fishing town turned holiday resort, with sandy beaches and a picturesque harbour. You'll be tempted to try out dinghy sailing, windsurfing and jet skiing. In summer, lie back on the sand and count the dotted white sails that fill the bay. Just two miles to the southwest, Porth Neigwl (Hell's Mouth) is one of Wales' best surfing beaches. Abersoch hosts a jazz festival each year in June.

The town also has boat trips to Bardsey Island (see page 61), and to St Tudwal Islands, a pair of small offshore islands bought in 1934 by Clough Williams-Ellis, the creator of Portmeirion, to preserve them from development. St Tudwal was a Breton who studied in Ireland before becoming a hermit on the island in the sixth century. Having prepared himself spiritually, he set out as a missionary for Brittany where he founded a monastery. The ruins of a small medieval priory stand on the more easterly of the St Tudwal Islands.

▼ Harbour in Abersoch

HIT THE BEACH

Abersoch has impressive dunes and lots of sand. There's also a motorboat exclusion zone for bathers and excellent water quality.

LEARN TO SAIL

Abersoch Sailing School

abersochsailingschool.co.uk
Abersoch, LL53 7DP | 07917 525540
Sailing tuition is available or you can hire a dinghy, kayak or pedalo.

SADDLE UP

Cilan Riding Centre

abersochholidays.net
Pwllheli, LL53 7DD | 01758 713276
The centre offers a great way to explore the area.

PLAY A ROUND

Abersoch Golf Club

abersochgolf.co.uk
Golf Road, Abersoch, LL53 7EY
01758 712622 | Opening times vary; call or check website for details

A lovely seaside links, with five parkland holes.

EAT AND DRINK

Porth Tocyn Hotel ◉◉

porthtocynhotel.co.uk
Bwlch Tocyn, LL53 7BU
01758 713303
This hotel was converted from a lowly terrace of lead miners' cottages into the homely, unstuffy country house that you'll find here today. Enjoy spectacular views over Cardigan Bay with the peaks of Snowdonia rising in the distance.

▶ PLACES NEARBY

Go surfing at **Porth Neigwl (Hell's Mouth)**, a southwest-facing rural beach popular with surfers and kayakers because of its wild Atlantic waves. Be warned: bathing can be very dangerous here as there are often strong undertows and cross-currents.

▶ Aberystwyth MAP REF 328 C1

Once known as the fashionable 'Biarritz of Wales', today this seaside town doubles as a lively and cosmopolitan university town. If you fancy a night out on the west coast, this is the town to hit. It's also best for shopping, being the retail hub for many local villages scattered between the mountains and the sea. Known to locals as 'Aber', it's located near to where the rivers Ystwyth and Rheidol join and is really quite isolated, with a largely Welsh-speaking population. Despite this, or because of it, it's exceedingly popular with holidaymakers. While here, you can stroll along its Victorian promenade, a gracefully curving seafront lined with pastel-shaded guest houses and hotels. The seafront ends at Constitution Hill, which can be climbed on foot or travelled more sedately by the Cliff Railway – 'a conveyance of gentle folk since 1896' – the longest electric cliff railway in Britain and the only one of its kind in Wales. It runs

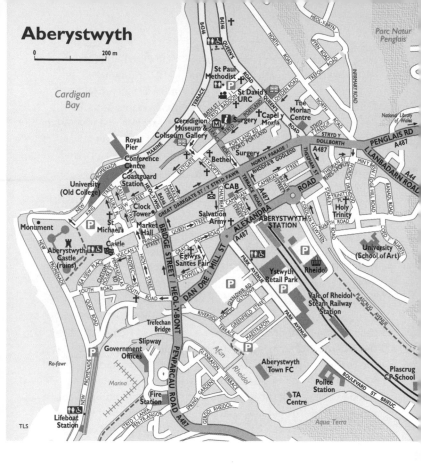

very slowly and gently up a steep gradient to the 430-foot-high summit. At the top is another attraction from the Victorian Age – a recreated camera obscura installed in 1985. Here you can look out over Cardigan Bay and see more than 25 mountain peaks.

As with so many other Welsh towns, Aberystwyth did not escape Edward I's castle-building craze. The now mainly ruined castle was erected in 1277 as part of his impregnable 'iron ring'. In 1404, the town and castle fell to Owain Glyndwr and for a short time Wales' parliament was based here. During the Civil War the castle was wrecked by Oliver Cromwell's forces. It was effectively blown up and left to disintegrate – no longer having any town walls or gates. In terms of other history, the town developed largely as a fishing hub, although lead mining also played a role.

The railway arrived in 1864 and so too did the tourists. Since the late 19th century, Aberystwyth has also been a major Welsh educational centre. Wales' first university opened in a seafront hotel in 1872, with 26 students and a staff of 3. The present university campus is spread out across the hillside above the town and during term time the usual 15,000-strong population of the town swells with an additional 10,000 students.

Nearby is the National Library of Wales, whose unrivalled collection of books and material relating to Wales and the Celtic countries contains venerable manuscripts of early Welsh poetry and laws. Being the largest library in Wales and over 100 years old, it is the country's leading research centre and incredibly popular with those studying family history. Its collections include books, manuscripts, archival documents, maps and photographs, as well as paintings, film, video and sound recordings. Try and catch one of the lectures or screenings that take place throughout the year, or one of the constantly changing exhibitions in the galleries and exhibition halls. The Welsh Language Society has its base in Aberystwyth and the town has played a prominent part in modern-day Welsh patriotism.

If you are here for a few days, next to Aberystwyth Station is the starting point of the narrow-gauge Vale of Rheidol Railway. Opened in 1902 as a narrow-gauge line to serve the lead mines, the timber industry and tourism, it steams its scenic way inland from Aberystwyth to Devil's Bridge. Here is a spectacular wooded gorge with three bridges, one on top of another (legend has it that the lowest one was built with the help of the Devil). The stunning Mynach Falls are also here, tumbling from a great height past the treetops into the depths of the gorge far beneath your feet.

▼ Aberystwyth

TAKE IN SOME HISTORY
Aberystwyth Castle
aberystwyth.com
New Promenade, SY23 2AU
01970 612125
Built in 1277 for Edward I
as part of his 'iron ring', this
castle stands overlooking the
harbour and took 12 years to
build. It was blown up and left
to disintegrate during the Civil
War and remains in much the
same state.

VISIT THE MUSEUMS AND GALLERIES
Ceredigion Museum and Coliseum Gallery
ceredigion.gov.uk
Aberystwyth, SY23 2AQ
01970 633088 | Open Apr–Sep
Mon–Sat 10–5, Oct–Mar 12–4.30
Displays here include the
furniture, archaeology,
agriculture and seafaring and
lead mining industries of the
people of Ceredigion.

National Library of Wales
llgc.org.uk
Penglais, SY23 3BU | 01970 632800
Open Mon–Fri 9.30–6, Sat 9.30–5
This is the place to come to
search through ancient Welsh
documents or trace your family
history. There are free guided
tours on Mondays at 11am and
on Wednesdays at 2.15pm.
Group guided tours available
by prior arrangement.

Oriel y Bont Gallery
orielybont.co.uk
4 Heol y Bont, SY23 1PY
01970 627307 | Open Mon–Fri
10–4.30, Sat 10–5

5 top free days out

▶ **The National Museum & Gallery**, Cardiff page 127

▶ **St Fagans National History Museum**, Cardiff page 294

▶ **National Wool Museum**, Drefach Felindre page 247

▶ **The National Library of Wales**, Aberystwyth see below left

▶ **The National Roman Legion Museum**, Caerleon page 111

Established in 2002, this gallery
and workshop has a great
range of original art, ranging
from the contemporary to the
more traditional.

Aberystwyth Arts Centre
aberystwythartscentre.co.uk
The University of Wales, Penglais
Campus, SY23 3DE
01970 623232 | Call or check
website for details

GET OUTDOORS
Devil's Bridge Falls
devilsbridgefalls.co.uk
Woodlands, Devil's Bridge,
Ceredigion, SY23 3JW
01970 890233
These world-famous falls
have attracted thousands of
visitors since the 18th century,
when Romantic poet William
Wordsworth was duly inspired
to write *To Torrent at the Devil's
Bridge* in its honour. Today the
Falls Nature Trail provides

visitors with a unique opportunity to explore this great natural feature in the Rheidol Gorge on foot.

TAKE A TRAIN RIDE
Vale of Rheidol Railway
rheidolrailway.co.uk
Aberystwyth, SY23 1PG
01970 625819
Catch the steam train from Aberystwyth to Devil's Bridge for a nostalgic experience. The three locomotives were built by the GWR in the mid-1920s.

PLAY A ROUND
Aberystwyth Golf Club
aberystwythgolfclub.com
Brynymor Road, SY23 2HY
01970 615104 | Open daily all year
This is a lovely undulating meadowland course, with testing holes including the 16th (The Loop, par 3), 17th (par 4) and 18th (par 3). There are good views over Cardigan Bay.

EAT AND DRINK
The Glengower Hotel
glengower.co.uk
3 Victoria Terrace, SY23 2DH
01970 626191
Just a stone's throw from the beach, the sun terrace at 'The Glen' – as it's affectionately known by the locals – offers fabulous views across Cardigan Bay where you might be lucky enough to spot one of the friendly local dolphins. This traditional free house serves a wide range of homemade food all day. It also has a good reputation for real ales, including beers from the award-winning North Wales brewery Purple Moose. Look out for the pub's Bank Holiday beer festival in late May.

Matt's Deli
Bow Street, Pendre (Penygarn), SY24 5BQ | 01970 358274
Slightly out of the centre, but well worth a visit, this little deli gets rave reviews. Although unobtrusive and quite small, the food is delicious. Come on a Sunday for a lunch-time roast.

▶ PLACES NEARBY
North of Aberystwyth is Borth, with its rescue zoo – a great place for kids on a rainy day – and a golf course.

Borth Animalarium
animalarium.co.uk
Ynisfergi, Borth, SY24 5NA
01970 871224 | Open Apr–Oct 10–6, Nov–Mar 11–4
This rescue zoo for unwanted animals makes a great family excursion. All kinds of exotic animals live here, including a lynx, meerkats, capuchin monkeys, prairie dogs and hamsters. Many come from other zoos and wildlife parks that could no longer house them, but some come from private owners.

Borth and Ynyslas Golf Club
borthgolf.co.uk
High Street, Borth, SY24 5JS
01970 871202 | Open daily 12–5
This traditional links course with superb scenery provides a tough challenge for players of all standards.

▶ Isle of Anglesey (Ynys Mon)

MAP REF 336 C3

Compared to the wilds of Snowdonia, the view over to Anglesey can look surprisingly flat and uninspiring. Don't be fooled. This island – the largest in England and Wales at 276sq miles – is a visitor's delight where you can enjoy miles of golden beaches and tiny villages. It has a great number of neolithic sites and castles and one of only two Welsh geoparks. Most of all, for a traveller, it feels somewhat off the beaten track and very authentically Welsh, as the language is so commonly spoken.

Historically, it's also this authenticity that's made the island stand out. Indeed, its ancient name is Mon mam Cymru, which means Mother of Wales. Anglesey has always had a spiritual and sacred element. The Celts considered it holy, and the Druids formed a stronghold here, offering human sacrifices during their standoff with the Romans in AD 60. It was the last part of Wales to fall. Whether or not some of the mystique vanished when it was linked to the mainland is debatable, but no one can deny the engineering feat of Thomas Telford's iconic 570-foot suspension bridge, erected in 1826. It has a 98-foot-high central span, allowing the passage of tall ships through the turbulent Menai Strait below. It was joined in 1850 by Robert Stephenson's Britannia Bridge, which carried a railway to mainland north Wales.

▼ Burial chamber at the entrance of Bryn Celli Ddu

Nowadays the island is relatively easy to get around, largely thanks to the new A55 expressway. Once here, you'll probably want to visit Beaumaris and its castle. The town has Anglesey's best infrastructure and services. Two low-key tourist centres can be found at Llanfair PG and Holyhead. It is also famous for its Halen Môn sea salt (halenmon.com).

If you love wildlife, head to South Stack cliffs, where you can see puffins, razorbills, fulmars, guillemots and choughs. Those interested in history should visit the Bronze Age burial mound at Bryn Celli Ddu (east of Llanddaniel Fab), with its stone entrance still intact.

If you want to hike, head to the breezy summit of Holyhead Mountain (708 feet/216m), which is the highest point in Anglesey and capped by an Iron Age fort. Alternatively, you can stroll along the dunes from Newborough Warren, in the southeast of the island, to the peninsula and lighthouse of Llanddwyn Island. Other highlights include Cemaes Bay rock pools, a delight for kids, and the Oyster Catcher restaurant and social enterprise scheme in Rhosneigr.

▼ The Menai Strait

GO BACK IN TIME

Bryn Celli Ddu Burial Chamber

cadw.wales.gov.uk

Nearest town: Llanddaniel Fab, Anglesey, LL61 6DQ

01443 336000

Open daily 10–4

The name of this site means 'the mound in the dark grove' and in neolithic times it was a henge with a stone circle, most likely used to plot the summer solstice. It was plundered in 1699, excavated in 1928 and is now in the hands of Cadw. Visitors can get inside the mound through a stone passage to the burial chamber and see a pillar, and a stone carved with a serpentine design.

10 top places to visit on Anglesey

▶ Bala MAP REF 334 B2

With Llyn Tegid – the largest natural lake in Wales – at its centre, you really won't be able to miss Bala. Here are the stats: it's four miles long, three-quarters of a mile wide and, in places, 140 feet deep. Amazingly, it is still capable of freezing over, most recently in the severe winters of 1947 and 1963. Not surprisingly, it's popular for water sports, especially when strong southwesterly winds whip up the waves into white horses. Anglers also love it here, as pike, perch, roach, trout and salmon are plentiful, but these waters are most famous for a type of freshwater herring called a 'gwyniad', believed to have been trapped here, or so it is believed, since the last ice age.

However, it's the lake's setting that makes it, surrounded as it is by the Aran and Arenig mountains, including Aran Fawddwy. At a mighty 2,969 feet (905m) it's Wales' highest mountain south of Snowdon. Once locals mistakenly believed nearby Cadair Idris to be a few feet higher and, jealous of its popularity, erected a huge cairn to redress the balance.

Venture into town and you'll find a wide main street of austere architecture, camouflaged by the brightly coloured signs of cafes, gift shops and inns. You'll also notice its strong religious roots in its many chapels and statues dedicated to both Dr Lewis Edwards, founder of the Methodist College, and Reverend Thomas Charles, one the founders of the British and Foreign Bible Society. In the 18th century the town was also known for making flannel, stockings and hosiery. The Bala Lake Railway, one of those splendid narrow-gauge steam railways for which the Welsh are justly famous, has its terminus on the south shore of the lake, just over half a mile from the town.

GO ROUND THE GARDENS
Caerau Uchaf Gardens
caerau-gardens.co.uk
Sarnau, Bala, LL23 7LG
01678 530493
Situated at well over 1,000 feet, these are the highest private gardens in Wales that are open to the public.

TAKE A TRAIN RIDE
Bala Lake Railway
bala-lake-railway.co.uk
The Station, LL23 7DD | 01678 540666 | Open Apr–Sep daily; closed certain Mondays & Fridays; call or check website for details Steam locomotives, which once worked in the slate quarries of north Wales, now haul passenger coaches the 4.5 miles from Llanuwchllyn, the railway's main station, along the lake to Bala. Some of the coaches are open so passengers can enjoy the beautiful views of the lake and mountains in all weathers.

GET ON THE WATER
National White Water Centre
ukrafting.co.uk
Frongoch, Bala, LL23 7NU
01678 521083
The Afon Tryweryn runs through Bala and is world famous for its white-water kayaking. Many international kayak and canoe events are held here.

GO FISHING
balaangling.co.uk
Bala and District Angling Association supplies permits on both rivers and lakes for coarse or game fish. Permits are available for a day, week or season; visit website for details.

▲ Boats on Bala Lake

▶ Bangor MAP REF 337 D3

One of the smallest cities in Britain, Bangor is known more for its buzzing university than anything else. In term time, its population of 12,000 swells with around 10,000 students. Old Bangor is a maze of streets leading down to the sea. Gwynedd Museum and Art Gallery can be found in town, and contains many culturally important artefacts and modern exhibitions.

Despite its great location on the Menai Strait, you might be less than impressed when you arrive – but although some say the centre has been destroyed by the soulless Deiniol shopping centre, the city has some appeal and is a useful transport hub, connecting people to Snowdonia and Anglesey.

Built in 1896 and stretching 1,476 feet out into the Menai Strait, the Victorian pier is popular for a stroll. Three miles east is the spectacular Penrhyn Castle, which despite having the appearance of an authentic Norman fortress was actually built in the early 19th century as a sumptuous family home.

TAKE IN SOME HISTORY
Bangor Cathedral
bangor.churchinwales.org.uk
LL57 1LH | 01248 353983
Open Mon–Fri 9–4.30, Sat 10.30–1
This ancient cathedral occupies one of the oldest ecclesiastical sites in Britain. It was founded in AD 530 by St Deiniol, who enclosed the sacred site inside a fence constructed by driving poles into the ground and weaving twigs and branches between them. The Welsh term

for this type of fence was 'bangor' – which is how the city got its name. The cathedral's earliest remains are from the 12th century, but these were largely destroyed during the Glyndwr rebellion and subsequent civil war. Much of today's architecture dates from the 19th-century reconstruction that was overseen by renowned architect Sir George Gilbert Scott. The tranquil site also has a small shop and exhibition centre.

Penrhyn Castle

nationaltrust.org.uk
LL57 4HT | 01248 353084
Open March–Nov; times vary, call or check website for details
Located in some of Wales' most picturesque countryside, this 19th-century neo-Norman castle resembles a large, sumptuous manor house. The architect behind it, Thomas Hopper, designed the imaginative fantasy structure for George Dawkins Pennant, a local slate-quarry owner, whose family made their fortune from Welsh slate and Jamaican sugar. Notable rooms include the Great Hall, which is heated by hot air, and the library with its heavily decorated ceiling. The grand staircase is quite startling in both its proportions – three storeys high – and its cathedral-like structure of lofty arches, carved stonework and stained glass. There is an industrial railway museum in the courtyard, a model railway museum and a doll museum. The whole ensemble is set in 40 acres of beautiful grounds between Snowdonia and the Menai Strait, overlooking the north Wales coast.

VISIT THE MUSEUM AND GALLERY
Gwynedd Museum and Art Gallery

gwynedd.gov.uk
LL57 1DT | 01248 353368
Open Tue–Sat; times vary, call or check website for details
This unique collection reflects the history of north Wales, paying particular attention to the Welsh identity and culture from the 18th century to the present day. A changing programme of arts and crafts, including works by local artists, touring exhibitions and historical displays, keeps the collections fresh and exciting. There's also a craft shop selling handmade jewellery, ceramics and glassware.

PLAY A ROUND
St Deiniol Golf Club

bangorgolf.co.uk
Bangor St Deiniol, Penybryn,
LL57 1PX | 01248 353098
Open daily all year; call or check website for details
This is a superb 18-hole, championship-standard golf course, but watch out for the tricky fourth hole. Founded in 1906, the club features a number of events throughout the year. The bar and restaurant both have great views of the Snowdonia ranges.

▶ Bardsey Island MAP REF 332 A3
see **Aberdaron & Bardsey Island,** page 61

▶ Barmouth MAP REF 333 E4

In summer, this Victorian seaside resort is heavily infiltrated by those seeking sun, sand and fun. Dodgem cars, funfair rides and chip shops all come alive to cater for its visitors – a Welsh Blackpool in miniature, if you like (though without the stomach-churning rollercoasters).

In the town, you can explore a web of stairs and alleyways leading up from the High Street to the old town, which is built haphazardly up the cliffs. Further up is Dinas Oleu (the Fortress of Light), the first property ever bequeathed to the National Trust, in 1895.

Whatever you think of the town, Barmouth is blessed with some wonderful sands. It's a blue-flag beach, meaning you can enjoy swimming or surfing in the waters. Across the Mawddach Estuary, Fairbourne also holds blue-flag status. This estuary boasts Wales' only surviving wooden rail viaduct, which has a handy pedestrian walkway alongside it. Behind the resort lies the Rhinogydd mountain range, where you can hike through some of the finest landscapes in Wales.

HIT THE BEACH

Barmouth has a sandy beach with blue-flag waters. South of the Mawddach Estuary is Fairbourne, a pebble-and-sand beach, ideal for swimming.

CATCH A PERFORMANCE
Dragon Theatre
dragontheatre.co.uk
Jubilee Road, LL42 1EF
01341 281697

LEARN TO SAIL
Merioneth Yacht Club
merionethyachtclub.co.uk
The Quay, Barmouth, LL42 1HB
01341 280000
The mainly southerly winds provide excellent sailing conditions. There is also a Celtic longboat rowing section.

▶ PLACES NEARBY
At Fairbourne you'll find a pony trekking centre and a fun steam railway.

Bwlchgwyn Farm Pony Trekking Centre
bwlchgwynfarm.co.uk
Fairbourne, LL39 1BX
01341 250107
Enjoy a horse ride along the gorgeous sands at Fairbourne.

Fairbourne Railway
fairbournerailway.com
Beach Road, LL38 2EX
01341 250362 | Open daily Feb–Oct; closed Mon and Fri term time; call or check website for details
This fantastic small steam train travels along the 2.5-mile coastal stretch at Fairbourne.

▶ Barry MAP REF 326 B6

'Oh, what's occurin?' If you were a fan of the TV sitcom *Gavin & Stacey*, chances are you'll have heard of Barry. This town, seven miles from Cardiff, was once one of the biggest ports in the world, established specifically to serve the nearby coalfields. Those living in the mining towns also became frequent visitors to this seaside town. You can still come here for the sand – although the beach is not a patch on many of the other Welsh beaches. You can also explore the amusingly named Barry Island Pleasure Park. Technically, Barry Island doesn't exist any more. It was joined to the mainland by a causeway in the 1880s.

ENTERTAIN THE FAMILY
Welsh Hawking Centre
welsh-hawking.co.uk
Weycock Road, CF62 3AA
01446 734687 | Open Wed–Mon 10.30–5
Be amazed by the speed of graceful falcons and the silent flight of an owl at this top hawking centre. In total, there are more than 200 birds of prey here, including eagles, hawks, owls, buzzards and falcons. The daily flying displays are hugely popular; you may even be able to get involved and have one of the birds land on your gloved hand. For the more timid, there are plenty of friendly tame animals to admire, including guinea pigs, horses and rabbits. The centre is situated in 20 acres of scenic Welsh parkland with ample parking.

GET OUTDOORS
Porthkerry Park
valeofglamorgan.gov.uk
Park Road, Barry CF62 3BY
01446 733589 | Open daily all year
This parkland contains 220 acres of woodland and meadows, leading down to a sheltered pebble beach and spectacular cliffs. Picnic sites, nature trails, a forest cafe and adventure playground add to the appeal.

PLAY A ROUND
Brynhill Golf Club
brynhillgolfclub.co.uk
Port Road, CF62 8PN
01446 720277 | Open Mon–Fri and Sat pm all year
This course is known for its prevailing west wind.

▼ Whitemore Bay, Barry Island

RAF St Athan Golf Club

rafstathangc.co.uk
Clive Road, St Athan, CF62 4JD
01446 751043 | Open daily all year
If you like your golf with the
added challenge of low-flying
jets, you'll enjoy playing a
round here. It's also a very tight
course with lots of trees.

St Andrews Major Golf Club

standrewsmajorgolfclub.com
Coldbrook Road East, Cadoxton,
CF63 1BL | 01446 722227
Contact club for opening times
A scenic, 18-hole parkland
course suitable for golfers
of all abilities.

EAT AND DRINK

Blue Anchor Inn

blueanchoraberthaw.com
East Aberthaw, CF62 3DD
01446 750329
This pretty, stone-built inn
has been trading almost
continuously since 1380, the
only break being in 2004 when
a serious fire destroyed the
top half of the building, forcing
its closure for restoration. The
interior is warmly traditional
and there's a selection of real
ales on tap. The food comes
highly recommended and you
can choose to eat in the bar
or restaurant.

▸ **PLACES NEARBY**

Close to Barry are wonderful
gardens in the little village of
Dyffryn, a castle near the
market town of Cowbridge, the
seaside town of Penarth (see
page 262) and the capital city
of Cardiff (see page 122).

10 top movies and TV shows filmed in Wales

▸ *Being Human*; 2011–2013
▸ *Clash of the Titans*; 2010
▸ *Die Another Day*; 2002
▸ *Doctor Who*; 2004–present
▸ *The Edge Of Love*; 2008
▸ *Gavin and Stacey*; 2007–2010
▸ *Harry Potter and the Deathly Hallows*; 2007
▸ *Merlin*; 2008–2012
▸ *Robin Hood*; 2010
▸ *Torchwood*; 2006–2011

Dyffryn Gardens

nationaltrust.org.uk
St Nicholas, CF5 6SU
029 2059 3328 | Open Apr–Oct
daily 10–6, Nov–Feb 10–4
Just to the west of Cardiff,
these Grade I-listed gardens
offer an outstanding example
of Edwardian garden design.
Covering more than 55 acres,
they feature formal lawns,
seasonal bedding plants and an
arboretum with trees from all
over the world. Within the
gardens lies Dyffryn House;
dating originally from the late
Edwardian times, it's now kitted
out in Victorian splendour and
open to the public. Thomas
Mawson, the leading landscape
architect of his generation,
designed the gardens between
1906 and 1914, commissioned
by visionary John Cory and his
son Reginald. Key sights
include the Pompeian Garden
with its impressive collection of
statuary and plants from South

Africa, China and Japan. Today, this early interest is reflected in the many impressive oriental trees and shrubs. In front of the house is a stunning water lily canal, surrounded by a great lawn. To the west is a series of garden rooms enclosed by yew hedges, each one with a different theme, such as the Roman garden and fuchsia garden. Beyond, winding walks lead through the informal west garden, where magnolias offer a magnificent display in spring and early summer. In its heyday the walled garden would have played a vital part in the daily life of the household, supplying exotic fruit, vegetables and flowers, but it fell into disrepair and was not accessible to the public for many years. An ambitious restoration scheme has brought this site back to life. About a quarter of the area is taken up by two new glasshouses, producing heritage fruit and vegetables in one and exotic plants, including cacti and rare orchids in the other. This garden is truly a feast for the senses.

Old Beaupre Castle
cadw.wales.gov.uk
St Hilary, Cowbridge, CF71 7LT
01443 336000 | Open daily 10–4
This ruined manor house was built around 1300 and remodelled during the 16th century to include the addition of the impressive gatehouse and porch.

▶ Beaumaris MAP REF 337 D3

One of the most beautiful of Edward I's masterpieces, moated Beaumaris Castle on Anglesey was built in the late 13th century to guard the approaches to the Menai Strait. The concentric walls with their circular towers were never completed to their full height, and the castle never saw military action. You can't help but be impressed by the great hall and chapel in the central tower. You can also enjoy the town's history with such attractions as the former gaol and courthouse, where you can see the grim cells and foreboding 19th-century courtroom.

TAKE IN SOME HISTORY
Beaumaris Castle
see highlight panel opposite

Beaumaris Gaol and Courthouse
visitanglesey.co.uk
Steeple Lane, LL58 8EP
01248 810921 | Open Easter–Sep
Sat–Thu 10.30–5

This may sound dry but it's actually a really interesting place to visit. It gives a fascinating insight into the world of Victorian prisoners. An audio tour dishes the dirt on how the courthouse and gaol operated, and gives authentic insight into social and judicial history, as well as the cases of

▶ Beaumaris Castle MAP REF 337 D3

cadw.wales.gov.uk

LL58 8AP | 01248 810361 | Open Mar–Jun daily 9.30–5, Jul–Aug 9.30–6,
Sep–Oct 9.30–5, Nov–Feb Mon–Sat 10–4, Sun 11–4

Sitting majestically on the shores of the Menai Strait, looking
from the island of Anglesey across to mainland Wales, this
powerful castle took more than 35 years to build, and even so
was never finished completely. It was the last of an ambitious
series of fortifications built by Edward I following his conquest of
Wales. Building began in 1295 with the construction of a wide
moat, high walls and strong towers. In the inner ring, two
massive twin-towered gatehouses were built, while the outer
ring comprised a wall 27 feet high, bristling with defensive
towers and its own protected dock. The rooms were furnished to
the highest standards and the whole thing thought impregnable.
However, this was never put to the test, and no siege machines
or artillery have ever been fired at or from its walls. Less than
20 years after building work stopped on the unfinished castle,
there were reports that it was already falling into decay.

real people. You can walk the dimly lit corridors and explore the cells.

TAKE A BOAT TRIP
Starida Sea Services
starida.co.uk
Little Bryn, Beaumaris, LL58 8BS
01248 810379
Head out from the Starida kiosk by Beaumaris Pier into the Menai Strait or to Puffin Island – a bird sanctuary and seal colony haven.

PLAY A ROUND
Henllys Golf Club
henllysgolfclub.co.uk
Henllys Hall, LL58 8HU
01248 811717 | Open daily all year
A mature parkland course with natural water hazards.

EAT AND DRINK
Bishopsgate House Hotel ◉
bishopsgatehotel.co.uk
54 Castle Street, LL58 8BB
01248 810302
This Georgian town house with its cheery mint-green facade looks out from the Beaumaris waterfront over the Menai Strait. The restaurant is full of old-world charm and enjoys a strong following with locals who come for the kitchen's quietly confident cooking, as well as a healthy showing of top-class local produce.

Ye Olde Bulls Head Inn ◉◉◉
bullsheadinn.co.uk
Castle Street, LL58 8AP
01248 810329
This 15th-century pub began life as a staging post and inn on the main route to Ireland, a stone's throw from the gates of Beaumaris' medieval castle. The bar takes you back to Dickensian times (in fact Charles Dickens himself stayed here), with antique furnishings, settles and artefacts on display, including the town's old ducking stool. The menu is exceptional and you can choose to eat in the brasserie or the restaurant, or simply enjoy one of the quality cask ales or a glass of champagne in the bar. Accommodation is available.

▸ PLACES NEARBY
Just a 20-minute drive from Beaumaris is Red Wharf Bay (see page 279). Further afield is Llanfair PG (see page 208).

▸ Beddgelert MAP REF 337 D5
This town is all about location, location, location. Tucked away between the Glaslyn and Colwyn valleys, Beddgelert is surrounded by wooded lower crags, rocky slopes, mountain lakes and the bluffs of Snowdon. The centrepiece of the village is a pretty twin-arched stone bridge over the lively Glaslyn River. Huddled around the bridge are stone-built cottages, inns, craft shops and cafes. It's so picturesque, Hollywood chose to shoot Ingrid Bergman's film *The Inn of the Sixth Happiness* here in the 1950s.

Beddgelert, which means 'Gelert's grave', takes its name from the Celtic saint Kelert. Some tourist literature would have you believe that Gelert was Llywelyn the Great's faithful dog, killed by his master, who mistakenly believed it had butchered his child. It seems, however, that the myth and the building of the grave were ploys by David Pritchard, the first landlord of the Royal Goat Hotel, built in 1803, to bring more visitors to his new establishment. To the north of the town is the Sygun Copper Mine, known as one of the wonders of Wales. To the south of the village, on the Aberglaslyn Pass and close to the Welsh Highland Railway track, 700-foot cliffs form a cavernous rocky gorge, through which the waters of the Glaslyn transform into violent white torrents. There's an adventurous riverside path here, from which you can see the water in all its glory.

GET INDUSTRIAL
Sygun Copper Mine
syguncoppermine.co.uk
LL55 4NE | 01766 890595
Open Mar–Oct 9.30–5, 27 Dec–2 Jan, Feb half-term holiday 10–4
Discover a spectacular audio-visual underground experience where you can explore the workings of this 19th-century copper mine and see the magnificent stalactite and stalagmite formations. Other activities include panning for gold, metal detecting and a children's playground. Marvel at the fantastic coin collection spanning the eras from Julius Caesar to Queen Elizabeth II, and visit the Time-Line Museum with Bronze Age and Roman artefacts.

EAT AND DRINK
Lyn's Café and Tea Garden
Church Street, Beddgelert, LL55 4YA | 01766 890374
Sited by the River Colwyn in Beddgelert, this cosy cafe has a splendid riverside garden where you can relax with a coffee or tea. Or choose from a menu of snacks, light meals and lunches, clotted cream teas and evening meals. The cafe is licensed in the evening, when a different atmosphere ensues.

Tanronnen Inn
tanronnen.co.uk
Beddgelert, LL55 4YB
01766 890347
Originally part of the Beddgelert Estate, this stone-built building, dating from 1809, was originally the stables for the passing coach trade. It opened as a beer house in 1830. The inn we see today has two attractive small bars serving Robinsons Ales, a large lounge with a roaring open fire, a dining room open to non-residents, serving home-cooked meals, and some overnight accommodation.

▶ PLACES NEARBY
Beddgelert is in the heart of the Snowdonia National Park (see page 299), and near Blaenau Ffestiniog (see page 94).

▶ Benllech MAP REF 336 C2

Benllech is a modern resort on Anglesey where you can enjoy a superb sandy beach with some decent cafes and facilities. You can also take a short walk southwards on the coastal path to Red Wharf Bay, where there's a huge expanse of sand, tidal mud and salt marshes stretching for 2.5 miles to Llandonna. The bay is absolutely superb for walking and birding – you'll more than likely spot redshanks, curlews, shelducks and oystercatchers. Anglesey's best pub, The Ship Inn (see Red Wharf Bay, page 279), and the best restaurant, The Old Boat House, are also here.

Close to Benllech is Red Wharf Bay (see page 279) and the pretty fishing village of Moelfre (see page 230).

▶ Betws-y-Coed MAP REF 337 F5

Betws-y-Coed, pronounced 'betoose ee koyd', is the most popular of all Snowdonia's inland resorts and the natural base for exploring the national park. Sheltered by the enormous Gwydir hillside forests and sited near the junction of three rivers – the Conwy, Lledr and Llugwy – it was built mostly in Victorian times when an artist colony set up here, attracted by the natural beauty. Some parts are older, and you might want to check out the 14th-century Church of St Michael's, one of the oldest in Wales. There's a museum at the railway station, which dates from 1868, boasting a miniature railway, shop and restaurant. The main street, Holyhead Road, has an excellent range of pubs and B&Bs. You'll see plenty of hikers in their wet-weather gear checking out the specialist outdoor shops. You can happily while away a few hours here picking up bargains. The tourist centre provides maps and advice on day trips in the area. Activities are best organised through the Plas y Brenin National Mountain Centre.

While here, you can also visit the cascading waterfalls – one flows beneath the Pont-y-Pair Bridge, which was built in 1468 at the heart of the town. Lying two miles west up the road, the Swallow Falls, best viewed from the north bank of the Llugwy, is another spectacular torrent. The Conwy Falls at the Penmachno end of the town are accessed from the car park of the Otter Restaurant and Café.

Betws-y-Coed also has great bridges. A mile or so away on the road to Capel Curig is the Miner's Bridge, where the miners crossed the river on a steep ladder to their work. Then there's Thomas Telford's iron Waterloo Bridge, built in 1815, which carries the A5 across the River Conwy. The town is also a great starting place for walks into the countryside.

TAKE IN SOME HISTORY
Ty Mawr Wybrnant
nationaltrust.org.uk

LL25 0HJ | 01690 760213

Opening times vary; call or check website for details

Ty Mawr was the birthplace of Bishop William Morgan (1545–1604), the first translator of the Bible into Welsh. This first edition appeared in 1588, before the King James Bible, with a revised version published in 1620. It is this later version that continues to be used in Wales today. The house has been restored to give an idea of its 16th-century appearance. The Wybrnant Nature Trail, a short walk, goes on for a mile.

VISIT THE MUSEUM
Conwy Valley Railway Museum
conwyrailwaymuseum.co.uk

Old Goods Yard, LL24 0AL | 01690 710568 | Open daily 10–5.30

The two museum buildings here have displays on the narrow- and standard-gauge railways of north Wales, railway stock and other memorabilia. There are working model railway layouts, a steam-hauled miniature railway in the grounds, and a 15-inch-gauge tramway to the woods. The quarter-size steam *Britannia* loco is also on display.

WALK THE HIGH ROPES
Tree Top Adventure
Llanrwst Road, LL24 0HA

ttadventure.co.uk

01690 710914 | Open spring, summer and autumn daily 9–4; winter 10–3

5 top steam railway trips in Wales

▶ **Brecon Mountain Railway,** Mid Wales page 228

▶ **Ffestiniog Welsh Highland Railways,** Snowdonia page 269

▶ **Gwili Steam Railway,** Carmarthenshire

▶ **Snowdon Mountain Railway,** Snowdonia page 196

▶ **Vale of Rheidol Railway,** Ceredigion page 76

Tree Top Adventure is home to the UK's premier high ropes course. It has the Skyride, Europe's highest and first five-seater Giant Swing, plus the Power-Fan plummet, the world's highest powerfan parachute simulator. There are also plenty of tree-top ropes courses for the kids.

EXPLORE BY BIKE
Beics Betws
bikewales.co.uk

Heol y Ficerdy, LL24 0AD

01690 710766 | Call or check website for details

Cycle through the Gwydyr Forest, taking any of the forestry tracks, miner's tracks or byway routes.

Plas y Brenin
pyb.co.uk

Capel Curig, LL24 0ET

01690 720214

This outdoors centre offers a range of courses in climbing, kayaking and mountain biking.

PLAY A ROUND

Betws-y-Coed Golf Club

betws-y-coedgolfclub.co.uk
LL24 0AL | 01690 710556
Contact club for opening times
An attractive course set
between two rivers with
stunning views of the Snowdon
mountain range; known as the
Jewel of the Nines.

EAT AND DRINK

Craig-y-Dderwen Riverside Hotel

snowdoniahotel.com
Betws-y-Coed, LL24 0AS
01690 710293
Built in the 1890s for an
industrialist, the partly
timbered house became a
favourite bolt-hole, and perhaps
inspiration too, for Sir Edward
Elgar. A hotel since the 1920s, it
has been carefully restored to
offer the full country-house
package, complete with
conservatory dining room views
of a riverside teeming with
wildlife (make a point of looking
out for the otters).

Llugwy River Restaurant@ Royal Oak Hotel ◉

royaloakhotel.net
Holyhead Road, Betws-y-Coed,
LL24 0AY | 01690 710219
The Royal Oak Hotel is the
tourist honeypot of Betws-y-
Coed, where ambling day
trippers and hardy hikers come
for refuelling. After a thorough
facelift, the Victorian coaching
inn now has a clean,
contemporary interior. The
kitchen staunchly supports
local suppliers and the concise
menu buzzes with interest,
including Eastern influences.
Game features in season.

Pinnacle Café

Capel Curig, LL24 0EN
01690 720201
This walkers' and climbers' cafe
serves good grub, including
all-day breakfasts, tea and hot
chocolate, jacket potatoes and
cakes. It's ideal for big pre-walk
or after-walk appetites. Next
to the cafe is a shop selling
food, drink, clothing and
walking supplies.

Ty Gwyn Inn

Betws-y-Coed, LL24 OSG
01690 710383
Located on the old London to
Holyhead road, the Ty Gwyn was
welcoming travellers long
before Thomas Telford built his
impressive cast iron Waterloo
Bridge over the River Conwy in
1815. Much of the original
17th-century character is
evident inside. The Ratcliffe
family has owned and run this
former coaching for the past
29 years. Real ales come from
as near as Conwy's Great Orme
brewery, as well as from much
further afield. The cooking
relies heavily on quality local
produce, including fresh
home-grown vegetables.

▸ **PLACES NEARBY**

The many attractions of
Snowdonia National Park (see
page 299) are close by, along
with Gwydyr Stables and the
delightful Swallow Falls, near
Betwys-y-Coed.

Gwydyr Stables

horse-riding-wales.co.uk
Ty Coch Farm, Penmachno,
near Betws-y-Coed | LL25 0HJ
01690 760248 | Open all year. Call
or check website for details
Horse-riding, pony trekking or
extended day trail rides.

Swallow Falls

Swallow Falls, near Betws-y-
Coed, is the most renowned
and popular display of natural water power to be found in
Snowdonia. Here, the beautiful
Afon Llugwy rages down from
the mountains through granite
chasms until il smashes
against the jagged rocks and
cascades between thickly
wooded banks to reach the
tranquil pool below. It's a
dramatic and unforgettable
sight for any visitor, where the
noise and the spray of the water
add to the experience.

▼ Swallow Falls

▶ Blaenau Ffestiniog MAP REF 337 E6

Arrive at Blaenau Ffestiniog in Snowdonia and you could be forgiven for thinking you were seeing nothing but slate. The houses are built from it, they're roofed with it and gardens and backyards are piled up with it. On a rainy day, the sky is also the same colour.

Locals don't mind though. Slate is Blaenau's heritage and they're proud of it. It's been mined and quarried from the Moelwyn and Manod mountains lying on either side of the town for two centuries. Its ghostly relics are still very much around. In nearby Cwmorthin you can take a track beneath the Moelwyn crags past a forlorn-looking lake into a valley devastated by quarries and mines. There you can still see rusting pulley wheels and the bogies of the old slate carts.

In recent years the town centre has been regenerated to create a decent shopping experience. A new bus station has been built along with new areas that allow visitors to sit back and enjoy the mountains that pop into view when the clouds lift. Slate is now being used to decorate the town and several structures have been engraved with poetry. Local sayings have also been engraved on slate set into the pavements throughout the centre of town.

Various walkways have been installed in the nearby forest, as well as a series of downhill mountain-bike trails. In 2014, Zip World also opened, offering a thrill similar to that already found in nearby Bethesda. If plans go ahead Blaenau Ffestiniog will also have the UK's first vélo-rail, popular in France.

▼ Ffestiniog Railway

GO UNDERGROUND
Llechwedd Slate Caverns
llechwedd-slate-caverns.co.uk
LL41 3NB | 01766 830306
Opening times vary; call or check
website for details
This is truly an adventure into
history. Take a guided tour on
the Miners' Tramway and
experience the life of the
Victorian quarrymen. Or travel
into the deep mine, where a
25-minute underground walk
reveals the social conditions in
which the miners lived as told
by 'the ghost of a Victorian
miner'. Recreated Victorian
shops, plus a licensed
restaurant and a pub complete
the experience.

SADDLE UP
E Prichard Pony
Trekking Centre
Felen Rhyd Fach, Maentwrog,
LL41 4HY | 01766 590231
The perfect way to enjoy
the fantastic scenery is
on horseback.

ZIP OVER A MOUNTAIN
Zip World Titan
zipworld.co.uk; bouncebelow.net
Llechwedd Slate Caverns, LL41 3NB
01248 601444
If you like speed and adrenalin,
you will love Europe's only
four-person zip line where you
can reach speeds of up to
70mph. Opened in 2014, and
known as Titan, it offers three
individual zip lines to complete.
The first gives panoramic views
of Snowdonia, the second is the
quickest line and has a huge
drop of 500 feet, while the third
finishes at the top of the hill,
overlooking Blaenau Ffestiniog.
It's run by the same company
that opened Zip World Velocity
in Penrhyn Quarry, Bethesda
in 2013.

▶ PLACES NEARBY
Blaenau Ffestiniog is in
the heart of the beautiful
Snowdonia National Park
(see page 299), and also close
to Beddgelert (see page 88).

▶ Blaenavon World Heritage Site

MAP REF 326 C2

Designated a UNESCO World Heritage Site in 2000, this town is renowned for its cultural significance and industrial heritage. Lying in southeastern Wales, at the source of the Afon Lwyd, it's set high on a hillside and has a population of around 6,349 – although at the height of its industrial prowess, this was more like 20,000. It grew up around an ironworks, opened in 1788, part of which is now a museum. The steel-making and coal-mining industries followed. The ironworks closed in 1900, and the coalmine in 1980, since when it has become a significant tourist attraction.

If you wish to learn about the industries that took place here, there are two main focus points. The first is the Big Pit National Coal Museum and the second is Blaenavon Ironworks. Big Pit is a genuine coalmine and one of Britain's leading mining museums. The biggest draw is going 300 feet underground with a miner to see what life was like for the thousands of men who worked on the coalface. On the surface you can also visit the colliery buildings, pithead baths and smithy. The ironworks – the setting of the award-winning BBC television series *Coal House* – is the best preserved blast furnace complex of its period and one of the most important monuments to have survived from the early part of the Industrial Revolution. During its heyday in the early 19th century, it was one of the biggest producers of iron in the world. Today you can view the extensive remains of the blast furnaces, the cast houses and the impressively restored water balance tower. Through exhibitions and reconstructions you can also learn about the international significance of the iron industry and the scientific processes involved in the production of iron. You can also build a picture of the social history of the time by viewing the reconstructed shop and row of workers' cottages.

In the town itself, you can also visit the Pontypool and Blaenavon Railway, the Blaenavon Male Voice Choir and many historical walks through Blaenavon's mountains. There you will most likely see red kites and paragliders, all enjoying the thermals. The people are friendly – many who live here today had ancestors who helped build this community.

GET INDUSTRIAL
Big Pit National Coal Museum
museumwales.ac.uk
NP4 9XP | 029 2057 3650
Open all year 9.30–5 (times vary in winter); call for underground guide tour availability
The UK's leading mining museum celebrated its 30th anniversary in 2013. The colliery was the workplace for hundreds of men, women and children for more than 200 years. The coal was used in furnaces and to light household fires across the world.

Blaenavon Ironworks
cadw.wales.gov.uk
North Street, NP4 9RN
01495 792615 | Open Apr–Oct daily 10–5; times vary in winter, call or check website for details
The Blaenavon Ironworks were a milestone in the history of the Industrial Revolution. Constructed between 1788 and 1799, they were the first purpose-built, multi-furnace ironworks in Wales. By 1796, Blaenavon was the second largest ironworks in Wales, eventually closing down in 1904.

Blaenavon World Heritage Centre
visitblaenavon.co.uk
Church Road, NP4 9AS
01495 742333 | Open all year Tue–Sun 9–5 and BHs.
Closed Xmas to New Year
The best starting point to any visit to Blaenavon is the centre, which provides an overview of how this industrial landscape became globally important. Traditional displays and modern videos illustrate the area's extraordinary history, focusing on a range of topics, including standards of living, geology and transport systems. Local artists and photographers frequently display their work in the changing exhibitions.

TAKE A TRAIN RIDE
Pontypool and Blaenavon Railway
pontypool-and-blaenavon.co.uk
NP4 9ND | 01495 792263
Call or check website for directions and opening hours
Take a trip along the Pontypool and Blaenavon Railway line, which used to haul coal and passengers up and down this prolific and historic valley.

INDULGE YOURSELF
Blaenavon Cheddar Company
chunkofcheese.co.uk
80 Broad Street, NP4 9NF
01495 793123
Here you'll find a range of handmade cheeses, some of which are matured down the Big Pit mineshaft. The staff also arranges guided walking and mountain bike tours.

EAT AND DRINK
Heritage Café
Church Road, NP4 9AS
01495 742339
This cafe at the Blaenavon World Heritage Centre offers hot meals, cakes and drinks, overlooking a mine, churchyard and miners' houses. In summer there are picnic tables.

▶ **Bodelwyddan Castle** MAP REF 338 B2

bodelwyddan-castle.co.uk

Bodelwyddan, LL18 5YA | 01745 584060 | Opening times vary;
call or check website for details

Set in 260 acres of magnificent parkland in Denbighshire, north Wales, this 19th-century mock castle, complete with turrets and battlements, is the Welsh headquarters of the National Portrait Gallery. It houses a large collection of Victorian portraits, including Victorian portraiture photographs. Interactive displays show how portraits were produced and used in the Victorian era. The Castle Gallery has a programme of temporary exhibitions and events, and there are large areas of formal garden and natural woodland. Imagine you're back in World War I and have a go in the practise trenches. Perfect for the whole family, it also has an adventure playground, garden maze, Victorian games room, old sweet shop and cafe.

Close to Bodelwyddan Castle is the summer tourist hotspot of Abergele (see page 69).

▼ Bodelwyddan Castle

▶ Bodnant Garden
see highlight panel overleaf

▶ Bosherston   MAP REF 323 D6

If you like Monet, you'll love Bosherston. The picturesque village is known for its lily ponds, or lakes. These were formed by the Stackpole Estate in three narrow limestone valleys in the late 18th and early 19th centuries, and are protected today as a National Nature Reserve. You reach them by crossing raised causeways. The lakes also support rare freshwater plants and a healthy population of otters, which feed on the eels, pike, perch, roach and tench that live in the lake. If you want to spot one, be aware: you may have to share your hide with one or more professional wildlife photographers, their long lenses trained on the water. Bats live here too, hunting for insects over the water, as do more than 20 species of dragon and damselfly. Breeding birds include herons, kingfishers, little grebes and moorhens while a dozen types of duck spend the winter on the lakes. Bosherton comprises a section of the Pembrokeshire Coast Path, which takes an inland detour here to avoid the army range. Southeast of Bosherston is a wonderful secluded beach at Barafundle Bay, which is well worth the walk. If the nature isn't tranquil enough, why not look around the Norman church of St Michael's – it has a fine medieval cross in the churchyard.

GET OUTDOORS

The excellent footpath network around Bosherton Lakes ensures you can enjoy the area at any time of year. A short circular route from Bosherston car park takes in the water lilies, which are at their best in June and July.

Stack Rocks and the Green Bridge of Wales

pembrokeshirecoast.org.uk

Probably the most photographed feature on the Pembrokeshire coastline is the Green Bridge of Wales (Pen-y-Holt), a huge natural arch formed by the collapsing of two coastal caverns. It can be viewed from the safe platform on Stack Rocks, also known as Elegug Stacks, after the Welsh word for guillemots. It's on military land and accessible only through organised walks run by the Pembrokeshire Coast National Park Authority.

HIT THE BEACH

Barafundle is regularly voted among the top beaches in the world for its great quality sand and water. It's a 10-minute walk from Stackpole Quay. Freshwater West, six miles west of the Stackpole Estate, is a great surf beach.

▶ Bodnant Garden MAP REF 337 F3

nationaltrust.org.uk
Conwy LL28 5RE | 01492 650460 | Opening times vary;
call or check website for details

Set high above the River Conwy, with spectacular views over the
magnificent Snowdonia range, Bodnant is considered by many
people to be the finest garden in Britain. It's famous for its
collections of rhododendrons, camellias and magnolias, which in
the spring and early summer create a dazzling kaleidoscope of
colour. In early summer there's also a long tunnel cascading with
laburnum racemes, and the Lily Terrace Pond, studded with many
rare water lilies. Bodnant may have initially been established in
1875, with the planting of conifers by wealthy industrialist chemist
Henry Pochin, but it was his daughter, the first Lady Aberconway,
who really extended it to include herbaceous borders and shrubs,
as well as trees. In 1949, the second Lord Aberconway gave the 80
acres to the National Trust. If you've only got a short amount of
time hit the Rose Terrace, offering what is probably the finest view
in the gardens, and the Croquet Terrace, which boasts a wisteria-
clothed fountain.

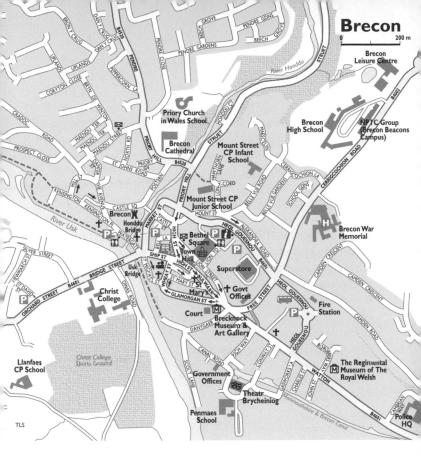

▶ Brecon MAP REF 330 C6

Brecon is a traditional mid-Wales' market town nestling in the foothills of the Brecon Beacons National Park in Powys. Found at the junction of two rivers, the Usk and the Honddu, it's always been a popular destination, largely due to its closeness to the national park. Although the Romans made their home here, Brecon's roots date back to the fifth century when it was governed by the Celtic chieftain Brychan, who gave his name to the town. The town grew in importance during Norman times when a Benedictine monastery, a castle and formidable town walls were built. In the Act of Union of 1536 Brecon was listed as one of four local capitals, and in 1542 Henry VIII set up a chancery here, installing the exchequer in the castle.

Today the castle is no more than a ruined wall set in the gardens of a hotel – the Castle of Brecon Hotel. It's a similar story for the town walls as only fragments remain. The town centre is a mixture of Georgian, Jacobean and Tudor architecture, with a network of narrow streets leading off the Bulwark. The 19th-century Shire Hall, with its Athenian-style columns, houses the lively Brecknock Museum and Art Gallery.

Meanwhile, Brecon's military history is well recorded at The Regimental Museum of the Royal Welsh in the Barracks. A market is held on Tuesday and Friday, and each August Brecon swings to its own jazz festival, one of the UK's premier jazz events. But whatever is going on, the one unmissable feature of Brecon is the twin peaks of Pen-y-Fan (2,907 feet/886m) and Corn Du (2,863 feet/873m). Your eyes can't help but be drawn up to their angular outlines, sculpted northern cliffs and shadowy cwms. Expect to see lots of walkers in their gear pottering around town and enjoying the many wonderful pubs.

TAKE IN SOME HISTORY
Brecon Cathedral
breconcathedral.org.uk
Cathedral Close, Brecon, LD3 9DP
01874 623857
Brecon Cathedral started life as the Benedictine Priory of St John the Evangelist, founded by the Normans in 1093, probably on the site of an older Celtic church. At the Dissolution of the Monasteries in 1538 it became Brecon's parish church. It only became a cathedral in 1923, on the establishment of the Diocese of Swansea and Brecon. It is now the mother church of the Diocese and offers a ministry of worship and welcome to all who visit.

VISIT THE MUSEUM
The Regimental Museum of The Royal Welsh
royalwelsh.org.uk
The Barracks, The Watton, LD3 7EB
01874 613310 | Open all year Mon–Fri 10–5, Apr–Sep Sat & BHs 10–4; call or check website for special Sun opening times
This military museum is dedicated to the South Wales Borderers and Monmouthshire

▼ Pen-y-Fan

Regiment (now the Royal Welsh). In more than 320 years of service, the regiment has gained 244 Battle Honours and 43 of its soldiers have received the Victoria Cross. It has been involved in many significant events in British military history.

CATCH A PERFORMANCE
Theatr Brycheiniog
brycheiniog.co.uk
Canal Wharf, Brecon, LD3 7EW
01874 611622
Brecon's centre for arts and entertainment has an excellent programme of events throughout the year.

EXPLORE BY BIKE
Bikes and Hikes
bikesandhikes.co.uk
Lion Yard, Brecon, LD3 7BA
01874 610071
This is a popular place to hire a bike, or go on an organised activity, such as climbing, caving or gorge walking.

TAKE A BOAT TRIP
Beacon Park Day Boats
beaconparkdayboats.co.uk
The Tollhouse, Canalside, LD3 7FD
0800 612 2890
Explore the beautiful Monmouthshire and Brecon Canal aboard a boat, available for hire by the day, half-day or hour.

PLAY A ROUND
Brecon Golf Club
brecongolfclub.co.uk
Newton Park, LD3 8PA
01874 622004 | Open all year daily

This is an easy-walking parkland course with good river and mountain scenery.

EAT AND DRINK
Giglios Coffee Shop
10-11 Bethel Square, LD3 7JP
01874 625062
A modern licensed coffee shop and restaurant in the heart of Brecon. Here you'll find excellent cream teas, gateaux and sandwiches.

Pilgrims Tea Rooms
pilgrims-tearooms.co.uk
Brecon Cathedral Close, LD3 9DP
01874 610610
Providing fresh homemade food and oozing charm, this is a great spot on a sunny day when you can sit outside under the cloisters or in the herb garden.

▶ PLACES NEARBY
Near to Brecon you'll find plenty of attractions, including a riding centre and a Georgian manor house. Slightly further afield is Llangorse Lake (see page 214) and the literary town of Hay-on-Wye (see page 182).

Cantref Riding Centre
cantref.com
Cantref, Brecon, LD3 8LR
01874 665223
Located in the foothills of the Brecon Beacons, this riding centre has been running for 40 years and caters for riders of all abilities.

The Castle Coaching Inn
castle-coaching-inn.co.uk
Trecastle, LD3 8UH | 01874 636354

This Georgian coaching inn sits on the old London–Carmarthen route in the northern part of the Brecon Beacons National Park. It has lovely old fireplaces and a remarkable bow-fronted window looking out from the bar, where an open log fire burns throughout the winter. Although it becomes lively on weekends, it is still – somehow – very relaxing. Two real ales on tap change weekly, ensuring a pint in tip-top condition. Wines and a good selection of Scottish and Irish whiskies are also served.

Peterstone Court ⊛

peterstone-court.com
Brecon Road, Llanhamlach, LD3 7YB
01874 665387

This handsome Georgian house overlooks the River Usk beneath the brooding peak of Pen-y-Fan. Blending eclectic

▼ Brecon village

contemporary style with period elegance, it boasts a fine restaurant serving dishes that use locally sourced ingredients. For those tired after a long day in the hills, it also has a lovely, pocket-sized spa. What a treat.

Star Inn

starinntalybont.co.uk
Talybont-on-Usk, LD3 7YX
01874 676635

This popular pub is found right next to the Monmouthshire and Brecon Canal and has an ever-changing choice of real ales – clocking up an impressive 500 plus guests a year. In mid-June and mid-October beer festivals pull in even more fans. Oh, and the food here is pretty special too.

The Usk Inn

uskinn.co.uk
Talybont-on-Usk, LD3 7JE
01874 676251

A short drive or walk from Talybont-on-Usk, on the picturesque Abergavenny to Brecon road, is the Usk Inn, which opened in the 1840s just as the Brecon–Merthyr railway line was being built alongside it. Over the years the pub has been transformed from an ordinary boozer into a country inn with a restaurant and guest rooms. The inn is a popular choice with canalfolk holidaying on the Brecon and Monmouthshire Canal, which passes through the village. It's also useful for access to the rest of South and mid-Wales.

▶ Brecon Beacons National Park

MAP REF 325 E2, 326 C1

breconbeacons.org

The National Park Visitor Centre, Libanus, Brecon, LD3 8ER | 01874 623366

Open daily summer 9.30–5.30; winter 9.30–4

This national park (Parc Cenedlaethol Bannau Brycheiniog) may not have the height and cliffs of Snowdonia, nor the sparkling sea of Pembrokeshire, but it's still got plenty to offer – including lots of thrills and plenty of space. Running from Llandeilo in the west to just past Abergavenny in the east, it covers the finest scenery in south Wales, from rolling, glacier-carved uplands to crashing waterfalls and green hills overlooking patchwork fields.

No doubt you'll be drawn to its most famous feature, the precipitous sandstone ridge of **Pen-y Fan** and high point at 2,907 feet (886m). It's found in the most well known part of the park, the central Brecon Beacons (Bannau Brycheiniog), an area that encompasses a group of flat-topped hills, as well as the Georgian town of Brecon (see page 101) and the mountain centre.

The park is divided into three other distinct areas. To the west, there is the wild, lonely **Black Mountain** (Mynydd Du), a bleak moorland expanse dominated by the craggy ridge of Carmarthen Fan. Lying between the A4067 and A470 is Fforest Fawr (Great Forest). The area is now a geopark (see page 164), due to its astonishing geology – its rocks are 480 million years old. It's also waterfall country, boasting a tremendous series of cascades along gorges. At one of these falls – **Sgwd yr Eira** – you can squeeze your way along a ledge behind the curtain of the fall. It also encompasses a large cave network, deep in the limestone rock.

The eastern flanks comprise the **Black Mountains** (Y Mynyddoedd Duon) – not the same as the Black Mountain in the west – that are made up of a series of ridges and lonely valleys. Here, the park encompasses

▼ The River Usk with the Black Mountains in the distance

the ruins of the stunning 13th–century Llanthony Priory (see page 67) and the second-hand bookshop town of Hay-on-Wye (see page 182), famous for its literary festival. This area is also a huge draw for mountain bikers wanting to test their speed, endurance and gravity on the Black Mountains Killer Loop, a 26-mile, cross-country ride that begins in Crickhowell (see page 155).

Similarly taxing rides can be found across the park, along with gentler counterparts. There are, in fact, 14 graded and waymarked bike trails, making it an 'easy' option for those who don't fancy biking while navigating from an Ordnance Survey map.

Walkers are also well catered for across the park. There are hundreds of walking routes, ranging from gentle strolls to big days out. The terrain is often used for Territorial Army and SAS training days and Duke of Edinburgh expeditions. Throughout the summer the park's staff organise guided walks and other activities. Walking cards, maps and route plans can be obtained from the Brecon town tourist office and the main park visitor centre near Libanus, located just to the west of Brecon town on the A470. It suggests great days out for people of all abilities. One of the trips involves a walk up **Sugar Loaf** – a conical mountain 1,995 feet (596m) high near Abergavenny (see page 66) – followed by a slurp of wine at its vineyard. Another involves a day in the Black Mountains, visiting Tretower Castle

▼ Cefn Cyff ridge

(see page 156) – the highest castle ruins in Wales – followed by an afternoon watching the skilled pilots of the Black Mountains Gliding Club soar along the mountain ridges. You can also take a trip on a vintage steam train, running alongside the Pontsticill and Pentwyn reservoirs, or drive up to Rhos Fach Common, tucked under Y Das Mountain, and make the most of the Black Mountain scenery. Alternatively, for those wishing to be independent and make their own routes, Ordnance Survey Outdoor Leisure maps 12 and 13 cover much of the park and have trails marked on them.

Daylight hours are not the only time to enjoy the park, however. One of the more peaceful and romantic activities it promotes is stargazing. With its quality dark skies and lack of light pollution from towns, this is one of the best places to spot the Milky Way, major constellations, bright nebulas and meteor showers. You may even lose count of the shooting stars that whizz overhead. The area is now the fifth destination in the world to be awarded International Dark Sky Reserve status, meaning it not only has great skies but also encourages people to enjoy, understand and protect them.

It's not just stars that come out at night, either. The park is home to many nocturnal animals, including barn owls, lesser horseshoe bats, foxes, badgers, dormice, hedgehogs, moths and insects. New research has revealed that light pollution disrupts many of these animals' navigational patterns. Come here and enjoy them.

▶ Bridgend MAP REF 325 F5

Bridgend, 22 miles west of Cardiff, is a town of around 40,000 people, many of whom commute into the capital for work. It's not really a tourist destination as such, with its two most notable features being the discounted designer shopping outlet McArthurGlen, located on junction 36 of the M4, and the Merthyr Mawr, a huge stretch of grassy sand dunes and a Site of Special Scientific Interest (SSSI), leading down to the sea. The area was a film location in *Lawrence of Arabia* (1962).

TAKE IN SOME HISTORY
Newcastle Castle
cadw.wales.gov.uk
Newcastle Hill CF31 4JN
01443 336000 | Open all year daily 10–4
The small castle dates back to the 12th century. It is in ruins, but a rectangular tower, a richly carved Norman gateway and massive curtain walls enclosing a polygonal courtyard can still be seen.

HIT THE BEACH
Managed by Natural Resources Wales, Merthyr Mawr is a great place to slide down the sand dunes. Nature lovers will enjoy the area as it is a designated SSSI owing to its abundance of plants and insect life. The sand dunes are actually the second highest in Europe, while the areas of dune woodland and scrub provide additional habitats, resulting in increased wildlife diversity. The site is also well known as a place where some nationally rare and unusual fungi species grow.

▶ PLACES NEARBY
Close to Bridgend is a choice of delightful inns and castles, plus several popular golf courses.

Coity Castle
cadw.wales.gov.uk
Coity, CF35 6BG | 01443 336000
Open all year daily 10–4
A fantastic stronghold dating from the 12th to 16th centuries, with a hall, chapel and the remains of a square keep.

Ogmore Castle
cadw.wales.gov.uk
CF32 0PA | 01443 336000
Open all year daily 10–4
Standing on the River Ogmore, the west wall of this castle is 40 feet high. A hooded fireplace is preserved in the three-storey keep and a dry moat surrounds the inner ward.

Coed-y-Mwstwr Golf Club
coed-y-mwstwr.co.uk
Bryn Road, Coychurch, CF35 6AF
01656 864934 | Open daily all year
Gently undulating parkland course with tree-lined fairways and small, well-protected greens. Playable all year due to a free-draining course.

Southerndown Golf Club
southerndowngolfclub.com
Ogmore-by-Sea, CF32 0QP
01656 880476 | Open all year daily
A downland-links championship course with rolling fairways and

fast greens. Golfers who successfully negotiate the four par 3s still face a testing finish with three of the last four holes played into the prevailing wind. The par 3 5th is played across a valley and the 18th, with its split-level fairway, is a demanding finishing hole.

Cross Inn

crossinncowbridge.co.uk
Church Road, Llanblethian, CF71 7JF
01446 772995
Much loved by visitors, this 17th-century former coaching inn is set in a picturesque corner of the Vale of Glamorgan's countryside, on the fringe of the ancient town of Cowbridge, just a few miles from the splendid Heritage Coast. A family-run pub, the Cross Inn has a cosy restaurant and comfortable, character bar with welcoming log fires and a convivial atmosphere. The chefs take great pride in developing daily menus of essentially British food with European influences. Fresh produce is sourced from local farmers and other reliable suppliers, with fish, prime Welsh steaks, poultry and other ingredients delivered every day. There's good bar food, as well as a frequently changing restaurant menu, specials boards and children's meals. Dogs are also very welcome.

Prince of Wales Inn

princekenfig.co.uk
Kenfig, CF33 4PR
01656 740356
Thought to be one of the most haunted pubs in Wales, this 16th-century, stone-built free house was once the seat of local government for the lost city of Kenfig. Just as remarkable, it is also the only pub in Britain to have held a Sunday school continuously from 1857 to 2000. A list of suppliers is available for those wishing to check the provenance of the ingredients. In the summer of 2013, HRH The Prince of Wales visited his namesake pub, which is part of his The Pub is the Hub organisation, and enjoyed half a pint.

Victoria Inn

Sigingstone, CF71 7LP
01446 773943
This family-owned inn stands near the top of an old village tucked away along country lanes in the Vale of Glamorgan, with the captivating coastline of the Bristol Channel a short hop away. Unusual, white-painted tiling on its upper half makes it instantly recognisable as you enter the village. There are photographs, prints and antiques everywhere in the beamed interior, while outside there's a beer garden. At the bar there's a range of south Wales real ales, including bitter from Evan Evans, Hancock's HB and beer from breweries in nearby Cardiff. The locally sourced menu, which is strong on seafood dishes, proffers modern twists on traditional mains.

▲ Roman army barracks, Caerleon

▶ Caerleon MAP REF 327 D4

Situated in the Usk Valley, just outside Newport, south Wales, Caerleon is a fairly nondescript town, famous for once being the site a permanent Roman legion. It housed the second Augustan Legion for 300 years, and their fort of *Isca Silurum* (the former name for Caerleon) was one of the most important in Wales. Today, substantial excavated remains can be seen despite locals having, on occasions, used the more accessible facing stones for their own building purposes. Most impressive is the great amphitheatre built around AD 80, the most complete excavated Roman amphitheatre in Britain. Capable of seating 6,000 spectators – the whole legion – ringside seats would have been a messy affair as gladiator and beast fought tooth and claw for their lives. The site also has the finest remains of a Roman barrack building in Europe, which housed 80 men.

VISIT THE MUSEUM
The National Roman Legion Museum
museumwales.ac.uk
High Street, NP18 1AE | 029 2057 3550| Open Mon–Sat 10–5, Sun 2–5
The museum illustrates the history of Roman Caerleon and the daily life of its garrison. On display are arms, armour and equipment, engraved gemstones, a labyrinth mosaic and finds from the legionary base at Usk. Phone for details of children's holiday activities.

GO BACK IN TIME
Caerleon Roman Fortress and Baths
cadw.wales.gov.uk
High Street, NP18 1AE
01633 422518 | Opening times vary; call or check website for details
Frigidarium, *tepidarium*, *caldarium* and *natatio* may sound like one of Harry Potter's spells but, in fact, these words describe the wide range of facilities on offer at the Romans' state-of-the-art leisure complex. In short, it had heated changing rooms, a series of cold and warm baths, covered exercise rooms and an open-air swimming pool.

PLAY A ROUND
Caerleon Golf Course
celtic-manor.com
The Broadway, NP18 1AY
01633 420342 | Open daily all year
This flat parkland course near Newport has beautiful views over the Usk, and two courses, one perfect for beginners. The Celtic Manor Resort (see page 250) – home to the 2010 Ryder Cup – took over management and investment in 2015.

EAT AND DRINK
The Bell at Caerleon
thebellatcaerleon.co.uk
Bulmore Road, NP18 1QQ
01633 420613
For more than 400 years this 17th-century coaching inn has stood in ancient Caerleon on the banks of the River Usk. Situated close to an ancient Roman burial ground (also believed by some people to be the location of King Arthur's kingdom, Camelot), the pub is particularly well known for its good range of local ciders and perrys alongside its Welsh and Breton dishes. Every year a real ale and cider festival is held here with barbecues and free entertainment.

▶ Caernarfon MAP REF 336 C4
Wedged between the rocky outcrops of Snowdonia and the Menai Strait is Caernarfon's big selling point – its astonishing castle. Indeed, if you're only going to pick just *one* castle to see in Wales, this should probably be the one. The town has also got other things in its favour, namely its proximity to the Snowdonia National Park and its strong cultural heritage, as most of the locals are Welsh speakers. History oozes out from the castle into the town. The old walled town has an abundance

of cobbled streets and a mixture of mostly Georgian and Victorian buildings, though some are older, such as St Mary's Church. The waterfront area also shows signs of gentrification, meaning the current slightly down-at-heel impression might soon be a thing of the past.

A town trail leaflet, available from the tourist information centre, will guide you from the Castle Square through the old gates, around the old red-light district of Northgate, where you'll see the 15th-century Black Boy Inn, the castle and the old Slate Quay. You might guess from the trail that Caernarfon was once a seafaring town. The Maritime Museum on Bank Quay near Victoria Dock adds to this, offering a history of seafaring and industry in the area. Exhibits include models of ships, photographs and artefacts.

TAKE IN SOME HISTORY
Caernarfon Castle
see highlight panel overleaf

VISIT THE MUSEUM
Segontium Roman Museum
segontium.org.uk
Beddgelert Road, LL55 2LN
01286 675625 | Open Tue–Sun
12.30–4; closed Mon except BHs
The museum tells the story of the conquest and occupation of Wales by the Romans and displays the finds from the auxiliary fort of *Segontium*, one of the most famous in Britain.

Combine a visit to the museum with an exploration of the Roman fort.

GET INDUSTRIAL
Inigo Jones Slateworks
inigojones.co.uk
LL54 7UE | 01286 830242
Open all year daily 9–5
Inigo Jones was established in 1861, mainly to make school writing slates. Today the company uses the same material to make architectural, monumental and craft products. A self-guided audio/

▼ The coast at Dinas Dinlle

video tour takes visitors around the slate workshops, and displays the various processes used in the extraction and working of Welsh slate.

TAKE A TRAIN RIDE
Welsh Highland Railway
festrail.co.uk
St Helen's Road, LL55 2YD
01766 516024 | Open Apr–Oct,
Santa trains in Dec; open between
Xmas and New Year; call or check
website for timetable
This is one of the Great
Little Trains of Wales
(www.greatlittletrainsofwales.
co.uk) and was voted Heritage
Railway of the Year in 2009.
A recently opened piece of
track now takes the line from
Caernarfon to Porthmadog.
Passengers can enjoy the
wonderful scenery of
Snowdonia from the comfort
of modern carriages. There
is a refreshment service on
all trains. A first-class
panorama vehicle, recently
named by Her Majesty the
Queen, is at the rear of
some trains.

HIT THE BEACH
Dinas Dinlle, near Caernarfon
is a good, sandy beach popular
for water sports.

CATCH A PERFORMANCE
Galeri
galericaernarfon.com
Doc Victoria, LL55 1SQ
01286 685250
Caernarfon's leading centre
for film, music, theatre, art
and dance.

5 top castles

▶ **Caernarfon Castle,
north Wales**
page 114
This World Heritage Site
is a brute of a fortress – it's
hard not to be impressed
with its polygonal towers.

▶ **Cardiff Castle**
page 126
Designed as a medieval
fairy-tale home, with
ornate fireplaces, gilded
ceilings and carved
animals throughout.

▶ **Castell Coch, Tongwynlais**
page 119
This red castle is a 19th-
century Gothic fantasy
situated on a steep hillside.
It is the castle of which
children dream.

▶ **Laugharne Castle,
Carmarthen**
page 192
This handsome old castle
stands in the sleepy
seaside town immortalised
by Dylan Thomas.

▶ **Powis Castle, mid-Wales**
page 319
Originally built around 1200,
this stunning castle is
equally famous for its
gardens, bursting with rare
plants, and its orangery.

PLAY A ROUND
Caernarfon Golf Club
caernarfongolfclub.co.uk
Aberforeshore, Llanfaglan,
LL54 5RP | 01286 673783
Open daily all year
An immaculately kept course
with excellent greens and
tree-lined fairways.

▶ Caernarfon Castle MAP REF 336 C4

cadw.wales.gov.uk

LL55 2AY | 01286 677617 | Open Mar–Jun, Sep–Oct daily 9.30–5, Jul–Aug
9.30–6, Nov–Feb Mon–Sat 10–4, Sun 11–4

In 1282, Llewelyn ap Gruffydd, the last native Prince of Wales, was
killed in an ambush, and Welsh resistance to English occupation
began to crumble. The victorious Edward I offered the Welsh a
prince who was born in Wales, could speak no word of English, and
whose life and reputation no one would be able to decry. He had in
mind his infant son, later Edward II, who became the first English
Prince of Wales. Edward was invested in Wales in 1301, and the
tradition has continued ever since. In 1969, Prince Charles was
invested as the current Prince of Wales in Caernarfon's courtyard,
watched by a worldwide television audience of millions.

Building of the castle started in 1283, but a decade later the
unfinished fortress came under attack during a Welsh rebellion,

and considerable damage was done. Believing he couldn't trust the native Welsh, Edward press-ganged English craftsmen and labourers to rebuild the castle, creating what still remains the grandest and most impressive of all the Welsh castles. Edward intended his castle to be not only a fortress, but also the seat of his government in Wales and his own official residence there. The massive building was also a clear statement of English victory over a defeated nation.

Caernarfon Castle is shaped like an hourglass. Great walls with stones in banded colours (inspired by the walls of Constantinople, which Edward admired while on a crusade) run between the great towers, topped by battlemented wall-walks. The defences of the castle were formidable. In order to gain access to the courtyard, visitors were obliged to cross two drawbridges, pass through five heavy doors and walk under six portcullises. A range of arrow slits and murder holes, through which an unpleasant array of deadly missiles could be hurled down onto unwelcome guests, protected the entire way.

EAT AND DRINK

Black Boy Inn

black-boy-inn.com
Northgate Street, LL55 1RW
01286 673604
Built around 1522, this is one of
the oldest pubs in Wales. It's
the perfect place for a pint of
Snowdonia Ale, relaxing in the
cosy, low-ceilinged rooms.

Seiont Manor Hotel ◉◉

handpickedhotels.co.uk/
seiontmanor
Llanrug, LL55 2AQ | 01286 673366
This charming grey-silver stone
building started life in the 18th
century as a working farmstead
and is now a prestigious
country house hotel. With the
Snowdonia National Park
nearby and Anglesey over the
water, there's no shortage of
country pursuits. You can catch
your own fish in the hotel's lake
(the River Seiont flows through
the 150-acre grounds) and get
the chef to cook it.

Snowdonia Parc Brewpub and Campsite

snowdonia-park.co.uk
Waunfawr, LL55 4AQ
01286 650409
In the heart of Snowdonia, a
short drive from Mount
Snowdon, this popular walkers'
pub is located at Waunfawr

Station on the Welsh Highland
Railway (see page 113 and page
270). There are steam trains
on site (the building was
originally the stationmaster's
house), plus a microbrewery
and campsite. Naturally, the
pub serves its own Welsh
Highland Bitter, along with
other ales. The Welsh Highland
Railway Rail Ale Festival is held
here in mid-May.

▶ PLACES NEARBY

You'll find the perfect place for
plane-spotting and the
university town of Bangor (see
page 81) close to Caernarfon.

Caernarfon Airworld Aviation Museum

airworldmuseum.co.uk
Caernarfon Airport, Dinas Dinlle,
LL54 5TP | 01286 832154
Open Mar–Jun daily 11–5,
Jul–Aug 10–6, Sep–Oct 11–5
The perfect outing for anyone
interested in flight, this
museum tells the story of the
RAF and the Mountain Rescue
Service. It has plenty of combat
aircraft, including the Hawker
Hunter, the Vampire and
Javelin, and you can sit inside
some of the cockpits. You can
watch aviation footage in the
small cinema and there is a
museum gift shop.

▶ Caerphilly MAP REF 326 C4

Just over the hill from Cardiff, this small town has produced
two great things – first a castle, and second a cheese. In terms
of the castle, it's enormous and one of the best preserved
specimens in Wales, second only in size to England's Windsor.
The site incorporates magnificent remains of its original water

defences and most of the inner, middle and outer walls. Work on it began in 1268 by Richard de Clare, Earl of Gloucester and Hereford, to defend his lands against the Welsh. This it did until the Civil War, when explosives used by besieging Parliamentary forces gave the southeast tower its precarious lean.

Caerphilly is also famous for its crumbly white cheese, which rivals other big names such as Cheddar and Leicester for taste and uniqueness. During the summer the town hosts The Big Cheese festival, while in winter there's the Festival of Light, which involves a procession with hundreds of lanterns through the centre of the town.

Sadly, despite these positive associations, the town is slightly rundown and is often looked down upon by its Cardiff neighbours. You won't see as many tourists here as the attractions might suggest.

TAKE IN SOME HISTORY
Caerphilly Castle
cadw.wales.gov.uk
CF83 1JD | 029 2088 3143
Open Mar–Jun, Sep–Oct daily
9.30–5, Jul–Aug 9.30–6, Nov–Feb,
Mon–Sat 10–4, Sun 11–4

When the huge water systems that make up a proportion of this castle's defences are taken into account, this is one of the biggest, and certainly one of the most spectacular, military complexes in Britain. In fact

▼ Caerphilly Castle

it's so big, it's best to appreciate it from a distance, taking in the vast outer walls, the lakes and the inner concentric castle itself.

After 1066, the Normans established themselves in southern Wales, leaving the unfarmable land in the north to the Welsh. In the mid-13th century, the last of the Welsh-born princes, Llywelyn the Last, decided that he should unite Wales under his own rule. He began to threaten the lands held by the Normans, causing Henry III to build a number of castles to protect them. One such castle was Caerphilly.

Work started in April 1268, funded by the wealthy, ambitious baron Gilbert de Clare, Earl of Gloucester and Hertford. Two years later, Llywelyn attacked. How much damage was actually done to the fledgling castle is not known, but de Clare ordered that building should be completed as soon as possible. When Llywelyn attacked again, in 1271, he was repelled and, although he claimed he could have taken the castle in three days, Caerphilly's defences were probably sufficiently developed to render this an idle boast.

▼ Castell Coch

The castle itself comprises a rectangular enclosure with outer and inner walls. The inner walls contain two great gatehouses and the remains of the great hall and domestic areas. The outer walls, well fortified with towers and gatehouses, gave additional protection to the inner ward and were surrounded by a moat. Beyond the moat to the east lay a further complex of defences in the form of great walls studded with towers. The artificial lake lent protection to the north and south sides, while a walled island defended the west.

After the death of de Clare's son, Caerphilly passed to Hugh Despenser, the favourite of Edward II. Edward himself took refuge here from his estranged wife and her lover, although he was forced to flee when she besieged the castle, leaving behind half his treasure and most of his clothes. Oliver Cromwell ordered Caerphilly to be slighted during the English Civil War. After the Civil War was over, local people stole Caerphilly's stones to build houses, and subsidence caused one of its towers to lean dramatically to one side.

▶ **PLACES NEARBY**

Close to Caerphilly is one of Wales' prettiest castles, while slightly further afield is Rhondda Heritage Park (see page 282) and a fascinating museum in Nelson.

Castell Coch

cadw.wales.gov.uk
Tongwynlais, CF15 7JS
029 2081 0101 | Open daily Mar–Jun & Sep–Oct 9.30–5, Jul–Aug 9.30–6, Nov–Feb Mon–Sat 10–4, Sun 11–4

Rising out of wooded parklands, popular with dog walkers and mountain bikers, is Castell Coch, a vast, elegant building with conical towers and a working drawbridge. Castell Coch ('red castle' in Welsh as it's built from red sandstone) is the quintessential fairytale castle. It was built during the 19th century, at a time when the Victorians were expressing a great interest in the past, especially in the Middle Ages. Designed by the architect William Burges for the third Marquess of Bute, it was never intended to be a permanent residence, but more for 'occasional occupation in the summer'. If the romantic exterior of the castle is impressive, then the interior is even more so — a breathtaking jumble of rich colours and minute attention to detail. There are fabulously decorated ceilings in many rooms, while the intricately painted wall panels are truly astounding. The total effect is the kind of exuberant gaudiness that is indisputably Victorian. There are some clever and quirky details evident in the wall decoration of the drawing room, such as painted ribbons that seem to support the family portraits, and the frog holding a bottle of cough mixture that is obviously meant to soothe the frog that has been placed in its own throat.

Although Castell Coch has a dungeon, it was never used except by actors – the castle has proved to be a popular ready-made film set. There are also fantastic views of it from the main road heading west out of Cardiff to Pontypridd.

Llancaiach Fawr Manor
llancaiachfawr.co.uk

Gelligaer Road, Nelson, CF46 6ER
01443 412248 | Open all year Tue–Sun, 10–5. Closed Mon (excluding BHs), 24 Dec–2 Jan
Step back in time at this fascinating living-history museum. The year is 1645 and you are invited into the manor to meet the servants of Colonel Edward Prichard – an interesting array of characters from the puritanical to the gossipy. Events run throughout the year, so check the website or call for more details.

▶ Caerwent   MAP REF 327 E4

If you're interested in history, visit Caerwent – the first town ever built in Wales. Pop in to see the remaining Roman walls, standing some 17 feet high in places, and the ruins of what would have been shops, a Romano-Celtic temple and the forum-basilica. Nowadays, it's sometimes used for open-air events and re-enactments. Recent finds suggest Roman occupation of some kind as late as AD 380. The Wales National Roman Legion Museum and Roman Baths Museum are also here. The town also has strong literary associations – Alfred Lord Tennyson wrote *Idylls of the King*, published between 1859 and 1885, while staying here.

GO BACK IN TIME
Caerwent Roman Town
cadw.wales.gov.uk
01443 336000 | Open daily 10–4; a facilitator is on site Tue and Thu at West Gate Barns
Take a complete circuit of the town wall of *Venta Silurum*, the tribal capital of the Silures, together with excavated areas of houses, shops and a temple.

GO ROUND THE GARDENS
Dewstow Gardens
dewstowgardens.co.uk
Caerwent, Caldicot, NP26 5AH

01291 431020 | Open 5 Apr–2 Nov daily 10–4
There are many gardens with secret rooms concealing architectural and floral delights but none, surely, with the magic and mystery of Dewstow. The white-painted, 19th-century house is surrounded by lawns, rock gardens, a string of pools linked by streams and a border bright with perennials and bulbs. Close by is a labyrinth of passages and pools, grottoes and caverns, waterfalls and rills, excavated and created by

one man's passion for ferns and tropical plants.

Henry Roger Keane Oakley, a director of the Great Western Railway, bought the Dewstow estate in 1893 and embarked on creating a natural-looking habitat for his extensive plant collection. It is thought that a manmade environment on this scale has no equal anywhere in the world.

GET OUTDOORS
Cwmcarn Forest and Campsite
cwmcarnforest.co.uk
Nantcarn Road, NP11 7FA
01495 272001 | Forest Drive: open Mar & Oct daily 11–5, Apr–Aug 11–7, Sep 11–6, Nov–Feb 11–4 (weekends only). Visitor Centre: Easter–Sep daily 9–5; Oct–Easter Mon–Thu & Sat–Sun 9–5, Fri 9–4.30; call or check website for details of Xmas and New Year opening times

Facilities here include barbecues, picnic and play areas, and forest and mountain walks. All this is in an area where some of the lush hillsides were once scarred and treeless slag heaps. There is a mountain bike trail and downhill track and a seven-mile scenic drive with spectacular views over the Bristol Channel and the surrounding countryside. Camping is available on site.

▶ **PLACES NEARBY**
Near to Caerwent is Caldicot Castle and Country Park (see below).

▶ **Caldicot Castle & Country Park** MAP REF 327 E4
caldicotcastle.co.uk
Church Road, NP26 4HU | 01291 420241 | Open 29 Mar–1 Nov, daily 11–5
Set in a 55-acre country park, Caldicot is an impressively restored 13th-century castle, built originally by Humphrey de Bohun, the Earl of Hereford. Its elaborate defences included portcullises, heavy gates and murder holes. Although the antiquarian J R Cobb restored the castle as a family home from 1855, much of the original stonework is still intact.

Other architectural details include latrine turrets, a hooded fireplace and window seats. Remember to take a look at the sculpted heads and ornate windows that decorate the turrets of the main gatehouse. The castle offers the chance to explore medieval walls and towers set in tranquil gardens and wooded country parkland. You can even play giant chess or draughts or sit astride a 12-pound, muzzle-loading canon in the courtyard. The River Nedern winds its way through the park and the wildlife pond is home to a variety of wildfowl. Oh – and don't forget to tell the children – the castle is reputed to be haunted by a number of ghosts. Who will you see before you leave?

▸ Cardiff MAP REF 326 C5

How many other cities have both an outstanding castle and a world-class stadium and events arena right in the thick of things? That's what Cardiff's got – plus great shopping (revamped in the past decade with a stylish, airy mall and large John Lewis) and an array of cool cafes, restaurants and bars. The urban medley creates a modern, buzzing city where buskers entertain the people. They are also there at night, trying to capture the benevolence of a cheery crowd who've been enjoying the city's nightlife, be it at a laidback local pub or a classy nightclub. In fact, the city has got a bit of a reputation for its nightlife – come the weekend, this hub of activity is a haven for fun-lovers from the valleys, arriving to enjoy everything from cheap shots to quality club nights, particularly along the main strip of St Mary Street. Cardiff knows how to party hard, so much so that both clubland and clubgoers can feel in need of a hangover cure come Sunday morning.

Drinking aside, this is a wonderful modern city but one that's never far from its roots. You can tell that by the number of statues around – some of them often sporting traffic cones on their heads. The Romans kicked things off, building a fort where the current castle stands in AD 75. The name Cardiff probably derives from the Welsh *Caer Taf* (fort on the River Taff). Later, the Normans built a moated castle on the site, whose 12th-century keep still survives in the grounds of the modern-day castle, and a small town began to emerge. As with so many Welsh castles, Owain Glyndwr left Cardiff ruinous, but it was rebuilt by Richard Beauchamp, the Earl of Warwick, and

▼ Welsh National War Memorial

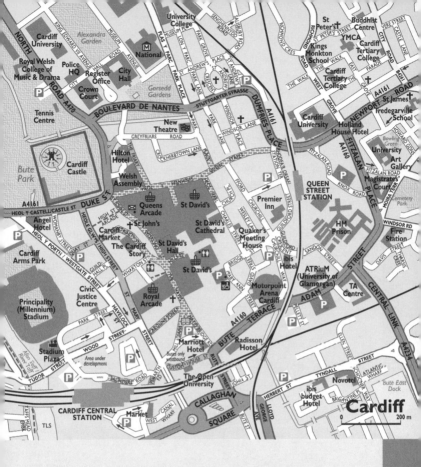

continued to serve as a residence for several centuries. There are not that many medieval reminders of the city and the only notable one is St John's Church, not far from the new shopping complex. By the turn of the 19th century, only 1,000 people were living here but the landscape changed dramatically with the Industrial Revolution.

The discovery of coking coal allowed the iron-smelting industry to flourish in the valleys to the north and Cardiff became the obvious choice as a port. At this time the wealthy Bute family, who were descendants of the royal Stuarts, moved here. They enlarged the docks and made Cardiff one of the world's largest coal- and iron-exporting ports, even building the canal for the shipment of iron from Merthyr Tydfil down to the capital. They also took possession of Cardiff Castle. The world's richest man – John Patrick Crichton-Stuart, third Marquess of Bute – commissioned William Burges to redevelop the living quarters into the Gothic Victorian style you see today.

The Butes continued their legacy in Cardiff and by 1840 the canal was supplemented by the new Taff Vale Railway. The second Marquess of Bute also completed Butetown's docks and, as other ports were not quite ready, it became the obvious choice from which to ship the seemingly never-ending supply of coal from the valleys.

By the end of the 19th century, the city was transformed, with a population of 170,000. Tiger Bay grew up populated by immigrants from all over the world. In 1905, Cardiff was granted city status and continued to grow, exporting millions of tons of coal. In 1910, the port saw the launch of Captain Robert Scott's ill-fated expedition to the South Pole. It couldn't last, however. The depression hit in the 1930s, and the city was badly bombed in World War II. The nationalisation of the coal industry saw the Butes leave town and donate the castle to the city.

▼ Bute Park

In 1955, the city was proclaimed the first ever capital of Wales, beating Caernarfon and Aberystwyth in the vote. It is filled with elegant buildings – a mix of Victorian and Edwardian – the most lovely being the classic Portland stone buildings of the Law Courts, City Hall and the national museum. They make up the civic centre and what is now the university area. The city is also very green, with the biggest open space being Bute Park, originally created as the private garden to the castle, which takes you from the castle to the banks of the River Taff.

On the riverside, you can catch a waterbus past the famous Cardiff Arms Park and the Principality Stadium (formally the Millennium Stadium) to Cardiff Bay, where the old dockyards have been transformed into a busy, thriving waterfront.

▶ Cardiff Castle MAP REF 326 C5

cardiffcastle.com

Castle Street, CF10 3RB | 029 2087 8100 | Open all year daily Mar–Oct 9–6;
Nov–Feb 9–5 (last entry 1 hour before closing)

Located in the heart of the city, Cardiff Castle enjoys a history
spanning 2,000 years. Initially, the Romans built a fortress here,
then, when the Normans arrived in the 11th century, they built a
motte about 40 feet high and topped with a wooden building. Later,
a 12-sided keep was erected, while a gatehouse and stairs were
added in the 15th century. Robert, the eldest son of William the
Conqueror, was held prisoner here for many years by his youngest
brother, Henry I, and died in the castle in 1134.

A short distance away from the keep is a magnificent Victorian
reconstruction. These buildings owe their existence to the rich
third Marquess of Bute. Bute had long been fascinated by history
and employed William Burges, an architect who shared his love of
the past, to construct a great palace in the style of a medieval
castle. Burges designed rooms as if they were part of a fairytale,
with intricately painted ceilings, elaborately marbled bathrooms,
spiral staircases and an impressive clock tower. The banqueting
hall is the largest room in the castle, and has a fine wooden roof,
liberally decorated with brightly coloured shields.

The high walls have murals showing scenes from the Civil War,
as well as a small painting of the Conqueror's son, Robert, gazing
wistfully from behind his barred prison window. The ornate clock
tower looks over the city, just as Big Ben does in London.

There are guided tours, a firing line exhibition, which tells the
history of the Welsh soldier over the last 300 years, and fabulous
banquets available all year. Booking is essential for the banquets.

TAKE IN SOME HISTORY
Cardiff Castle
see highlight panel opposite

National Museum Cardiff
museumwales.ac.uk
Cathays Park, CF10 3NP
029 2039 7951 | Open Tue–Sun
10–5
Home to spectacular collections
from Wales and all over the
world, the museum showcases
displays of art, archaeology,
geology and natural history all
under one roof. The archaeology
gallery traces life in Wales from
the earliest humans who lived
there 230,000 years ago.
Explore the past through
themes such as conflict, power,
wealth, family and the future
– are we really so different
today? Discover the stories
behind some of Wales' most
famous artworks and enjoy
changing displays from the
collection of Impressionist and
post-Impressionist paintings.
You can even have a close
encounter with The Big Bang or
see the skeleton of a new
species of dinosaur, related to
Tyrannosaurus rex.

CATCH A PERFORMANCE
Chapter Arts Centre is an
ambitious multi-platform
cultural space, with a cafe and
bar, while you'll find a rich
programme of events at
St David's Hall.

Chapter Arts Centre
chapter.org
Market Road, CF5 1QE
029 2030 4400

St David's Hall
stdavidshallcardiff.co.uk
The Hayes, CF10 1AH
029 2087 8444

EXPLORE BY BIKE
Pedal Power
cardiffpedalpower.org
02920 390713
Call or check website for
bike pick-up locations.

CLIMB THE WALLS
**Boulders Indoor Climbing
Centre**
bouldersuk.com
St Catherines Park, Pengam Road,
CF24 2RZ | 029 2048 4880
A variety of indoor climbing
activities is available here for
all ages.

GO BOUNCING
Go Air Trampoline Park
goairtrampolinepark.co.uk
Ty Glas Avenue, Llanishen, CF14 5YQ
Check website for details
Like to jump? Why not bounce
across 100 interconnected
trampoline beds suitable for
ages six and upwards at
Cardiff's new Air Trampoline
Park. It's a brand new all-
weather indoor jumping court
inside a 22,000-square-foot
venue. The space will also
accommodate a dodge ball
arena, rebound fitness areas
and a three-lane-long
trampoline that allows free
jumping into a foam pit to
practise skills.

WATCH A MATCH
Principality Stadium Tours
see highlight panel overleaf

PLAY A ROUND
St Mellons Golf Club
stmellonsgolfclub.co.uk
CF3 2XS | 01633 680408
Call for details
A parkland course on the eastern edge of the city – the two finishing holes are superb.

EAT AND DRINK
Bully's ●●
bullysrestaurant.co.uk
5 Romilly Crescent, CF11 9NP
029 2022 1905
'Shabby chic, eclectic' is the self-styled description of Bully's: walls crammed with pictures, gilt mirrors and framed restaurant menus and bills; wooden tables, Persian rugs on the floor and books everywhere. The kitchen relies on Welsh produce and devises menus that show a clear French influence.

Moksh
moksh.co.uk
Bute Crescent, CF10 5AN
029 2049 8120
Contemporary Indian fusion cooking is nothing new, but this kitchen takes it to the next level by throwing elements of molecular wizardry into the mix. The setting is suitably modern, with glass screens separating chunky unclothed tables beneath a trippy night sky ceiling, and the food has a sense of fun.

Park House ●●
parkhouserestaurant.co.uk
20 Park Place, CF10 3DQ
029 2022 4343

Once a private club, Park House is one of the Welsh capital's finest pieces of architectural extravagance. Designed by William Burges, one of the premier practitioners of the Gothic revival, it overlooks the gardens of the National Museum of Wales. The restaurant inside is decorated in pinks and peaches against a background of solid oak panelling, and has a pianist and singer on weekends. The menu is lengthy and ambitious.

Park Plaza Cardiff ●
lagunakitchenandbar.com
Greyfriars Road, CF10 3AL
029 2011 1111
In the centre of the city, not far from the castle and the Principality Stadium, the Park Plaza offers contemporary comfort with plenty of imaginative design features. A floor-to-ceiling wine wall divides the bar from the Laguna restaurant, where a sleek wood-surfaced tone predominates, and the generously portioned brasserie food is deservedly popular.

Pettigrew Tea Rooms
pettigrew-tearooms.com
West Lodge, Bute Park, CF10 1BJ
029 2023 5486
This is a relaxed spot for an afternoon tea, or a full Welsh breakfast, located in Bute Park's newly restored gatehouse. The cafe offers friendly service, loose tea, delicious homemade cakes and plenty of gluten-free options.

▶ Principality Stadium Tours

MAP REF 326 C5

principalitystadium.wales
Westgate Street, Gate 4, CF10 1NS | 029 2082 2228 | Open Mon–Sat 10–5,
Sun 10–4
Built in the late 1990s, the Principality (Millennium) Stadium is now
the heart of Welsh rugby; if you're lucky enough to be in town on a
match day, the atmosphere from within the stands can't be beaten
(though you'll probably have to book tickets in advance). If rugby
isn't your thing – and if it isn't, don't tell the Welsh – the stadium
also hosts football matches, music events and exhibitions. It's the
second-largest stadium in the world to have a fully retractable
roof, and boasts a resident hawk to keep away the seagulls and
pigeons. The stadium changed its name from the Millennium
Stadium to the Principality Stadium at the beginning of 2016.

▲ Llandaff village green and cathedral

5 top places to party in Cardiff

▶ **Aura:** This is for serious clubbers – house music and a state-of-the-art sound system.

▶ **Glam:** A stylish bar with a huge dance floor, overlooked by a DJ booth.

▶ **Metros:** This underground cellar bar is Cardiff's most popular alternative venue.

▶ **Oceana:** One of Cardiff's biggest clubs, which plays the latest chart music.

▶ **Retro:** A great night out if you like your old-school classics.

▶ **PLACES NEARBY**

Llandaff

Although Llandaff is just a couple of miles from Cardiff's centre and officially part of the capital these days, this ancient, tranquil city seems a world away. Set on the banks of the River Taff, its main attraction is the beautiful Llandaff Cathedral, standing on one of the oldest Christian sites in Britain. In the sixth century, St Dyfrig, followed by St Teilo, founded a community here, close to a forge where the Romans crossed the river. Nothing remains of the original church but a Celtic cross that stood nearby can still be seen.

Llandaff Cathedral

llandaffcathedral.org.uk
Llandaff, CF5 2LA | 029 2056 4554
Open all year Mon–Sat 9–7, Sun
7–7pm

The present cathedral dates
from 1107 but it suffered heavily
during the Reformation and
Civil War and was even used as
a beer house and a cattle shed.
Almost derelict in the 18th
century and badly damaged by
a World War II bomb, it was
slowly rebuilt in the late 19th
century. This job was entrusted
to architect George Pace, who
painstakingly sought to blend
old with new, while adding a
new sense of spaciousness to
the cathedral, which was
largely done by installing many
clear glass windows.

Caesars Arms

caesarsarms.co.uk
Cardiff Road, Creigiau, CF15 9NN
02920 890486

Just 10 miles from Cardiff, this
smart dining pub and farm shop
is tucked away down winding
country lanes. Inside the
whitewashed building you'll
find an appealing bar and
dining area, and fine
countryside views from the
heated patio and terrace.
Besides excellent ales from
Felinfoel Brewery, the pub
also produces honey from
its own beehives. Vegetables
and herbs from its garden
are used in the kitchen, and
there's a smokehouse. The
inn prides itself on its selection
of fresh fish, seafood, meat
and game.

Kings Arms

kingsarmspentyrch.co.uk
22 Church Road, Pentyrch,
CF15 9QF | 029 2089 0202

In a leafy village on the
outskirts of Cardiff, this
Grade II listed pub has a
flagstoned snug, exposed
lime-washed walls and a log
fire in the lounge. The menus
and daily blackboard specials
promote seasonal Welsh
produce, and the Sunday roasts
are very popular.

Llanerch Vineyard

llanerch-vineyard.co.uk
Hensol, Pendoylan, Vale of
Glamorgan, CF72 8GG
01443 222716

This is a working vineyard in
picturesque countryside with
a restaurant, bistro, boutique
vineyard hotel rooms, self-
guided vineyard tours and
cookery classes. Try the great
signature Welsh wines.

Restaurant James Sommerin
❀❀❀

jamessommerinrestaurant.co.uk
The Esplanade, Penarth, CF64 3AU
029 20706559

James Sommerin is chef-
patron of a snazzy restaurant
with cracking views of the
Severn Estuary. Indoors, it's a
picture of understated
contemporary style. Sommerin
uses precisely engineered
cooking techniques that take
the finest, locally sourced
materials as a starting point.
Choose between the a la carte
menu or the five- or seven-
course tasting menus.

▲ Wales Millennium Centre

▶ **Cardiff Bay** MAP REF 326 C6

Since redevelopment began in the 1990s, Cardiff Bay has
grown to be almost a town in its own right. Although just a
mile from the city centre, it's often treated as a separate
destination and visited independently. You may want to visit
for the ice cream parlour right on the seafront, or for one of
the many pizza houses. Equally, you may want to drink a coffee
in the large foyer of the Wales Millennium Centre, listening
to one of the local choirs or bands perform there for free
most weekends.

Whatever you choose to do here, you cannot escape the
history. The discovery of coking coal allowed the iron-smelting
industry to boom in the south Wales valleys during the
Industrial Revolution and this was the main port of choice. The
Bute family enlarged the docks and made Cardiff into one of
the world's largest exporters of coal and iron. Tiger Bay, the
area between the dock and city, became one of the roughest
but most lively multicultural centres in the world, producing

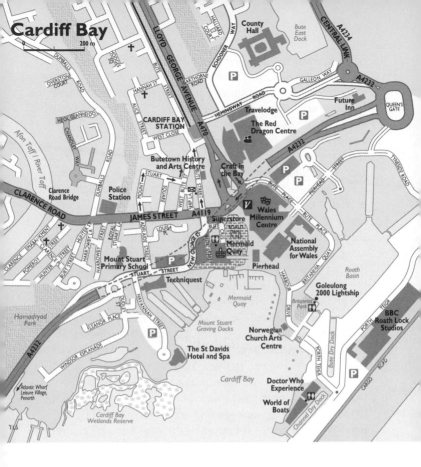

Cardiff Bay

200 m

none other than legendary singer Dame Shirley Bassey. Sailors from all corners of the globe patronised the pubs with names like the Bucket of Blood and the House of Blazes. By the 1970s, when the coal industry had been decimated, Cardiff's waterfront had sunk into an industrial wasteland of deprivation and decay, while Tiger Bay had lost its soul. With this in mind, the presiding Welsh Secretary, Nicholas Edwards, announced the establishment of the Cardiff Bay Development Corporation, its mission being to put Cardiff back on the international map and create a thriving maritime city. The harbour at Cardiff had one of the world's most expansive tidal ranges of up to 46 feet between low and high tide, rendering it completely inaccessible for up to 14 hours a day. The idea was to build a barrage that would create a 500-acre freshwater lake out of the bay. Although it brought vehement opposition from Friends of the Earth, the RSPB and local residents, who thought this would be an ecological disaster for the thousands of birds whose wetland and mudflat habitats would be submerged beneath the lake, the Welsh Office believed that the scheme would be the catalyst for a complete dockside development and persisted with the plans to cover the silvery mud. In 1993, the Cardiff Barrage Act was passed. The £220-million project included three locks for ships to pass through, sluice gates to control the water level in the lake, and a fish pass to allow the sea trout and salmon to access their spawning area in the Taff and Ely rivers. To compensate for the loss of wildlife habitat, 1,000 acres of farmland were flooded in the Gwent Levels, 15 miles to the east, to create a freshwater marsh.

The barrage was completed in 1997, along with eight miles of waterfront development, the biggest of its kind in Europe. The area now houses many attractions. Techniquest Science Discovery Centre promotes science and maths in an exciting and palatable way. The Welsh Assembly building – designed by Richard Rogers with energy conservation in mind – stands at the Pierhead, and Butetown History and Arts Centre provides a fun and interactive experience. Close by is the Wales Millennium Centre (see page 135), an international arts centre with restaurants, cafes and a theatre that offers the best in dance, music and drama. Built from local slate, the centre has a bilingual inscription: 'In these stones horizons sing' and *Creu gwir fel gwydr o ffwrnais awen*, which in English means 'creating truth like glass from the furnace of inspiration.' Shunning the modern look is the Norwegian Church, where Roald Dahl's parents worshipped – it's now an exhibition and arts centre with a cosy waterfront cafe. You can also go on a guided tour of the barrage, or take a boat trip or sailing lessons. A popular water taxi takes people to and from the bay, city centre and Penarth, while in the nearby Atlantic Wharf Village there's an international standard swimming pool and ice rink. Despite the huge environmental concerns over the redevelopment, the bay is still good for birding. Long-legged waders such as the grey heron, the egret – a small white heron-like bird – and the cormorant, another heron-like bird with a black coat, can be seen waiting patiently and silently for their fish suppers to swim by. The wetland reserve by the Taff Estuary also hosts great crested grebes and snipe.

VISIT THE MUSEUMS AND GALLERIES

Craft in the Bay

makersguildinwales.org.uk
The Flourish, Lloyd George Avenue,
CF10 4QH | 029 2048 4611
Open daily 10.30–5.30
Located opposite the Wales Millennium Centre, this shop and gallery is home to the prestigious Makers Guild, a craftmakers' cooperative formed in 1984 to bring together and promote and recognise the best of Welsh craft talent. It has an international reputation for craft and applied art.

The Norwegian Church Arts Centre

norwegianchurchcardiff.co.uk
Harbour Drive, Cardiff Bay,
CF10 4PA | 029 2087 7959
Open daily 9–6

This is a landmark building in Cardiff Bay with panoramic views over the waterfront. Formerly a church for Norwegian sailors, the iconic building dates back to the Industrial Revolution, when Cardiff Docks was the world's greatest exporter of coal. It now hosts events, classes and exhibitions. There is also a popular tea room.

Wales Millennium Centre

wmc.org.uk
Bute Place, Cardiff Bay, CF10 5AL
029 2063 6464

Visit Wales' leading arts centre housing theatre space for musicals, opera, ballet and dance, as well as cafes. It's the home of eight arts organisations, including the national orchestra and national opera, dance, theatre and literature companies.

ENTERTAIN THE FAMILY
Doctor Who Experience
see highlight panel overleaf

Techniquest

techniquest.org
Stuart Street, CF10 5BW
029 2047 5475 | Open daily
term-time 9.30–4.30, school
holidays 10–5

There's always something new to explore at this exciting science discovery centre, located in the heart of Cardiff Bay. Journey into space in the planetarium, enjoy an interactive Science Theatre Show or experience one of the 160 hands-on exhibits. Techniquest's planetarium has a new projector allowing visitors to see the night sky as never before. There's also a Science Theatre staging curriculum-linked shows for school parties during term time and shows for all the family at other times. Visit the website for details of events running throughout the year.

TAKE A BOAT TRIP
Bay Island Voyages
bayislandvoyages.co.uk
Mermaid Quay, lower board walk,
CF10 5BZ | 029 2078 2733

A great way to explore is to take an adventure boat trip on a RIB around Cardiff Bay.

5 top activities for rainy weather

▶ **Techniquest Science and Discovery Centre,** page 135

▶ **Sand-board at Merthyr Mawr**, page 108

▶ **Take a ride on a narrow-gauge steam train** (greatlittletrainsofwales.co.uk)

▶ **The National Museum,** Cardiff, page 127

▶ **Anglesey Sea Zoo**, page 226

▶ Doctor Who Experience

MAP REF 326 C6

doctorwhoexperience.com
The Red Dragon Centre, Hemingway Road, CF10 4JY | 020 8433 3162
Open all year 10–5 (last admission 3.30); closed most Tue in off-season

Fans of *Doctor Who* will already recognise many Cardiff Bay locations from the popular BBC television series, but the Doctor Who Experience takes things a step further by inviting visitors to become the Doctor's companion on a time-travelling adventure confronting classic monsters from series past. Eleventh Doctor Matt Smith filmed special scenes to be played as you journey through time and space.

Once your enemies have been vanquished, there's an extensive exhibition of props, artefacts and costumes ranging from 1963 right through to the present day, along with Daleks, Weeping Angels, Ood, Cybermen, and even a TARDIS.

▶ Cardigan   MAP REF 323 E1

Found on the estuary of the River Teifi, Cardigan is a special place to visit, combining historic culture with a cool trendy edge and outdoor vibe. It's largely one long strip of road – and a perfect example of how an independent high street should look. You won't find a shut shop or anything looking in need of some TLC. Indeed, Cardigan has seen great gentrification of late. Now you'll find boutique B&Bs, upmarket pubs, decent butchers, organic delis and antiques shops. You'll also find it's got a young hip crowd inspired by the outdoors scene, itself inspired by the river.

In summer, a great place to visit is Pizza Tipi, an open-air hangout right on the River Teifi, often hosting live music, while those into art should check out the work of Aneurin Jones – a Cardigan resident and one of Wales' foremost artists (see aneurinjones.co.uk for information).

The castle, once privately owned, is now in the hands of the local council and has reopened after having undergone extensive refurbishment. Another site is the 17th-century, six-arched bridge over the Teifi where, on occasions, ancient handmade coracles can be seen plying for salmon and sea trout. A weekly market is still held beneath the arches of the 19th-century Guildhall.

Most importantly for those travelling with kids, Cardigan boasts the best old-fashioned sweet shop around – Yum Yum, located on the high street – where you'll find favourite treats that will bring back memories of yesteryear. And Cardigan does do great fish and chips.

TAKE IN SOME HISTORY
Cardigan Castle
cardigancastle.com
SA43 1JA | 01239 615131
Open daily all year 10–4
Built in the 12th century, Cardigan Castle was an important stronghold in the ancient Welsh kingdom of Ceredigion and played a vital role in the history of the country. Decades of neglect left the site of the castle in ruins but, after years of local campaigning, it is now in public hands. Following an extensive £11 million restoration, the castle reopened to the public in spring 2015 as a community, recreational and educational hub. Now it is a centre for learning the Welsh language, culture and crafts, as well as providing a focus for environmental and horticultural studies. There is a heritage centre with educational facilities, rooms to hire for training and educational purposes, an Eisteddfod garden with a wet-weather dome, an open-air concert area, a restaurant and self-catering luxury accommodation.

ENTERTAIN THE FAMILY
Yum Yum
yumyumsweets.co.uk
6 Pendre, SA43 1JL | 01239 621201
Open Mon–Sat 9–5.30
Situated on the high street, Yum Yums is a child's paradise. In this old-fashioned sweet shop you can choose your favourite treat and buy it weighed out into a bag by the quarter pound. It has more than 500 jars of loose sweets.

5 top volunteering holidays

▶ **Cardigan Bay Marine Wildlife Centre:** Summer volunteers are recruited to help with surveying on land and boat, beach cleaning and educational activities.

▶ **CAT (Centre for Alternative Technology), Machynlleth:** Short-term or summer placements doing bird monitoring or woodland work.

▶ **Felin Uchaf, Pwllheli:** A creative educational centre offering year-round volunteering.

▶ **National Trust:** Opportunities available at a variety of locations; activities include gardening, surveying and archaeology.

▶ **RSPB:** Voluntary and practical conservation placements are available at a variety of sites around Wales.

HIT THE BEACH
Choose from either the pebbly Gwbert or the glorious sandy Poppit (see page 292), with views across the estuary towards Cardigan Island.

GET ON THE WATER
Cardigan Bay Active
cardiganbayactive.co.uk
Granary Warehouse, Teifi Wharf, Castle Street, SA43 3AA
01239 612133
Set up in 2011, this activity centre offers coasteering, sea kayaking, paddle boarding and white-water rafting for kids and grown-ups. Land adventures such as bush craft and climbing are also available.

▶ PLACES NEARBY
Near to Cardigan you'll find a wildlife centre, farm shop and railway, plus the towns of Cilgerran (see page 147), St Dogmaels (see page 291) and Fishguard (see page 165).

Welsh Wildlife Centre
welshwildlife.org
The Welsh Wildlife Centre, Cilgerran, Cardigan, SA43 2TB | 01239 621600
Open Mar–Dec daily 10–5
In a futuristic glass and timber building on the Teifi Marshes Nature Reserve, this centre is a great place from which to explore the surrounding area. The nature reserve covers woods, meadows, reed beds and marshes along the River Teifi, as well as a former slate quarry and railway bed. The diversity of habitats gives rise to an abundance of wildlife,

including otters and one of the largest British colonies of Cetti's warblers. A footpath around the marshes is dotted with hides on ground and treetop level, from which to spot elusive kingfishers or otters. For kids, there's an adventure playground and an enormous wicker badger to climb all over and explore. The centre has the wonderful Glasshouse cafe and a well-stocked gift shop. There's also an exhibition telling the story of how the ancient Teifi Marshes were created.

Llwynhelyg Farm Shop

llwynhelygfarmshop.co.uk
Sarnau, Llandysul, SA44 6QU
01239 811079 | Open Mon–Sat 9–6
Described as a 'food-lovers paradise', this farm shop has won a host of awards for the quality and diversity of its produce, the majority of which is sourced from the locality and around Wales. Products include home-grown potatoes and salad crops from the farm, fruit and vegetables from local specialist growers and delicious homemade cakes, desserts, pies and quiches. The shop is particularly known for its extensive range of Welsh artisan cheeses – it stocks 80 different types.

Teifi Valley Railway

teifivalleyrailway.org
Station Yard, Henllan, Llandysul,
SA44 5TD | 01559 371077
Call or check website for timetable
This is a narrow-gauge tourist railway located at Henllan, about four miles to the east of Newcastle Emlyn. It also boasts a model railway, about 400 yards long, picnic tables in a children's play area and a crazy golf course, so it's an all-round family attraction. Seasonal events take place throughout the year.

▶ Cardigan Bay MAP REF 323 E1, 333 D5

Cardigan also gives its name to its surrounding bay – Cardigan Bay. Just to clarify things, the county now uses the Welsh word for Cardiganshire – Ceredigion, pronounced with a 'dig'. The bay itself is a large inlet of the Irish Sea and stretches from Bardsey Island (see page 61) in the north to Strumble Head (see page 304) in the south. With many beaches and a unique marine life, it's the place to come for spotting bottlenose dolphins, porpoises and Atlantic grey seals. The area is also a Special Area of Conservation (SAC), designated under European law to protect its species and habitats. The Ceredigion coastal path is also a major attraction.

Much of the surrounding land is fertile farmland, dotted with towns and seaside resorts such as Fishguard, New Quay, Aberaeron, Aberystwyth, Borth, Aberdyfi, Barmouth and Porthmadog. It's also a section of coast that major rivers flow into, including the Afon Glaslyn, Teifi, Rheidol, Dyfi, Aeron, Dysynni and Mawddach. Historically, the area supported a strong maritime industry. Cardigan, in particular, was a major hub, once having more than 300 ships registered in its port, seven times as many as Cardiff. Due to being something of a backwater, in many ways this area remains charmingly unspoilt. The nearby heather-clad Preseli Hills (see page 273) are an additional delight.

Carmarthen   MAP REF 324 B1

Carmarthen may be a town of cultural provenance and history – claiming to be one of the oldest settlements in Wales – but in reality there's not as much to see here as you might assume, and it isn't really a tourist stop. The Romans built a fort here, but it was largely destroyed and, unlike many others, hasn't been rebuilt. A few crumbling walls are all that really remain. Between the 16th and 18th centuries it was thought of as Wales' chief city, but the population dwindled in the mid-19th century as workers moved to the coalfields in south Wales.

The town is said to be the birthplace of the Arthurian wizard, Merlin. Legend also had it that when a particular tree called 'Merlin's Oak' fell, it would be the downfall of the town as well. In order to stop this from happening, the tree was dug up when it died. Pieces can be found under glass at the Carmarthenshire County Museum.

VISIT THE MARKET
Carmarthen Market
carmarthenmarket.co.uk
Open Mon–Sat, 9.30–4.30;
outdoor market every Wed & Sat
Carmarthen Market is a perfect place to see a collection of crafts all under one roof – antiques stalls, engravers and home-produce outlets.

PLAY A ROUND
Carmarthen Golf Club
carmarthengolfclub.com
Blaenycoed Road, SA33 6EH
Open daily all year
A well-maintained heathland course with tricky greens and a magnificent clubhouse.

EAT AND DRINK
Y Polyn ◉◉
ypolyn.co.uk
Nantgaredig, SA32 7LH
01267 290000
This welcoming country pub is furnished in true rustic style with bare wood tables, and the happy buzz of customers is testimony to the success of the cooking. There is no desire to innovate for its own sake, just reliable local ingredients cooked with bravura.

▶ PLACES NEARBY
Close to Carmarthen is a county museum, the National Botanic Garden of Wales (see

page 241) and Dylan Thomas' home town of Laugharne (see page 191).

Carmarthenshire County Museum

carmarthenmuseum.org.uk
The Old Palace, Abergwili, SA31 2JG
01267 228696 | Open Tue–Sat
10–4.30

Housed in the old palace of the Bishop of St Davids and set in seven acres of grounds, the museum offers a wide range of local subjects to explore, from geology and prehistory to butter making, Welsh furniture, local pottery, fine paintings, love spoons and folk art. It also holds temporary exhibitions.

▶ Carreg Cennen Castle   MAP REF 325 D2

cadw.wales.gov.uk
Near Trapp, 4 miles south of LLandeilo, SA19 6UA | 01558 822291
Open all year daily Apr–Oct 9.30–6.30, Nov–Mar 9.30–4

Of all Wales' castles, this is regularly voted the most 'dramatically situated' and the most romantic ruin. It's found within the Brecon Beacons National Park (see page 105) in a spectacular position – standing proud above a limestone precipice, the 295-foot drop forming a natural defence. Despite this, the Welsh rebel Owain Glyndwr took the castle in the 15th century, and the Yorkists later destroyed it during the Wars of the Roses to prevent its use as a Lancastrian base.

Despite being in a ruinous state since 1462, it is still an impressive sight. It was originally an Anglo-Norman stronghold, designed to repel Welsh advances. Today it still has six towers of differing shapes, including a great twin-towered gatehouse on the north side and three drawbridges over deep pits. The inner court comprises a hall, kitchens, chapel and the so-called 'King's Chamber'. In it is a well-carved stone fireplace and ornate windows facing impressive views. Be sure to check out the passageway cut into the cliff, which leads to a natural cave beneath the fortifications. A freshwater spring rises in the cave, which would have been useful during dry weather when the castle would have had difficulty collecting rainwater to fill the cisterns.

The castle is under the care of Cadw, who have stabilised and, to a limited extent, restored some of the remains. You need to be fit to enjoy it though – it's accessed via a steep climb up the hill from Castell Farm, near the car park. A large threshing barn has been converted into tea rooms and a shop, while the majority of the farm buildings, around a traditional farmyard, retain their agricultural purposes. Since 1982 these have formed part of a farm park with rare and unusual breeds of cows and sheep.

▶ Castell Henllys Iron Age Fort MAP REF 323 E2

castellhenllys.com

Pant-Glas, Meline, SA41 3UT | 01239 891319 | Open all year daily Easter–
Oct 10–5, Nov–Mar 11–3 (last entry 30 mins before close); closed 24–31 Dec

There's no other way to describe this site other than a
wonderful one-off. Nestled deep in the Pembrokeshire Coast
National Park (see page 260), this Iron Age hill fort, dating
back 2,400 years, allows you to step back in time. Excavations
began in 1981. Since then, three roundhouses have been
reconstructed with hazel wattle walls, oak rafters and thatched
conical roofs. A forge, smithy and looms can also be seen, with
other attractions such as trails and a herb garden. A main draw
for many visitors is being able to sit inside a roundhouse and
grind flour to make bread, just as the Celts used to do. Check
the website or call for details of special events.

▶ Ceiriog Valley MAP REF 335 D2

'A little bit of heaven on Earth' is how the last British Liberal
Prime Minister, Lloyd George, described the Ceiriog Valley. Yet,
despite its stunning scenery and easy accessibility – being only
a few miles from the English border and the busy A5 – this
valley is something of a secret. It lies immediately south of the
Vale of Llangollen, and has been dubbed 'little Switzerland' for
its lush green hills, dotted with small farms that wouldn't go
amiss in a Constable landscape. It's also given rise to three

◀ Castell Henllys Iron Age Fort

notable Welsh poets – John Ceiriog Hughes (1832–87), Huw Morus (1662–1709) and Rev Robert Ellis (1812–75). Hughes, commonly known as 'Ceiriog', is known as the 'Robert Burns of Wales', while Morus, even before he turned 30, was already the most famous poet in Wales. His ballads, written in support of Charles I, were so evocative that Cromwell sent a detachment to silence him. Ellis was an Eisteddfod-winning poet and Minister at Glyn Ceiriog for many years.

The village of **Glyn Ceiriog** is the largest in the Ceiriog Valley. It expanded in the 19th century with the mining of slate and other minerals in the area. Here you can see the remnants of a slate-carrying tramway. You can also visit **Llanarmon Dyffryn Ceiriog**, the most beautiful village in the valley, with a church, two old-world pubs and several whitewashed cottages clustered around a picture-postcard square. Lying by the junction of the River Ceiriog and a tributary, the Gwrachen, the village takes its name from the fifth-century missionary St Garmon. A mound in the churchyard, known as 'Tomen Garmon', is a Bronze Age burial mound, which is believed to be the place where the missionary once stood to preach.

GET OUTDOORS
Pistyll Rhaeadr
see page 265

EXPLORE BY BIKE
Hit the Hills
hitthehills.com
0800 978 8579
Mountain bike the Berwyns with this national bike-ride specialist.

SADDLE UP
Andy Pughe Pony Trekking
ponytreks.co.uk
Pont-y-Meibion, Pandy, Glyn Ceiriog, Llangollen, LL20 7HS
01691 718686
With ponies and horses to suit all ages and abilitites, this is a fantastic way to explore the beautiful Ceiriog Valley. A whole host of other activities are also available, including clay-pigeon shooting and quad biking. Visit the website for details.

GO WALKING
Head off along Offa's Dyke Long Distance Footpath or up the Berwyn Mountains.

EAT AND DRINK
West Arms
thewestarms.com
Llanarmon Dyffryn Ceiriog, LL20 7LD | 01691 600665
The West Arms is cosy and welcoming with its beamed ceilings and roaring log fires. The food is of international standard with dishes such as local organic lamb braised in cider. Hungry already?

▶ Chepstow MAP REF 327 F4

Chepstow is a busy market town, close to the major hubs of Newport and Cardiff, and also Bristol in England. Located on the River Wye, it is also just two miles from the huge River Severn estuary and the old Severn crossing – the white bridge, rather than the newer peppermint-green one. Its name derives from the old English *ceap stowe*, meaning marketplace or trading centre. Although some might be slightly down on this town, it does have a splendid Norman castle, perched dramatically on a cliff top above the Wye.

Just outside the town is Chepstow Racecourse – one of Britain's finest – which has hosted the Welsh National each year since 1949. The town is also a gateway for exploring the beautiful border countryside, with scenic routes up to Tintern and the Forest of Dean.

Although the town initially developed around its castle, the Middle Ages also saw it become an important port for the import of wines and the export of timber and bark. In the late 18th century, the town was a focus of early tourism as part of the Wye tour. Shipbuilding was also important – during World War I, one of the first national shipyards was established here – as was heavy engineering. Bridges and now wind turbines were frequently built here.

TAKE IN SOME HISTORY
Chepstow Castle
cadw.wales.gov.uk
Chepstow, NP16 5EY
01291 624065 | Open Mar–Jun, Sep–Oct daily 9.30–5, Jul–Aug 9.30–6, Nov–Feb Mon–Sat 10–4, Sun 11–4

One of the first stone castles ever constructed in Britain, Chepstow was begun in 1068, just two years after the invasion of England by William the Conqueror. It was of great strategic importance and William entrusted one of his best generals, William FitzOsbern, who became Earl of Hereford, to build the castle and control the Marches. The site is naturally protected on one side by cliffs plummeting into the River Wye, and on the other by a valley. The very first building was a simple, two-storeyed rectangular keep. In the 12th century, its defences were improved and the castle extended. Although Chepstow was never besieged in medieval times, it played an important role in the Civil War, coming under siege twice while it was being held for King Charles I. After this, its importance declined and it fell into the romantic ruin it is today.

PLAY A ROUND
St Pierre, A Marriott Hotel and Country Club
stpierregolf.com
St Pierre Park, NP16 6YA
01291 625261 | Open daily all year

The course at this Marriott Hotel and Country Club is set in 400 acres of delightful parkland and there are two 18-hole golf courses on offer here – the oldest being one of the finest in the country.

▶ **PLACES NEARBY**

Chepstow is close to the magnificent Tintern Abbey, an excellent vineyard, which offers wine-tasting, and the attractive gardens at Veddw House.

Tintern Abbey

cadw.wales.gov.uk
NP16 6SE | 01291 689251
Open all year Mar–Jun, Sep–Oct daily 9.30–5, Jul–Aug 9.30–6, Nov–Feb Mon–Sat 10–4, Sun 11–4
The ruins of this Cistercian monastery church, founded in 1131 by Walter de Clare, Lord of Chepstow, are still surprisingly intact. The monastery was established in 1131 and became increasingly wealthy well into the 15th century. During the Dissolution it was closed and most of the buildings were completely destroyed. During the 18th century many poets and artists, including William Wordsworth, came to see the ruins and recorded their impressions in words and art. It is still a wonderful sight, accentuated by the green wooded valley and neighbouring river.

Parva Farm Vineyard

parvafarm.com
Tintern, NP16 6SQ
01291 689636 | Open Nov–Mar daily 11.30–4, Apr–Oct 1–5.30
Parva Farm is a privately owned vineyard producing award-winning wines, meads and sparkling wines. Some 4,500 vines, planted in 1979, now grow on this south-facing hillside overlooking the River Wye. It's believed the site was where monks from Tintern Abbey grew grapes, and possibly the Romans before them. Drop by for a tour of the vineyard, take a picnic in the

▼ Chepstow Castle

gardens and be sure to try one of the range of Welsh wines, with the most popular being the Bacchus dry white, Pinot Noir rosé and Dathliad sparkling wine. The shop sells locally produced preserves, honey, ales and perry.

Veddw House Garden

veddw.com

The Veddw, Devauden, NP16 6PH

01291 650836 | Open Jun–Aug Sun only 2–5

Although not quite as famous as the National Botanic Garden of Wales, Veddw is every bit as special. In particular, journalists and reviewers who come here often cite it as their favourite. Located five miles northwest of Chepstow, in border country, it comprises mazes, ornamental grasses, and distinct gardens, such as the cornfield garden and hedge garden, with clipped yew trees and vegetable garden. There's also the froth garden, planted with pink roses, geraniums and hydrangeas.

The Woodlands Tavern Country Pub & Dining

hotelchepstow.co.uk

Llanvair Discoed, NP16 6LX

01633 400313

Below Gray Hill, near the Roman fortress town of Caerwent, this friendly pub is popular with walkers, cyclists and fishermen. They like it, not just because it's close to the Wentwood Forest and plentiful rivers, but also because it has a good selection of Welsh real ales, such as Wye Valley, Felinfoel and regularly changing guest beers. In addition, there's a menu of modern British food. The Sunday roasts are popular.

▶ Chirk MAP REF 335 E2

This is one for canal enthusiasts. Prepare to be gobsmacked by Thomas Telford's magnificent 10-arched aqueduct, built in 1801 to convey the canal more than 70 feet above the bottom of the valley. As if that's not enough, alongside it is an even taller viaduct, built by Henry Robertson in 1840 to carry the railway. Both were used to carry coal from the once-thriving Flintshire coalfields.

The other main feature of Chirk is its 14th-century castle, which stands proudly overlooking the town and the Ceiriog Valley (see page 142). It is one of the few built by Edward I to survive intact, with the exterior still boasting its original squat towers, dungeon and forbidding walls. Inside, however, much has changed. The Myddelton family, resident since 1595, added staterooms, tapestries, a 17th-century Long Gallery, and medieval decorations. Check out the dungeon. As well as exploring the castle, check out the beautiful grounds and their lovely circular wooded walk.

147

CILGERRAN

TAKE IN SOME HISTORY
Chirk Castle
nationaltrust.org.uk
LL14 5AF | 01691 777701
Castle open Mar–Oct daily 11–5;
garden Feb–Mar Sat–Sun 10–4;
estate all year daily 10–5
This magnificent fortress of the
Welsh Marches is the last
Welsh castle from Edward I's
era that is still inhabited.

▶ PLACES NEARBY
Close to Chirk are the towns
of Wrexham (see page 320)

and Llangollen (see page 210),
as well as riding stables
near Oswestry.

Springhill Farm
Riding Stables
springhillfarm.co.uk
Selattyn, Oswestry, SY10 7NZ
01691 718406 | Opening times vary;
call or check website for details
Overlooking the Ceiriog
Valley, the Springhill Farm
stables have instant access to
off-road riding across attractive
tracks, fields and bridleways.

▶ Cilgerran MAP REF 323 F2
Cilgerran is on the northern border of Pembrokeshire between
St Dogmaels (see page 291) and Cenarth. The village itself
stretches along the banks of the River Teifi. The main attraction
is the castle, a small construction that is quite triangular in
shape. It was built around 1223 by William Marshall, Earl of
Pembroke, in a dominant position high above the River Teifi,
and was captured and recaptured many times. Today, it
features two wooden bridges that cross the defensive ditches.
Much of the outer wall is missing although most of the two
circular towers remain. There are also some small rooms and
dark passageways to explore.

Other attractions in the village include annual coracle races.
This event started in 1950 and still attracts competitors from
all over the world. The churchyard of St Llawddog is also of
some interest, due to its megalithic standing stone. West of the
village is Cilgerran Gorge where three slate quarries once
flourished. It now provides a base for river activities, largely
operated by Cardigan Bay Active (see Cardigan, page 137).

TAKE IN SOME HISTORY
Cilgerran Castle
cadw.wales.gov.uk
SA43 2SF | 01239 621339
Opening times vary; call or check
website for details
Perched high on a spectacular
crag, this 13th-century ruined
castle has a suitably romantic

air. It makes a great backdrop
to the annual coracle regatta
where local fishermen in their
one-person boats compete
against each other in various
contests on the River Teifi.
Take the Wall Walk to really
appreciate the castle's stunning
strategic location.

▶ Colwyn Bay MAP REF 337 F3

A charming traditional Victorian resort, Colwyn Bay has some fine architecture and a long promenade, unfortunately shared by the parallel railway line. This promenade follows a vast sweep from Old Colwyn to Penrhyn Bay and gives easy access to the beaches, jetties for sailing and fishing and the harbour at Rhos-on-Sea. You can also pedal along a cycle track linking these places. The sands are golden and the water quality getting better all the time – the aim is to get blue-flag status.

The bay is close to the renowned Welsh Mountain Zoo, several golf courses and many areas ideal for climbing and walking. The tiny chapel of St Trillo, built in the sixth century on the beach in Rhos-on-Sea, is worth viewing. The chapel measures only 15 feet by 6 feet and stands over a holy well. It's reputed that Madoc – son of Owain Gwynedd – began his voyage of discovery from here to the Americas in 1170, more than three centuries before Columbus.

ENTERTAIN THE FAMILY
Welsh Mountain Zoo

welshmountainzoo.org
Old Highway, LL28 5UY
01492 532938 | Open Apr–Oct daily 9.30–6, Nov–Mar 9.30–5

This caring conservation zoo is set among beautiful gardens with panoramic views. Visitors are encouraged to roam the wooded pathways, relax on the grassy slopes or spend a day learning about endangered species, including snow leopards, chimpanzees, red pandas and Sumatran tigers. There are daily shows by the zoo's penguins, birds, sea lions and chimps, along with various events throughout the year.

PLAY A ROUND
Old Colwyn Golf Club

www.oldcolwyngolfclub.com
Woodland Avenue, Old Colwyn, LL29 9NL | 01492 515581
Open Sun–Fri

Designed by renowned golf course designer and patriotic Scot James Braid, this wonderfully hilly nine-hole meadowland course is full of character. There are great views of the Irish Sea and Colwyn Bay from the greens.

EAT AND DRINK
Pen-y-Bryn

brunningandprice.co.uk/penybryn
Pen-y-Bryn Road, LL29 6DD
01492 533360

Looks can be deceiving and, while this unprepossessing 1970s building may look like a medical centre on the outside, inside there's a handsome interior with friendly atmosphere, local ales, a decent wine list and cracking pub food. Make sure you check out the stunning rear garden and terrace, both of which enjoy panoramic views over the sea.

▶ Conwy MAP REF 337 F3

Conwy is one of the great treasures of Wales, a place where history parades itself around every corner. Three fine bridges – Thomas Telford's magnificent suspension bridge of 1822, Robert Stephenson's tubular railway bridge, and a newer crossing – all stretch over the estuary beneath the castle, allowing both road and the railway into this medieval World Heritage Site. Pride of place goes to the castle. It dates back to 1287 when Edward I built it as part of his 'iron ring' to repress the rebellious troops of Llywelyn the Great. In the town centre, a statue of the revered Welsh prince dominates Lancaster Square.

Conwy is the most complete walled town in Britain and extremely impressive. The walls themselves are six feet thick and 35 feet high, with three original gates and numerous towers. The walkway along the top of the walls offers splendid over-the-rooftop views of the castle, the estuary and the rocky knolls of the nearby village of Deganwy. At the wall's end, steps descend to the quayside where fishermen sort their nets and squawking seagulls steal scraps. It's a great place to stop for a while and take in the surroundings. In summer, there is a good selection of boat trips, some just around the estuary, others further afield to Anglesey. You might think this quayside is a bit rundown, with its flaky paint and slightly unloved vibe – particularly if compared to neighbouring Llandudno – but regeneration is happening and there are a few fine old buildings to admire, chiefly the half-timbered Aberconwy House, the large mansion of Plas Mawr and St Mary's Church, built on the site of a Cistercian abbey.

▼ Conwy

TAKE IN SOME HISTORY
Conwy Castle
see highlight panel opposite

Aberconwy House
nationaltrust.org.uk
LL32 8AY | 01492 592246
Opening times vary; call or check
website for details
Dating from the 14th century,
this is the only medieval
merchant's house remaining in
the area. Furnished rooms and
an audio-visual presentation
show daily life in the house.

Plas Mawr
cadw.wales.gov.uk
High Street, LL32 8DE
01492 580167 | Open 31 Mar–Sep,
Tue–Sun 9–5, also BH Mon (last
admission 45 mins before closing)
Built between 1576 and 1585 for
local merchant Robert Wynn,
Plas Mawr (Great Hall) is
regarded as the finest surviving
Elizabethan town house in
Britain. The house and gardens
have been restored to their
original appearance.

Smallest House
thesmallesthouseingreatbritain.co.uk
The Quay, LL32 8BB | 07925 049786
Open summer 10–dusk, winter 10–4
The Guinness Book of Records
lists this as the smallest house
in Britain. Just six feet wide by
ten feet high, it is furnished in
the style of a mid-Victorian
Welsh cottage.

GET INDUSTRIAL
Conwy Suspension Bridge
nationaltrust.org.uk
LL32 8LD | 01492 573282
Open Mar–Oct daily 11–5 (last
admission 4.30)
Designed by Thomas Telford,
one of the greatest engineers
of the late 18th and early 19th
century, this was the first
bridge to span the river at
Conwy. The bridge has been
restored and the toll house
furnished as it would have been
a century ago.

GO BACK IN TIME
Castell Caer Lleion
To the east of Conwy, on the
peak of Conwy Mountain, is an
easily accessible Iron Age hill
fort, which has spectacular
views of the north Wales
coastline. Here you'll find the
remains of around 50 stone
roundhouses enclosed by thick
stone walls. It can be accessed
on foot by various footpaths,
and by road via the Sychnant
Pass and Mountain Road.

HIT THE BEACH
One mile west of the town is
Conwy Sands, a great sandy
expanse with plenty of dunes.

GO SURFING
Surf Snowdonia
surfsnowdonia.co.uk
Conwy, LL32 8QE | 01492 353123
Park open daily 8.30am–11.30pm;
Wavegarden 10am–sunset
Fancy catching a wave? Try this
perfect lozenge-shaped fresh
lagoon, with a two-metre-high
barrelling wave that starts at
the centre of the lagoon, peels
perfectly for more than 150
metres, and dissipates softly
as it hits the shore. Surf

▶ Conwy Castle   MAP REF 337 F3

cadw.wales.gov.uk
LL32 8AY | 01492 592358 | Open all year Mar–Jun, Sep–Oct 9.30–5,
Jul–Aug 9.30–6, Nov–Feb, Mon–Sat 10–4, Sun 11–4
Although this castle may be slightly overshadowed by Caernarfon,
it is still one of the best in Wales and Edward I's most expensive
castle. Construction of this massive fortress began in 1283 and was
completed around 1287. During this very short time, the town's
defences were also built, taking in some 0.75 miles of walls, with
22 towers and 3 gateways.

Snowdonia is a revolutionary world-first inland surf lagoon and the UK's most compelling outdoor adventure destination.

PLAY A ROUND
Conwy (Caernarvonshire) Golf Club
conwygolfclub.com
Beacons Way, Morfa, LL32 8ER
01492 592423 | Open daily all year
This true links course offers visitors real golfing enjoyment in stunning scenery.

CROSS THE BRIDGE
Conwy Suspension Bridge
nationaltrust.org.uk
Conwy, LL32 8LD
Designed by Thomas Telford, one of the greatest engineers of the late 18th and early 19th century, this was the first bridge to span the river at Conwy. The bridge has been restored and the toll house furnished as it would have been a century ago.

EAT AND DRINK
Castle Hotel ●●
castlewales.co.uk
High Street, Conwy, LL32 8DB
01492 582800
Built on the site of a Cistercian abbey and with a Victorian bell-gabled facade of local green granite and red Ruabon bricks, this hotel aims to be 'boutique'. The restaurant, Dawsons, has a contemporary style and offers modern British cooking. Local flavour is big on the menu.

▼ Statue of Owain Glyndwr, Corwen

▶ PLACES NEARBY
Conwy is close to an RSPB
nature reserve and the towns of
Llandudno (see page 202) and
Colwyn Bay (see page 148).

RSPB Nature Reserve Conwy
rspb.org.uk/conwy
LL31 9XZ | 01492 584091

Explore the quiet nature trails,
get close up with birds and
other wildlife, or simply enjoy
a cup of coffee while enjoying
the fantastic views. There are
lots of activities for big and
small people alike here, and
various events are held
throughout the year.

▶ Corwen MAP REF 338 C5

Located on the banks of the River Dee, Corwen is a tiny town
with a population of roughly 3,000. It's best known for its links
with Owain Glyndwr, who proclaimed himself Prince of Wales
from his nearby manor of Glyndyfrdwy on 16 September 1400.
So began his 14-year rebellion against English rule. In 2007, a
life-size bronze statue of the prince mounted on his battle
horse was installed in the town's square. Besides this famous
Welsh ruler, the town – which grew up as a centre for cattle
drovers – is known for the motte of its Norman castle, the
13th-century Church of St Mael and St Sulien. Today, the main
economy is based around farming.

SEE A LOCAL CHAPEL
Rug Chapel
cadw.wales.gov.uk
Rug, LL21 9BT | 01490 412025
Open Apr–early Nov Wed–Sun 10–5,
BH Mon 10–5
Rug Chapel was built in 1637.
This rare, little-altered private
chapel is decorated in a highly

elaborate fashion and set in a
wooded landscape. The chapel's
modest exterior gives little hint
of the interior where local
artists and carvers were given
a free rein, with spectacular
results – see the altar rails,
family pews, painted gallery
and bench ends.

▶ Criccieth MAP REF 333 D2

This small seaside town in Cardigan Bay styles itself as the
'pearl in Wales, set on the shores of Snowdonia'. It's popular
with families and the main attraction is the ruins of Criccieth
Castle, with extensive views. In the centre lies Y Maes,
part of the medieval town common. The town is known for its
summer fairs and also for the pride it takes in its aesthetics –
it won the Wales in Bloom competition every year from 1999
to 2004. It's also associated with the former British Prime
Minister David Lloyd George, who grew up in the nearby village
of Llanystumdwy.

TAKE IN SOME HISTORY
Criccieth Castle
cadw.wales.gov.uk
LL52 0DP | 01766 522227
Open Apr–Oct daily 10–5, Nov–Mar
Fri–Sat 9.30–4, Sun 11–4
In 1404, Owain Glyndwr took
Criccieth Castle from the
English by force. Shortly
afterwards, however, it was
badly damaged in a fire and
never really used again. Today,
the castle is in ruins, although
its commanding position on a
promontory overlooking the
picturesque Tremadog Bay
gives an idea of the status it
once must have enjoyed.
A massive gatehouse still
presents a forbidding face to
the world, while the thickness
of its crumbling walls gives
it an aura of strength
and permanence.

PLAY A ROUND
Criccieth Golf Club
cricciethgolfclub.co.uk
Ednyfed Hill, LL52 0PH
01766 522154 | Open daily all year
A hilly course on high ground
with generous fairways and
natural hazards. The ninth tee
has panoramic views.

▼ Criccieth Castle

EAT AND DRINK
Bron Eifion Country House Hotel ⊕
broneifion.co.uk
LL52 0SA | 01766 522385
Set in landscaped gardens with views over Snowdonia and the coastline of the Llyn Peninsula, Bron Eifion is a small Victorian country house in the classic style. Inside, its period features have survived unscathed and include the impressive Great Hall with a minstrels' gallery. The Garden Room restaurant aims for a more contemporary look and serves up Modern Welsh cooking.

Caffi Cwrt Tearoom
Y Maes, Criccieth LL52 0AG
Try tea, sandwiches and homemade cakes in this charming, old-fashioned, 18th-century cottage, which used to be a Court of Petty Sessions, located just off the village green. The cottage has beamed ceilings and the tea garden has a view of the castle.

▶ **PLACES NEARBY**
Close to Criccieth is the LLoyd George Museum and the pretty holiday resort of Porthmadog (see page 268).

Lloyd George Museum and Highgate
gwynedd.gov.uk/museums
Llanystumdwy, LL52 0SH | 01766 522071 | Open Mon before Easter, daily 10–5.30, Apr–May Mon–Fri 10.30–5 (also Sat in Jun), Jul–Sep daily 10.30–5, Oct Mon–Fri 11–4; other times by appointment
Explore the life and times of World War I prime minister David Lloyd George in this museum. Highgate, his boyhood home, has been recreated, and is as it was when he lived there (1864–80), along with his Uncle Lloyd's shoemaking workshop.

▶ **Crickhowell** MAP REF 326 C2
An upmarket town close to the English border in Powys, Crickhowell has a fine 19th-century high street selling a wide variety of goods. The shops include many family-run businesses as well as an artisan chocolatier and an artists' cooperative art gallery. The town is set close to Table Mountain – Crug Hywel in Welsh, from which the town takes its name – and some stunning Welsh countryside. It is the perfect spot for a weekend away, with plenty of luxury holiday cottages to rent nearby and fine walking in the Black Mountains area of the Brecon Beacons National Park (see page 105). The Green Man music festival takes place in nearby Glanusk Park each August.

PLAY A ROUND
The Old Rectory Country Hotel and Golf Club
rectoryhotel.co.uk
NP8 1PH | 01873 810373
Open Mon–Sat all year
This is a sheltered course with easy walking.

EAT AND DRINK

The Bear ◉

bearhotel.co.uk

High Street, Crickhowell,
NP8 1BW | 01873 810408

The old stagecoach doesn't run past here any more, but an enduring testament to the last time it did is present in the form of a Victorian timetable in the bar. The Bear goes back further than that, though, to the reign of Henry III in the 1430s, when it must have been as much a local beacon as it is now, at the heart of the Brecon Beacons National Park. Its traditional interiors and ancient arched cellar where the beers are kept are all part of the deal, as is vibrant modern food with the emphasis on regionally sourced ingredients.

5 top cool natural wonders

▶ **Dan-yr-Ogof National Showcaves**
page 157
Explorers have uncovered 10 miles of underground lakes, stalactites and stalagmites and magnificent passages and chambers.

▶ **The Drowned Forest of Wales**
Head to Borth Beach in Ceredigion at low tide to see the remains of a 6,000-year-old forest.

▶ **Glyder Fach, Snowdonia**
page 299
This dramatic mountain (3,261 feet/993m) is crowned by a famous cantilever rock, a massive precariously balanced slab that's a favourite spot for climbers.

▶ **Pistyll Rhaeadr, Powys**
page 265
With a drop of nearly 246 feet, this is the tallest waterfall in Wales.

▶ **Wolf's Leap, Cambrian Mountains**
This tight rocky canyon on the River Irfon, near Abergwesyn, is a perfect spot for wild swimming.

▶ **PLACES NEARBY**

Crickhowell is close to the market town of Abergavenny (see page 66), as well as Tretower Court and Castle. A great local walk climbs up the Sugarloaf Mountain – suitable for children (four and upwards).

Tretower Court and Castle

cadw.wales.gov.uk
NP8 1RD | 01874 730279
Open Apr–Oct daily 10–5, Nov–Mar Fri–Sat 10–4, Sun 11–4

This delightful site comprises a stone Norman tower, with walls nine feet thick, a splayed-out bottom to make it difficult to undermine, and tiny arched windows. It stands among trees in the beautiful Usk Valley. There's also Tretower Court, built in the early 15th century. You can admire the magnificent wooden ceiling in the hall and the gallery's sliding shutters. The building is mostly well preserved, although some parts have been reconstructed. There is also a recreated 15th-century garden within the castle grounds.

▶ Dan-yr-Ogof National Showcaves MAP REF 325 F2

showcaves.co.uk

Abercrave, Swansea SA9 1GJ | 01639 730284 | Open Apr–2 Nov daily 10–3

Fancy a spot of caving? Jeff and Tommy Morgan did, way back in 1912. They were the duo that first had the courage to explore this complex of caves under the Brecon Beacons, using candles to light their way and arrows in the sand to find their way back. What they discovered was an array of stalactites and stalagmites, but they were prevented from penetrating too far into the mountain by a lake. Not a pair to be deterred, they soon returned, this time with coracles – traditional one-man fishing boats used on the rivers of west Wales. They crossed one lake, then carried on to cross three more. Eventually, they discovered more magnificent passages and chambers – only to be stopped in their tracks by a very tight space. This hurdle wasn't surmounted until 1963, when Eileen Davies, a local girl and member of the South Wales Caving Club, struggled through it. She and others have now found over 10 miles of unique caves.

Visitors can tour many of these caves, including Bone Cave, where 42 Bronze Age skeletons were found, and the Dome of St Pauls in Cathedral Cave, where waterfalls feed into an underground lake. Cavers believe that this is the tip of the iceberg and that there is still much to discover.

▶ Denbigh MAP REF 338 B3

Lying north of Ruthin and south of St Aseph in north Wales, Denbigh can be found in the wide and verdant Vale of Clwyd dividing the rolling Clwydian Hills. It's a medieval county town that grew up around the glove-making industry.

Denbigh means 'little fortress', probably referring to the original hilltop castle belonging to the ancient Welsh princes, rather than the large Norman castle you see today. After defeating the Welsh in 1282, Edward I granted the town to his friend, the English nobleman Henry de Lacy, who became the first Lord of Denbigh. The castle and its town walls were completed not long afterwards, at which point the action really started, culminating in a successful six-month siege of Royalist troops during the Civil War. Although the castle fell into decay not long afterwards, there's still much to see, including the gatehouse, fronted by two polygonal towers, and walls that give tremendous views of the town and valley.

Beneath the castle, Denbigh has many historical nooks to explore. Narrow alleys such as Back Row thread through the medieval part of the town, revealing buildings from the 15th century. You can also see the remains of a 14th-century

Carmelite friary, and the walls of an unfinished cathedral dreamed up by Dudley, Earl of Leicester, favourite of Queen Elizabeth I, but abandoned on his death in 1588.

From Denbigh you can also explore the local Clwydian Hills, which have long been popular with walkers who delight in the heather ridges. Moel Famau, which means 'mother mountain', at 1,818 feet (554m) is the highest of the range. Its summit monument was built in 1810 to celebrate the jubilee of King George III. The square tower and spire were wrecked by a violent gale 50 years later, and the place lay in ruins until 1970, when it was tidied up. To the west, and clearly in view from the ridge, are the concentric earthwork rings of Maes y Gaer, just one of many ancient fortifications on the range.

TAKE IN SOME HISTORY
Denbigh Castle
cadw.wales.gov.uk
LL16 3NB | 01745 813385
Open Mar–Oct daily 10–5;
winter hours vary, call or
check website for details
Even in decay this tower exudes power and importance. Its most impressive feature is its great gatehouse, although the centuries have not treated it kindly. There is also a statue of Edward I, now very weathered. An unusual feature is the steeply sloping barbican that protected the back of the castle.

EXPLORE BY BIKE
Ride North Wales
ridenorthwales.co.uk
C/O Denbighshire Countryside
Service, Loggerheads CP, near
Mold, CH7 6LT | 01352 810614
This mountain biking specialist covers much of north Wales, including the Clwydian Hills, a 22-mile-long chain of hills between Prestatyn and Llandegla. It's the ideal way to explore and enjoy the countryside.

PLAY A ROUND
Denbigh Golf Club
denbighgolfclub.co.uk
Henllan Road, L16 5AA
01745 814159 | Open daily all year
This parkland course in the Vale of Clwyd provides a testing and varied game.

▶ PLACES NEARBY
Close to Denbigh is a lovely craft centre at Ruthin, and further away, to the northeast, the seaside town of Abergele (see page 69).

Ruthin Craft Centre
ruthincraftcentre.org.uk
Park Road, Ruthin, LL15 1BB
01824 704774 | Open daily all year
10–5.30
As one of the leading craft centres in Britain, Ruthin has three on-site galleries, a number of artists in residence and interesting changing exhibitions. There are many workshops teaching a range of crafts. There's also contemporary work for sale from some of the country's leading craftworkers.

▶ Dolaucothi Gold Mines MAP REF 329 D5

nationaltrust.org.uk

Pumsaint, Llanwrda, SA19 8US | 01558 650177 | Open mid-Mar to Jun, Sep–Oct daily 11–5, Jul–Aug 10–6

Between Lampeter and Llandovery in a remote part of mid-Wales lies Britain's only known Roman gold mine. In fact, it may date back as early as the Bronze Age. It was also in use from Victorian times until the 1930s.

You can take a long guided tour (children under five are not permitted) exploring the Roman/Victorian caves and passages. Wearing a helmet and carrying a lamp for the underground section, you can also try your hand at panning for gold. Look out for the Roman axe marks still visible in the rock at the entrance to the mining passage.

Please note, underground tours involve steep slopes so sturdy footwear is essential.

▶ Dolgellau MAP REF 333 F4

Ten miles east of Barmouth, Dolgellau sits snugly among rural pastureland in the shadow of Cadair Idris. Climbing and walking on this mountain is the main attraction here. Steeped in Celtic legends and myths, Cadair Idris (the Seat of Idris) is the most romantic of the Welsh peaks. Though not quite reaching the heights of central Snowdonia, it has fine crag-bound tarns, sheer rock faces and wide-sweeping views across what seems like the whole of Wales. It's also set in a green, fertile landscape of oak woods, dashing streams and pretty stone cottages dotted across pastoral foothills. The main starting points for walks are Minffordd, which lies just north of Tal-y-llyn, and Pont Dyffrydan car park on the Old Cader Road, the start of the route known as the Pony Path.

As for the town itself, it began life in the 12th century but very little remains from that era – even the old parliament building, *Cwrt Plas yn Dre*, where Owain Glyndwr plotted the downfall of the English in 1398, was pulled down in 1881. The town grew during the 18th and 19th centuries from the proceeds of the wool industry – celebrated every year in the local 'Wool Race' – and also a gold rush. At its peak, more than 500 men were employed in the gold and copper mines in the hills around Dolgellau.

The town once had a significant Quaker community. Rather grimly, a museum in Eldon Square tells how they were persecuted. Rowland Ellis, one of their number, emigrated to Pennsylvania in 1686, where he founded the famous Bryn Mawr women's college at the University of Pennsylvania.

VISIT THE MUSEUM
Quaker Heritage Centre
gwynedd.gov.uk
Sgwar Elson, Dolgellau
01341 424680 | Open summer
daily 10–6, winter Thu–Mon
10–5; check council website to
confirm opening times
This centre tells the story of the
local Quaker community that
lived here, of their persecution
and emigration to Pennsylvania.

HIT A TRAIL
Mawddach Trail
mawddachtrail.co.uk
The 9.5-mile Mawddach Trail
between Dolgellau and
Barmouth is a biking or walking
trail along an old railway line,
encompassing woodland,
saltings, the stunning
Mawddach Estuary and some
spectacular bridges. There are
plenty of birds to spot en route.

▼ Foel Cynwch, Dolgellau

PLAY A ROUND
Dolgellau Golf Club
dolgellaugolfclub.com
Pencefn Road, LL40 2ES
01341 422603 | Open daily all year
One of the most beautiful courses in Wales and a great place to enjoy nine holes.

EAT AND DRINK
Bwyty Mawddach Restaurant ⬢
mawddach.com
Pen-y-Garnedd, Llanelltyd, LL40 2TA | 01341 421752
This old granite barn has been transformed into a simple, modern restaurant. Spread over two floors, there are exposed beams in the vaulted ceiling upstairs, slate floors on the ground floor, and a glass frontage that gives views over the Mawddach Estuary and Cadair Idris. Dishes are well prepared and hearty.

▶ PLACES NEARBY
Close to Dolgellau is an abbey, the ruins of a castle, and the brilliant bike park at Coed-y-Brenin.

Castell y Bere
cadw.wales.gov.uk
Llanfihangel-y-Pennant, Abergynolwyn | 01443 336000
Open all year daily 10–4
Ten miles from Dolgellau lies this Welsh castle. Once very powerful, Castell y Bere controlled one of the primary routes through central Wales, but today the major road runs further south and the castle is abandoned and lonely. Little remains and only foundations represent the original buildings. Built by Llywelyn the Great in the 1220s, it is probable that the castle was intended to be more a step towards securing his position as Prince of Wales in the minds of his warring compatriots than a stand against the invading Normans. The castle was roughly triangular, following the shape of the rock, with towers at each angle. The entrance was defended by an impressive array of ditches, as well as a drawbridge and a portcullis. During Edward I's wars against the Welsh princes, Castell y Bere was besieged and damaged. It was completely abandoned by 1295.

Cymer Abbey
cadw.wales.gov.uk
LL40 2HE | 01443 336000
Open Mar–Oct daily 10–5, Nov–Mar 10–4
The abbey was built for the Cistercians in the 13th century, and appears to have been left unfinished. The church is the best-preserved building, with windows and arcades still visible. The other buildings have been plundered for stone, but low outlines remain.

Cycle hire at Forest Visitor Centre
beicsbrenin.co.uk
LL40 2HZ | 01341 440728
Coed-y-Brenin is a great place for bike rides and is Wales' first trail centre with technical routes and beginner trails.

▶ **Dolwyddelan Castle** MAP REF 337 E5

cadw.wales.gov.uk

LL25 0JD | 01690 750366 | Open Nov–28 Mar Mon–Sat 10–4,
Sun 11.30–4, 29 Mar–Sep Mon–Sat 10–5, Sun 11.30–4, Oct–Mar
Mon–Sat 10–4, Sun 11.30–4

This sturdy three-storey tower seems almost insignificant
among the sweeping hills of the Welsh countryside. Its precise
origins are obscured by time, but the Princes of Wales built
the castle to guard the ancient pathway that ran from
Meirionnydd to the Vale of Conwy. It's said that one of Wales'
most famous princes, Llywelyn the Great, was born here
around 1173.

Edward I's forces captured Dolwyddelan Castle in 1283
during his Welsh campaign. Seeing its great strategic value,
the king had it refortified and manned by English soldiers.
The castle itself was originally a single rectangular tower
of two storeys but was later given an extra floor and a

▼ Dolwyddelan Castle

battlemented roof line. Later still, thick walls were added to form an enclosure with another rectangular tower, all protected by ditches cut into the rock. Although the Welsh were responsible for building the castle, the design was borrowed heavily from the Norman style. There was a first-floor entrance, protected by a drawbridge. It is now cared for by Cadw.

EAT AND DRINK

Elen's Castle Hotel

hotelinsnowdonia.co.uk

Dolwyddelan, Betws-y-Coed,

LL25 0EJ | 01690 750207

Elen's Castle was once owned by the Earl of Ancaster, who sold it to his gamekeeper. The latter opened it as a coaching inn specialising in hunting parties around 1880. It is now a family-run pub featuring a traditional bar with a wood-burning stove and the intimate Siabod Restaurant, which has breathtaking views of the mountains and Lledr River. Wherever possible produce for the kitchen is sourced locally. Water from the onsite Roman well is said to have healing properties.

▶ Elan Valley   MAP 330 B3

elanvalley.org.uk

Located to the west of Rhayader (see page 280) in Powys, this river valley is often known as the Welsh Lake District. It was created between 1893 and 1952 to provide water for the city of Birmingham, and comprises dams and reservoirs along the Cambrian Mountains. Initially, the scheme caused controversy as it flooded several existing communities of around 100 people. However, enough time has now passed for the lakes themselves to be recognised as attractions.

The dams are worth an ogle, being built in elaborate Victorian style. Together they now supply around 70 million gallons of water daily for Birmingham and parts of south and mid-Wales.

The area is also famous for its scenery. More than 80 per cent of it comprises Sites of Special Scientific Interest (SSSIs) and there are more than 80 miles of nature trails and footpaths. You can also cycle here along the popular Elan Valley Trail, making a loop from Rhayader around the reservoirs. It's also used by walkers and horse-riders and is even suitable for buggies and wheelchairs. The valley is also rich in wildlife, especially the red kite, identified by its large wing span and forked tail. More information can be found at the Elan Valley Visitor Centre, which has an exhibition, cafe and maps and information on the local wildlife.

Erddig MAP REF 339 E4

nationaltrust.org.uk
LL13 0YT | 01978 355314 | Open all year daily Apr–Oct 11–5,
Nov–Mar 11–4

Enjoy Downton Abbey with its upstairs, downstairs life? If so, then you'll be sure to love Erddig, an 18th-century house and country park located close to Wrexham in north Wales (see page 320). Whether you consider it to be an architectural masterpiece or not, it offers great insight into the real life of a gentry family over the course of 250 years. The extensive downstairs area contains a unique collection of servants' portraits, while the upstairs rooms are an amazing treasure trove of fine furniture, textiles and wallpapers. Outside, an impressive range of outbuildings includes stables, a smithy, joiner's shop and sawmill. It's the tour that's the best bit, though. It begins at the working end of the estate, where the carpenters, blacksmiths, stable hands and laundry maids toiled away. The workshops are fully equipped and the sawmill has a display of photographs and a video showing the extent of the restoration work carried out at Erddig through the centuries.

After passing through the kitchens and servants' hall, you reach the grand neoclassical rooms occupied by the Yorke family until the 1970s. They are still furnished with wonderful collections of gilt and silver furniture amassed by John Mellor, ancestor of the Yorkes, who bought Erddig from its original owner in 1716. Perhaps the most remarkable piece of furniture is the shining gold and cream state bed, complete with Chinese silk hangings. The bed was very nearly lost when the house was in a bad state of repair; rain poured through the collapsing plaster ceiling of the bedroom through the canopy and into buckets placed on the bed. However, after two years in the conservation department of the Victoria and Albert Museum, this magnificent piece of furniture has been restored to its original condition. In contrast are the sparsely furnished attic bedrooms where the maids slept, and the nearby workroom where they spent their rare moments of leisure.

Fforest Fawr Geopark MAP REF 325 F2

fforestfawrgeopark.org.uk
Brecon Beacons National Park Authority, Plas y Ffynnon,
Cambrian Way, Brecon, Powys, LD3 7HP | 01874 620415

So much of Wales is tied up in its geology and that's what makes this geopark so important and special. Which story do you want to hear? The one about rocks taking 500 million years to form? Or how ice and volcanic eruptions shaped the landscape? Or how about the Industrial Revolution, hacking away at precious minerals? Fforest Fawr – meaning 'great forest' – is a vast area of upland country, including mountain and moorland, woods and meadows, that forms part of the Brecon Beacons National Park. Stretching from Llandovery in the north to Merthyr Tydfil in the south, Llandeilo in the west to Brecon in the east, it covers miles of mountain, moorland, woods, meadows, lakes and rivers. It also encompasses the Dan-yr-Ogof National Showcaves (see page 157) and the Brecon Beacons' mighty reservoirs.

Fforest Fawr was made Wales' first European geopark in 2005. Its aim is to promote and support sustainable tourism and local economies, while safeguarding the natural environment. There are a variety of activities on offer. Most involve geo-tourism and are educational, including schools programmes, guided walks and museum exhibitions. Information can be obtained on the area's geology, wildlife, archaeology, legends, history and much more. For more information, contact the park warden.

▷ Fishguard MAP REF 323 D2

Located on Wales' west coast, between Cardigan and St Davids, Fishguard was built in 1906 as a rival to the great shipping ports of Liverpool and Southampton, although it never reached that potential. The town still remains a busy port and the main sailing place in north Pembrokeshire; however, it's largely overlooked, as most people simply use it as a base to pass through on their way to and from Ireland. Despite this, it has great appeal as a small seaside town with attractive fishermen's cottages dotted along the shoreline, a harbour and some decent pubs and places to eat. Perhaps its biggest claim to fame is that it's the setting for the 1971 film adaption of Dylan Thomas' *Under Milk Wood*, starring Richard Burton and Elizabeth Taylor. It also featured – albeit briefly – in John Huston's 1956 version of *Moby Dick*, starring Gregory Peck.

Fishguard is also known as the setting of the last foreign invasion of Britain in 1797. It was an unlucky coincidence. Led by Irish-American William Tate, four large vessels carrying French convicts and mercenaries intended to land at Bristol and march to Liverpool, keeping England busy while the French occupied Ireland. But bad weather blew them ashore at Carregwastad, just north of Fishguard, where they attempted to steal local poultry and get drunk. In the end they were efficiently caught by local farmers' wives brandishing pitchforks and were made to surrender in the local hostelry, the Royal

Oak Inn, where evidence of this ridiculous saga can still be seen today.

The Royal Oak continues to plays an important part in village life today and is one of the venues for the Fishguard Folk Festival held each year in May. During the day, performances at this excellent event are perfect for families, while more raucous skits take place at the pub in the evenings. Music master classes are also offered.

CATCH A PERFORMANCE
Theatr Gwaun
its4u.org.uk
West Street, Fishguard, SA65 9AD
01348 873421
This is a community theatre-cum-cinema run mainly by volunteers. It offers a rich programme of film, music and events throughout the year.

5 top cycling tours

▶ Weave your way through the Wye Valley, Cambrian coast and Snowdonia with **Bicycle Beano** (bicyclebeano.co.uk)

▶ Tootle around Anglesey with **Crwydro Môn** (angleseywalkingholidays.com/cycling.html)

▶ Go all over Wales – even on an electric bike – with **Drover Holidays** (droverholidays.co.uk)

▶ Try a six-day, self-guided tour in the Black Mountains with **PedalAway** (pedalaway.co.uk)

▶ Get rough and really mucky in rural Wales with **Wheely Wonderful Cycling** (wheelywonderfulcycling.co.uk)

EXPLORE BY BIKE
Pembrokeshire Bikes
pembrokeshirebikes.co.uk
1 Rushacre Enterprise Park, Redstone Road, Narberth, SA67 7ES
01834 862755
This cycle hire company is based in Narberth but offers a delivery service to Fishguard.

GO FISHING
Yet-y-Gors Fishery
yet-y-gors.co.uk
Manorwen, Fishguard, SA65 9RE
01348 873497
Has two coarse lakes plus still-water fly-fishing for trout.

SADDLE UP
Llanwnda Riding and Trekking
llanwndastables.co.uk
Penrhiw Fach, Llanwnda, Goodwick, SA64 0HS | 01348 873595
This is a great place to enjoy trekking, riding or hacking.

▶ PLACES NEARBY
Newport (see page 253) and Cardigan (see page 137) are both close to Fishguard, as well as the enticing Harp Inn pub.

The Harp Inn
theharpatletterston.co.uk
31 Haverfordwest Road, Letterston SA62 5UA | 01348 840061

▲ Fishguard's Old Harbour

Formerly a small working farm and home to a weekly market, this 15th-century free house remained largely unchanged for 500 years. The building has a stylish conservatory restaurant where diners can enjoy dishes using fresh local produce. Alternatively, the bar lunch menu offers a good selection of classic pub meals. Try one of the real ales on tap. Enjoy lunch in all areas with your children. Some of the old farm buildings have been converted into accommodation.

....

▶ Flint MAP REF 339 D2

East of Rhyl and west of Liverpool, Flint has always occupied a strategic position on the western shore of the Dee Estuary. The castle, built between 1277 and 1284, was the first of Edward I's creations to be built during his campaigns to control the Welsh. Owain Glyndwr tried to capture it in his 1400 revolt but failed. The town itself is believed to be one of – if not the – oldest charters in Wales, dating from 1284.

TAKE IN SOME HISTORY
Flint Castle
cadw.wales.gov.uk
CH6 5PH | 01443 336000
Open all year daily 10–4
Building work on Flint Castle started in 1277, and the huge workforce – believed to be around 2,300 labourers – was paid handsomely, largely owing to the fact that building a castle in such a hostile land was hard and dangerous work. The castle itself was a rectangular enclosure with four round towers at the corners, and was further protected by additional walls, a moat and some deep ditches. One of the round corner towers was larger than

the others and protected by a moat. It also had its own kitchens, living quarters and chapel. Today, this once vitally important castle leads a quiet life hidden behind the modern town, standing lonely and forgotten on the marshy shores of the River Dee, and bypassed by tourists heading west.

PLAY A ROUND
Flint Golf Club
flintgolfclub.co.uk
Cornist Park, Flint, CH6 5HJ
01352 732327 | Open Mon–Sat and Sun pm
A parkland course with woods and streams and views of the Dee Estuary and Welsh hills.

▶ PLACES NEARBY
Attractions near Flint include an abbey and inn, and the towns of Rhyl (see page 286), Prestatyn (see page 274) and Mold (see page 231).

Basingwerk Abbey
cadw.wales.gov.uk
Greenfield Valley Heritage Park, Greenfield, CH8 7GH
01443 336000 | Open all year daily 10–4

Founded around 1131 by Ranulf de Gernon, Earl of Chester, the first stone church dates from the beginning of the 13th century. During the Middle Ages a thriving artistic community grew up around the abbey. The last abbot surrendered the house to the Crown in 1536. The abbey is close to the heritage park visitor centre.

Black Lion Inn
theblacklioninn.uk.com
Babell, CH8 8PZ | 01352 720239
A building surely cannot survive for 700 years without acquiring the odd ghost or two, and this former coaching inn is reputed to have plenty, including that of a Canadian man forever asking if he can come in. From its rural location it commands stunning views, and over recent years has become a destination restaurant in north Wales. The bar has comfy sofas to sink into with a glass of one of the locally brewed cask ales. The menu is modern British. Wednesday is pie night. The last Wednesday of each month is Celtic Music Night, and there's a beer festival in September.

▶ Glamorgan Heritage Coast   MAP REF 325 F6
glamorganheritagecoast.com
Heritage Coast Visitor Centre, Dunraven Bay, Southerndown, Bridgend, CF32 0RP | 01656 880157
Stretching between Porthcawl (see page 267) and east **Aberthaw** on the coastline of south Wales, not far from Cardiff, Glamorgan Heritage Coast was one of Britain's first designated heritage coastlines, the other two being Dorset and Suffolk. The project, launched in 1973, covers a 14-mile stretch of coastline incorporating Porthcawl, **Dunraven Park**, **Monknash**

Coast, **St Donats** and **Summerhouse Point**. It covers cheerful beach holiday resorts, such as Porthcawl and Barry Island (see page 84), and also striking coastal countryside and lush green hills. The aim is to conserve the 'unique character of its landscape and habitats' for future generations.

If you are interested in walking, this area will appeal for its Heritage Coast Walk. It starts at **Newton Point**, just round the twin beaches of **Sandy Bay** and **Trecco Bay**. South of here and at the mouth of the River Ogmore are the immense sand dunes of **Merthyr Mawr Warren**, the setting for some scenes in the 1962 classic film, *Lawrence of Arabia*.

Further along the coast, at **Southerndown**, the unusual cliffs consist of horizontally bedded limestone alternating with softer shales. Around Dunraven, where they face the prevailing southwesterly winds, the cliffs are unstable and deeply eroded into stripy bands. At **Nash Point**, more striking geology is on show, and many different types of snail shells can be found fossilised in the rock. At the cliff tops, rare meadow and maritime species flourish, while by the Nash Point Lighthouse lies a rare colony of the tuberous thistle, undiscovered here until 1977.

The sparkling white lighthouse was erected in 1832 to warn incoming vessels about the treacherous sandbanks lying at the entrance to the Bristol Channel. This was the last manned lighthouse in Wales, in operation until 1998. Now, the former keepers' cottages are let out as holiday accommodation. There are public tours of the lighthouse, and it is one of the few operational lighthouses to be licensed for weddings. It might look like the ultimate romantic wedding destination, but be warned – the foghorn is tested at least twice a month. Elsewhere on the south-facing coastline around St Donats, the cliffs are sheltered and wearing away much more slowly than those near Dunraven.

The main landmark here is **St Donats Castle**, which dates from around 1300. American newspaper magnate William Randolph Hearst entertained high society here in the 1920s and 1930s, with Charlie Chaplin and John F Kennedy among his guests. In 1962, it became the home of Atlantic College, an international school for 16- to 18-year-olds.

At Summerhouse Point, near Llantwit Major, the remains of a stone-built octagonal summer house from around 1730 are set within an Iron Age hill fort. The Heritage Coast Walk ends at **Limpert Bay**, just before Breaksea Point, the most southerly extremity of Wales. For more information head to the visitor centre at Dunraven Park.

▶ The Gower Peninsula MAP REF 324 C4

With its first-class amenities and Britain's first designated Area of Outstanding Natural Beauty in 1956, the Gower offers roughly 70 square miles of unspoiled coastline, castles and villages. The perfect holiday destination, it is the ideal place to surf, kite surf or boogie board, with stunning beaches and pretty inland areas. There are also four National Nature Reserves and ample gardens, parks, cycle-paths and bridleways. The gateway city of Swansea (see page 306) is regularly voted Britain's number-one city for lifestyle.

The peninsula's coastline has two sides to its personality. The northern shore has a low-lying coastline fringed with saltings and marshland. Further east are the sands at **Penclawdd**, where hardy villagers still come to pick cockles. But the most impressive part of the peninsula lies in the far west around Rhossili (see page 283), where sweeping beaches, accessible only on foot, stretch north, overlooked by **Rhossili Down**, the highest point on Gower at 633 feet. The land ends in the narrow promontory of **Worm's Head**. In the south and southwest, towering limestone cliffs are broken by a succession of sheltered sandy bays, including **Langland** and **Three Cliffs Bay**, and also larger beaches such as Port Eynon, Rhossili and **Oxwich Bay** – another key highlight of the Gower. Lying on the south coast, there is a National Nature Reserve with one of the most diverse coastal habitats in Britain, including salt and freshwater marshes and lagoons set behind the beach and sand dunes. It also supports more than 600 species of flowering plant.

The village of **Oxwich** lies at the western edge of the bay. It's very charming, with thatched and whitewashed cottages, and has been important since the Norman de la Mare family built a castle here. Their tombs can still be seen in the lovely church of St Illtyd, which stands deep in woodland at the edge of the bay, some way from the village.

Further around the coast is Three Cliffs Bay. You'll see why it's so named – it consists of glorious golden sands set beneath the stunning, almost vertical limestone strata of three cliffs. The popular climbers' crags are the start of a fine stretch of superb cliff scenery extending past the houses of Southgate to **Pwlldu Head**. Pwlldu means Blackpool, but that's where the similarity with England's version ends, for you'll find yourself looking down from this massive headland to a pebble storm beach at the head of the lovely wooded limestone gorge of the Bishopston Valley. Further round still and you'll come to the more commercial **Caswell Bay**. Surfers love this sandy cove overlooked by pines and self-catering apartments. Next up is The Mumbles, where the world of the Gower begins to collide with that of urban Swansea (see page 306). A pier, amusement parlours, ice-cream kiosks and cafes might make country lovers want to retreat rather quickly back to the real Gower, although the children will want to stay, play and eat. You might also want to stop by Mumbles Pier, once a destination for the world's first passenger train service, on a horse-drawn railway from Swansea that was used for carrying coal. Converted for steam trains, then electric trams, it ran from 1807 until 1960.

Although most people come for the beaches, Gower also has two caves – Minchin Hole and Paviland. The latter lies between Rhossili and Port Eynon and is where, in 1823, the Reverend William Buckland, a professor of geology at Oxford University, found a fossilised and anatomically modern human skeleton laid out with seashell and mammoth-bone jewellery and scattered with a red ochre dye. Owing to these adornments, it became known as the 'red lady of Paviland'. Buckland thought 'she' was Roman, but modern techniques have established that it was in fact the remains of a young man who died approximately 33,000 years ago.

Inland Gower is mostly heath and grazing farmland broken up into tiny parcels of fields, but it has its fair share of attractions, with a smattering of little villages, such as **Reynoldston**, situated on the Cefn Bryn ridge from where there are far-reaching views of the peninsula. You can walk along here, enjoying fine views of the entire peninsula before retiring to the King Arthur Hotel – a delightful country pub – for a pint. Around one mile to the northwest of the village, on the next rise, is Arthur's Stone (*Maen Ceti*), an unusually large neolithic chambered tomb consisting of 10 uprights and a massive, 30-tonne capstone. The ruins of 14th-century **Weobley Castle** are also here. Although it was strongly fortified, with further modifications made in the 16th century, the castle later fell into decline and was used as a farmhouse. An exhibition on the site traces its history.

▶ Rhossili Bay

TAKE IN SOME HISTORY
Oxwich Castle
cadw.wales.gov.uk
Gower, Swansea, SA3 1ND
01792 390359 | Open Apr–Oct
daily 10–5
On the Gower Peninsula, this
Tudor mansion is a testament
in stone to the pride and
ambitions of the Mansel
dynasty of Welsh gentry. In the
E-shaped wing is an exhibition
on Gower and 'Chieftains and
Princes of Wales'.

Weobley Castle
cadw.wales.gov.uk
West Castle Farm, Llanrhidian,
Swansea, SA3 1HB | 01792 390012
Open 29 Mar–Oct daily 9.30–6,
Nov–Mar 9.30–5
There aren't many places left
where you can stand at the
same window as others did half
a millennium ago and see the
same unspoiled view. The vista
from Weobley – pronounced
Web-lee – over the north Gower
marshlands and mudflats has
hardly changed in centuries.
This 12th-century manor house,
rich in intricate decorations,
has an exhibition on Weobley
and other historic sites.

PLAY A ROUND
Fairwood Park Golf Club
fairwoodpark.com
Blackhills Lane, Gower, Swansea,
SA2 7JN | 01792 297849
Open daily all year
This parkland championship
course – the flattest and
longest in Swansea – is
considered to be the most
beautiful in southwest Wales.

EAT AND DRINK
Britannia Inn
britanniainngower.co.uk
Llanmadoc, SA3 1DB
01792 386624
The Britannia's attractive
whitewashed and flower-
bedecked exterior features a
terrace with lovely Gower
views. Inside, chunky wooden
furniture and beamed ceilings
contribute to a welcoming
ambience. Beer gardens front
and back are home to a variety
of pets. The fixed-price lunch
menu is indicative of the quality
fare on offer.

Fairyhill ◉◉
fairyhill.net
Reynoldston, SA3 1BS
01792 390139
For a restorative retreat, this
lovely 18th-century country
house is hard to beat. It's got
bags of style and an interior
kitted out to befit a modern
country house. It's also set in 24
acres of delightful grounds,
with mature woodland, a lake
and trout stream, so there's
plenty of room to shake off
other guests without venturing
too far from base. The
restaurant makes excellent use
of the produce from the region
and delivers a refined
experience that doesn't feel in
the least bit stuffy, with Welsh
Black beef, salt marsh lamb,
Penclawdd cockles and fresh
fish, most from a 10-mile radius
around the Gower.

King Arthur Hotel
see Parkmill, page 258

▶ Greenwood Forest Park MAP REF 337 D4

greenwoodforestpark.co.uk

LL56 4QN | 01248 670076 | Open Feb half term, mid-Mar to Oct daily
10–5.30; Dec–Feb Enchanted Wood Barn only

If you're travelling in north Wales with a tribe of young ones,
it would seem churlish not to stop here. Located within easy
distance of Bangor, Anglesey, Betws-y-Coed and Porthmadog,
it's the perfect place to let off steam with its many imaginative
activities. Highlights include a 230-foot sled run, jungle boat
ride and mini tractors. Kids can also build dens, ride the green
dragon rollercoaster or try longbow archery. The park is filled
with animals from peacocks to rabbits. It has an arboretum
and gardens, a sculpture trail and a rainforest boardwalk.

▶ Grosmont, Skenfrith & White Castle, Monmouthshire

Grosmont Castle MAP REF 327 E1

cadw.wales.gov.uk

NP7 8EQ | 01443 336000 | Open all year daily 10–4

Skenfrith Castle MAP REF 327 E1

cadw.wales.gov.uk

NP7 8UH | 01443 336000 | Open all year daily 10–4

White Castle MAP REF 327 E2

cadw.wales.gov.uk

NP7 8UD | 01600 780380 | Open all year daily 10–4

In their bid to control the borderlands of Monmouthshire –
an area otherwise known as the Marches – the Normans built
a triangle of castles: Grosmont, Skenfrith and White. At first,
they were simple wooden structures strengthened by
earthworks, but when the lively Welsh refused to stop
attacking them, it was decided more permanent fortresses
were needed. It came down to one of King John's barons, the
Earl of Kent, Hubert de Burgh, to provide them. Of course,
things failed to run smoothly and he lost them twice to the
Welsh. The upshot of this was that these castles had two
main building phases.

Grosmont, for instance, was begun in 1201 with the building
of the rectangular hall, while the gatehouse and round towers
were only added in his second reign of ownership, between
1219 and 1232. Grosmont is also associated with Jack O'Kent,
a local folk hero. The Devil vowed to take O'Kent, whether he

was buried in the church or outside it. For that reason, O'Kent arranged to be buried under the wall of the village church, so that he was neither inside nor out.

Skenfrith Castle is not quite as impressive. Built on the River Monnow to command one of the main routes in and out of England, it has a round keep set inside an imposing towered curtain wall, but is largely ruined.

The third castle – the White Castle – was so named for its white rendering, although this can no longer be seen. It stands on a low hill, protected by high curtain walls, six drum towers and a deep water-filled moat.

In 1941, Rudolf Hess, Adolf Hitler's second in command, flew to Scotland to try to negotiate a peace treaty with Britain. Treated as a prisoner of war, he was moved to Wales and held for a while at a hospital near White Castle. He was sometimes taken to feed the swans in the castle moat.

The views from the battlements over the surrounding countryside to the Black Mountains are stunning. In reality, so is all the scenery in this area – consisting largely of a patchwork of low hills, hidden valleys, fields criss-crossed with hedgerows and small belts of woodland. If you're feeling fit, there is a fantastic circular walk around the castles, taking in a route of about 20 miles, beginning at Grosmont.

EAT AND DRINK

The Bell at Skenfrith ◉
skenfrith.co.uk
Monmouthshire, NP7 8UH
01600 750235
This 17th-century coaching inn is one of the most famous restaurants in Monmouthshire, located on the banks of the River Monnow. Character oozes from the fully restored oak bar. There are flagstone floors, comfortable sofas and old settles, while upstairs are 11 individually decorated bedrooms. Real ales come from Kingstone, Wickwar and Wye Valley breweries and cider from the village's own Apple County. The award-winning restaurant skilfully uses organic herbs and vegetables from its own kitchen garden in its regularly changing menus.

Part y Seal
partyseal.co.uk
Grosmont, NP7 8LE | 01981 240814
This traditional country house operates as a tea room, serving morning coffee, light lunches and afternoon teas, all using home-grown seasonal produce from their organic kitchen gardens when available. The gardens are also open to the public, so you can have a look inside the greenhouses. There's also excellent B&B accommodation too.

▲ Harlech's dunes

▶ Harlech   MAP REF 333 E2

Harlech is a seaside resort lying in Tremadog Bay within the boundaries of the Snowdonia National Park, south of Porthmadog on the west coast of Wales. The big draw is its castle but you can also come to enjoy its sandy beaches. The castle itself stands on a 200-foot crag and is regularly dubbed the most 'dramatic' castle in Britain. Although the outer walls are badly damaged, the inner curtain wall and their great round corner towers are well preserved. Built for Edward I around 1280, the castle would have been protected by sea cliffs, although the sea has since receded to reveal coastal plain and sand dunes. In the spring of 1404, Welsh leader Owain Glyndwr gathered his forces against the mighty fortress of Harlech, but the castle was too strong to be taken in a battle and so Glyndwr began a siege. For many months the castle garrison held out, despite Glyndwr's efficient blockade of all the supply routes. Food ran low, then disease broke out. After some soldiers made an unsuccessful escape bid, Glyndwr stood at the castle's gate and demanded surrender.

Harlech was Glyndwr's home and headquarters for the next four years, and it is possible he even held a Welsh parliament here. Finally, in 1409, Henry IV sent a powerful force to recapture the castle and stamp out the rebellion. After a short siege, the castle fell. Glyndwr's wife and children were taken prisoner, and although Glyndwr himself escaped, the fall of Harlech marked the beginning of the end for him. Within four years he had disappeared.

In contrast to the impressive castle, Harlech itself is actually quite small. The old quarter lies on the hillside by the castle, while the holiday quarter, including a hotel, campsites, apartments and the railway, spreads across the plains. Visitors come here for the magnificent beaches, which are positioned with the purple ridges of Snowdonia spanning the skyline. Behind the village, narrow country lanes wind through the impressive Rhinog Mountains, a range that consists of thick beds of gritstone and shale formed in the Cambrian era – some of the world's oldest surface rocks. You can attempt to walk along the ridge but be warned, it's full of deep canyons that act as obstacles. Boulders and scree from the eroded gritstone slabs are frequently covered with knee-deep heather, making the territory somewhat ankle-breaking.

Harlech's also known for its famous marching song, *Men of Harlech*. Inspired by a seven-year siege during the 15th century Wars of the Roses, it remains important in Welsh culture, and became widely known when it featured in the 1964 film *Zulu*.

TAKE IN SOME HISTORY
Harlech Castle
see highlight panel opposite

GET OUTDOORS
Morfa Harlech
This is a large system of sand dunes, salt marshes and mudflats reaching out into Tremadog Bay. Rich in flora, it even contains the purple-pink flowers of the pyramidal and green-winged orchids. The mudflats in the north are good for wading birds and wildfowl. Polecats have been spotted here, as have many species of butterfly, including the dark-green fritillary. Today, Morfa Harlech is considered one of the most important actively growing dune systems in Britain and a National Nature Reserve. As such, it is highly protected and permits are required to stray off the beach and away from the rights of way. It also forms part of Morfa Harlech and Morfa Dyffryn Special Area of Conservation (SAC), Morfa Harlech SSSI and the Pen Llyn a'r Sarnau SAC.

HIT THE BEACH
Harlech has a straight beach with miles of golden sand, and is ideal for swimming.

CATCH A PERFORMANCE
Theatr Harlech
theatrharlech.com
St David's Hill, LL46 2PU
01766 780667
A great theatre, presenting quality shows and concerts to suit all tastes.

PLAY A ROUND
Royal St David's Golf Club
royalstdavids.co.uk
LL46 2UB | 01766 780361
Open daily all year
This is a championship links with easy walking.

▶ Harlech Castle MAP REF 333 E2

cadw.wales.gov.uk
LL46 2YH | 01766 780552 | Open Mar–Jun, Sep–Oct daily 9.30–5, Jul–Aug
9.30–6, Nov–Feb Mon–Sat 10–4, Sun 11–4
This great castle, the site of so many battles and sieges, was
one of Edward I's 'iron ring'. Unlike Beaumaris (see page 86),
on which building continued for 35 years, Harlech was completed
within just seven years (1283–90). Master builder James of
St George (1230–1308) personally supervised the building, and
it doesn't take much imagination to envisage what a remarkable
feat of engineering was required to erect such a vast fortress
in such a short space of time.

EAT AND DRINK

Cemlyn Restaurant and Tea Shop
cemlynteashop.co.uk
Stryd Fawr, Harlech, LL46 2YA
01766 780425
This award-winning tea shop serves more than 20 varieties of tea, along with coffees, delicious homemade cakes and sandwiches. Try local specialities such as Bara brith, a wonderfully Welsh kind of fruit cake. If it's sunny, spread out on the terrace for spectacular views of Harlech Castle, Cardigan Bay and the mountains beyond.

▶ Haverfordwest & St Brides Bay MAP REF 322 C4/B4

Located in the heart of Pembrokeshire, several miles inland from St Davids, is the county town of Haverfordwest. It was sited on the Western Cleddau, one of the two wide rivers that flow into the Milford Haven, and was once a thriving port with barges, small steamships and coasting vessels regularly docking on the quayside. The castle, built in the 12th century by the first Earl of Pembroke, Gilbert de Clare, dominates the town from a lofty crag above the river. As a Norman stronghold, Haverfordwest was attacked and burned to the ground by Llywelyn the Great, but the castle survived, as it did when it was besieged in 1405 by Owain Glyndwr.

There wasn't to be a third time lucky, though. Oliver Cromwell ordered its destruction following the Civil War, and that's pretty much what happened. Despite this, the substantial walls and keep are still impressive – second only to Pembroke in this region. Today Haverfordwest is a thriving market town and the main shopping centre for the area. Many shops and

▼ Coast path at Marloes

cafes line the quayside. If you have a few hours to while away, try the town museum, which is housed in the castle off Church Street, and the recently excavated ruins of the Augustinian Priory of St Mary and St Thomas the Martyr, a short walk from the centre of town.

The town is an excellent base from which to explore Pembrokeshire's West Coast and St Brides Bay. This is a huge arch of a bay, facing the Atlantic and stretching from Ramsey Island off St David's Head in the north to Skomer Island off Marloes Peninsula in the south. Due to its endless amount of glorious beaches, it's a perfect haven for families, water-sports lovers and surfers. Popular beaches are Newgale and Broad Haven – great for surfing, windsurfing and exploring natural arches and stacks. Then there's Little Haven, a pretty village with a slipway used by the lifeboat, and a beach that's popular with sea anglers. Most spectacular is Marloes Sands, where violent earth movements have thrust the rock strata upwards to form steeply angled rocky cliffs.

Not all the action is on the coast, however. Ramsey Island (see page 290), Skomer Island and Skokholm Island (see page 297) are wonderful attractions a few miles offshore. Skomer, itself, is a Wildlife Trust Nature Reserve, and Ramsey Island, an RSPB Nature Reserve. Skokholm is smaller and home to fantastic birdlife such as rare cloughs. Boats run regularly to Ramsey and Skomer. You'll more than likely spot seals and dolphins en route.

GET OUTDOORS
Scolton Manor Museum and Country Park
pembrokeshire.gov.uk
Scolton Manor, SA62 5QL
01437 731328 (museum)
01437 731457 (park) | Museum open Easter–Oct daily 10.30–5.30; country park Apr–Oct 9.30–5.30, Nov–Mar 9.30–4.30

A traditional Victorian country house five miles north of Haverfordwest, Scolton Manor is now the site of the county museum. The house itself has been sympathetically restored to provide visitors with a taste of Victorian society and style, both above and below stairs. The 60 acres of surrounding park and woodland have been used as a country park since the 1970s. The staff endeavours to conserve wildlife, as well as creating opportunities for visitors to enjoy what's on offer.

HIT THE BEACH
Broad Haven Beach and Marloes are popular with families and watersports lovers.

GET ON THE WATER
Newsurf
newsurf.co.uk
Newsurf, Newgale, SA62 6AS
01437 721398 | Open daily all year

A water-sports specialist, dealing in surfboards, kayaks and coasteering.

TAKE A BOAT TRIP
Wildlife Trust South and West Wales
welshwildlife.org
Cilgerran, Cardigan, Pembrokeshire
SA43 2TB | 01239 621600
For trips to Skomer and Skokholm, telephone the booking office at the Wildlife Trust South and West Wales.

SADDLE UP
East Nolton Riding Stables
noltonstables.com
East Nolton Farm, Nolton Haven,
SA62 3NW | 01437 710360
Ride along the beach and feel the wind in your hair. Zorbing is also available for those so inclined.

LEARN TO KITE SURF
The Big Blue Experience
bigblueexperience.co.uk
Flat 1 Newgale House,
Newgale, Haverfordwest
SA62 6AS | 07816 169359
The local beaches are a great place to learn to kitesurf, kiteboard or powerkite. Classes and courses are available for all levels.

PLAY A ROUND
Haverfordwest Golf Club
haverfordwestgolfclub.co.uk
Arnolds Down, SA61 2XQ
01437 764523 | Open daily all year
This flat parkland course challenges golfers of all handicaps. Tailored packages are available for visitors.

EAT AND DRINK
Wolfscastle Country Hotel ◉◉
wolfscastle.com
Wolf's Castle, SA62 5LZ
01437 741225
Local legend has it that the great Welsh rebel leader Owain Glyndwr may be buried in the field alongside this old stone country hotel. The place sits on a promontory overlooking the Pembrokeshire countryside and makes the most of its historical location. The menu comprises modern classic dishes cooked with confidence and flair.

▶ PLACES NEARBY
Close to Haverfordwest are two stunning castles, while further afield is Milford Haven (see page 229)

Llawhaden Castle
cadw.wales.gov.uk
Llawhaden, SA67 8HL
01443 336000 | Opening hours vary, call or check website
The castle was first built in the 12th century to protect the possessions of the Bishops of St Davids. The 13th- and 14th-century remains of the bishops' hall, kitchen, bakehouse and other buildings can be seen, along with a deep moat.

Picton Castle
pictoncastle.co.uk
The Rhos, SA62 4AS
01437 751326 | Open Mar–Oct daily 10.30–5
Enjoy the idyllic gardens and 13th-century collections at this fine stately home.

St Brides Inn
saintbridesinn.co.uk
St Brides Road, Little Haven,
SA62 3UN | 01437 781266
An ideal stop for walkers on the nearby Pembrokeshire Coastal Path, St Brides Inn has an indoor ancient well and a pretty floral beer garden. Fresh fish is always available, together with locally caught lobster and crab, in season.

The Swan Inn
theswanlittlehaven.co.uk
Point Road, Little Haven, SA62 3UL
01437 781880

This free-house pub is 200 years old and sits perched above a rocky cove overlooking St Brides Bay. It buzzes with chatter and people enjoying well-kept real ales and a good choice of wines in the comfortably rustic bar, furnished with old settles, polished oak tables and leather armchairs. There's also an intimate dining room, with an elegant contemporary-style restaurant upstairs. The menu is modern British, with a commitment to seasonal and local produce.

▼ Little Haven and Broad Haven Beach

▶ **Hay-on-Wye** MAP REF 331 E5

This may be a small town but Hay-on-Wye has a global reputation. Lying in the northeast corner of the Brecon Beacons National Park by the sleepy banks of the River Wye, it's a very special place. First off are the surroundings. It's sheltered by the sweeping slopes of the Black Mountains and has Radnorshire to the north, filled with flower-decked meadows and rolling green hills.

Second is its well-established reputation for secondhand books. This movement began under the leadership of local maverick Richard Booth. He opened his eponymous bookshop in the 1960s, stocking it with literary delights. Rather as Owain Glyndwr proclaimed himself Prince of Wales, Booth then proclaimed himself 'King of Hay', all the while campaigning for the support of bookshops to revive rural areas. It was an ambition that's been more than realised by Hay-on-Wye – today you can browse around 30 bookshops, selling everything from poetry to cookery books to old novels. In 1988, the town also launched its festival of literature and culture, which has since grown into a event attracting huge names and the hottest authors, as well as tourists from all over the world.

Walk the maze of narrow streets and you'll discover many fascinating old buildings, including a 19th-century market. There are plenty of reminders of the town's turbulent history, switching between the English and Welsh on countless occasions. The town is also a popular destination for walkers, as it's on Offa's Dyke Path and the Wye Valley Walk.

HIT THE FESTIVAL

Hay-on-Wye Literary Festival
hayfestival.com
The Drill Hall, 25 Lion Street,
Hay-on-Wye, HR3 5AD
01497 822620
No one summed up this festival better than Bill Clinton in 2001, calling it the 'Woodstock of the mind'. Held annually at the end of May, the festival draws global speakers to talk on everything from politics to publishing to the performing arts. The 2015 line-up included Stephen Fry, Sandy Toksvig and Charlotte Rampling.

EAT AND DRINK

Old Black Lion Inn ⍟
oldblacklion.co.uk
26 Lion Street, Hay-on-Wye,
HR3 5AD | 01497 820841
Situated close to the Lion Gate, one of the original entrances to the old walled town of Hay-on-Wye, this charming 17th-century whitewashed inn has bags of character. It is believed that parts of the building date back to the 1300s. The oak-timbered bar is furnished with scrubbed pine tables, comfy armchairs and a log-burning stove, perfect for savouring a pint of Old Black Lion Ale. The

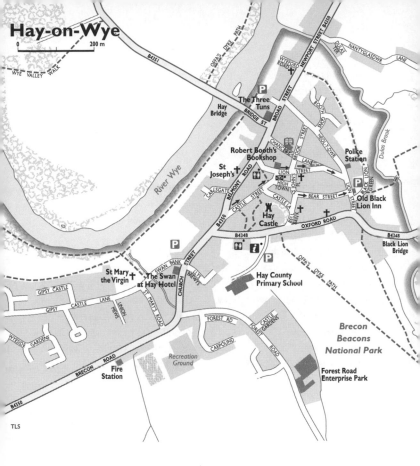

inn has a long-standing reputation for good food – witness the AA Rosette – and has a pretty dining room overlooking the garden terrace.

The Swan-at-Hay Hotel

swanathay.co.uk

Church Street, Hay-on-Wye, HR3 5DQ | 01497 821188

The Swan is a family-run hotel of grey stone with flower-bordered lawns to the rear, with relaxed and welcoming service in the bistro-style dining room, even when it's busy. Local produce is at the core of the kitchen's business, and the concise menu is an appealing mix of contemporary ideas.

The Three Tuns

three-tuns.com

4 Broad Street, Hay-on-Wye, HR3 5DB | 01497 821855

Despite a devastating fire a few years ago, this 16th-century pub has attracted an eclectic roll call of famous, even infamous, visitors, from musician Jools Holland and singer Marianne Faithfull to the Great Train Robbers. In the bar is an old settle, reclaimed from the fire and restored for that welcome pint of Wye Valley Bitter or Butty Bach. The frequently changing menu uses produce sourced from local farmers and butchers, and the bread is home-baked.

▶ **PLACES NEARBY**

Near Hay-on-Wye is an outdoor centre, several places to eat and the exquisite Llanthony Priory (see page 67).

Black Mountain Activities and Adventure Centre

blackmountain.co.uk

LD3 0SD | 01497 847897

Get active with Black Mountain Activities – try your hand at white-water kayaking, gorge walking, raft building, land carting, abseiling, mountain biking, paintballing or archery.

The Boat House

wyevalleycanoes.co.uk

Glasbury-on-Wye, HR3 5NP

01497 847213

Hire a canoe, a kayak or a double kayak, and paddle down the River Wye. Next door to the centre is the River Cafe, which welcomes all river users.

The Harp Inn

theharpinn.co.uk

Glasbury, HR3 5NR

01497 847373

A pub since the 17th century, this comfortable inn overlooks the River Wye and is just a few miles from Hay-on-Wye. In the bar, grab a table and enjoy a pint of one of several local real ales, including Mayfields Glasbury Undaunted, specially brewed for the pub. The tempting menu offers classic dishes, pizzas and an interesting specials board. Regular music events include monthly folk and Irish sessions, and occasional jazz nights.

Llangoed Hall ◉◉◉

llangoedhall.co.uk

Llyswen, LD3 0YP | 01874 754525

Surrounded by 17 acres of the lush green Wye Valley, this grand house has pristine lawns, manicured gardens, a kitchen garden and maze. The interior has a luxurious traditional finish, with original features and fine furniture, creating a sophisticated old-school atmosphere. It uses locally sourced produce from Llangoed's own organically run kitchen garden, and what doesn't come from their own land is sourced with due diligence. Choose from the à la carte or tasting menus (including a cracking veggie version) and expect polished modern British cuisine.

▶ **Holyhead & Holy Island** MAP REF 336 A2/A3

Ask anyone of a certain age with links to Ireland what their thoughts are of Holyhead and they will most likely groan and recount terrible stories of driving through the night to get here in order to catch a ferry to Dublin. It may be the biggest town on Anglesey but this is largely what it's known for – being a transport hub. The rise in cheap flights, however, has diminished this need and visitor numbers have reduced accordingly. However, regeneration designed to enhance 'leisure and tourism' is slowly happening, particularly around the harbour. It's got a decent maritime museum, as well as Penrhos beach.

At 719 feet (216m), Holyhead Mountain is one of the best viewpoints in Anglesey, taking in the distant coast of Ireland to the west, the Isle of Man to the north and the jagged peaks of Snowdonia to the southeast. Nearer to hand are a wealth of prehistoric remains and the rocky island of South Stack, with its gleaming white lighthouse – a popular visitor attraction. Also on the wild southwest coast of the island lies another beach, Trearddur Bay. Here the coastline is heavily indented, with rocky promontories and low cliffs enclosing small sandy beaches. In the central region, there is one superb, sweeping sandy cove, overlooked by a yacht club, the lifeboat station and the huge whitewashed Trearddur Bay Hotel, which is at the centre of all things local. To the north of Trearddur the rough and rugged coastline becomes truly spectacular.

Holyhead itself is located on Holy Island, a seven-mile stretch of land separated from the mainland by a narrow channel and connected by a four-mile bridge. It's been deemed 'holy' since a Cornish bishop called St Cybi lived here in the sixth century.

VISIT THE MUSEUM

Holyhead Maritime Museum
holyheadmaritimemuseum.co.uk
Newry Beach, LL65 1YD
01407 769745 | Open Easter–Oct
Tue–Sun & BHs 10–4
Step back in time at the oldest lifeboat station in Wales (c.1858), which houses a wonderful collection of exhibits. Telling the enthralling maritime history of Holyhead, this museum has detailed models of ships from 100 years ago and offers history on local shipwrecks and the lifeboat men who saved so many lives. Standing beside it is a World War II air raid shelter housing a permanent exhibition, 'Holyhead at War', where you can even test the air raid warning siren.

▼ South Stack Lighthouse

GET OUTDOORS
RSPB Nature Reserve
South Stack Cliffs
rspb.org.uk/reserves/southstack
Plas Nico, South Stack, LL65 1YH
01407 762100 | Visitor Centre open
all year daily 10–5; Ellins Tower open
Easter–Sep 10–5

Set at the most westerly extremity of the Isle of Anglesey, South Stack is a rocky island crowned by a lighthouse, providing the first hint of land for boats coming from Ireland. Constructed in 1809, the lighthouse is open to visitors. You can climb to the top and tour the engine room and exhibition area. Access from the mainland is by a dizzying footbridge, some 400 steps down massive, 200-foot cliffs.

In May and June, watch out for the thousands of nesting seabirds, including puffins, guillemots and razorbills which throng the cliffs. The RSPB visitor centre at Ellins Tower has telescopes, binoculars and live TV links for viewing the birds without disturbing them. This is also one of the few places in the UK where choughs live and breed.

HIT THE BEACH
There are two beaches in this area – Trearddur Bay, with big sands and seas ideal for canoeing and surfboarding, and Penrhos, another great beach.

PLAY A ROUND
Holyhead Golf Club
holyheadgolfclub.co.uk
Lon Garreg Fawr, Trearddur Bay,
LL65 2YL | 01407 763279
Open daily all year

An undulating seaside course providing players with a varied and testing game, and some delightful views of Snowdonia. The fairways are bordered by gorse, heather and rugged outcrops of rock.

EAT AND DRINK
Wavecrest Cafe
Church Bay, LL65 4ET
01407 730650

With little choice in the area, it's great to find this cafe – a no-nonsense place, offering great food at reasonable prices. The staff are friendly and the puddings are delicious. The cheese and onion pie is the owner's speciality; the cafe is licensed too.

▶ Kidwelly Castle MAP REF 324 B3
cadw.wales.gov.uk
SA17 5BQ | 01554 890104 | Open Mar–Jun, Sep–Oct daily 9.30–5, Jul–Aug
9.30–6, Nov–Feb Mon–Sat 10–4, Sun 11–4

Kidwelly is a small town located about 10 miles northwest of the main Carmarthenshire hub of Llanelli. Lying on the River Gwendraeth above Carmarthen Bay, it was first established in the 12th century. Today its main attractions include the former quay – now a nature reserve – a Norman parish church and an industrial museum.

Most important of all, however, is the impressive castle. Founded by the Normans in 1106, it is a forbidding grey beast that rises above a pretty waterway. Its history has been tempestuous. It was Roger de Caen, the Bishop of Salisbury, who first put up earthworks on the site, some of which can still be seen in the semicircular ditch that curves around the present castle. In 1231, Llywelyn the Great attacked the Norman castle, causing considerable damage. It was rebuilt to withstand one further attack in the 1250s, but most of the building that remains today dates from the 1270s.

The main castle forms a rectangle, with great circular towers at each corner. A semicircular wall sweeps around one side and the site is protected by defensive earthworks. Unusually, the great gatehouse is not a part of the inner walls, but forms part of the outer walls. The most likely reason for this is that there was not enough firm ground inside the castle to support such a large building. Instead, the interior consists of many small rooms, chambers and interconnecting passages, all of which help make this castle a tremendous example of medieval architecture and style. The castle was used as a location for the 1975 film *Monty Python and the Holy Grail*.

HIT THE BEACH

Cefn Sidan is an eight-mile stretch of sandy storm beach. It's a great place for spotting jellyfish.

▶ **PLACES NEARBY**

Close to Kidwelly is an industrial museum and Pembrey Country Park (see Llanelli, page 208).

Kidwelly Industrial Museum
kidwellyindustrialmuseum.co.uk
Broadford, Kidwelly, SA17 4LW

01554 891078 | Open 25 May–28 Sep, Tue, Thu & Sat 10–5; other times vary, call or check website for details

Two of the great industries of Wales are represented in this museum: tinplate and coal mining. The original buildings and machinery of the Kidwelly tinplate works are now on display to the public. There is also an exhibition of coal mining with pithead gear and a winding engine, while history of the area occupies a separate exhibition.

▶ **Knighton** MAP REF 331 E2

Known as the 'town on the dyke', Knighton stands right on the border, halfway between Ludlow in Shropshire and Llandrindod Wells in Powys. At its heart – literally on the eighth-century dyke – stands a motte-and-bailey castle, the only place along its route that is straddled by a building. Elsewhere, the town's main street ascends gently to a fine Victorian clock tower where, back in the early 19th century, men could effectively obtain a divorce by 'selling' their wife at the place where the clock tower now stands. Town tours will point that out to you, as well as other historical features, such as a section of Offa's Dyke, and Bryn y Castell – one of the two Norman castle mounds in Knighton. Market Street is worth a look, boasting Georgian houses and businesses with traditional shopfronts, a far cry from the brightly coloured plastic ones on most modern high streets. It also has countless narrow streets to explore, known locally as 'The Narrows'. The town is an excellent base for walking – either the disputed border area of the Marches or the Offa's Dyke Path. The Offa's Dyke Centre on West Street can help with information and advice.

It's worth noting that you can travel to Knighton by the Heart of Wales Railway, which runs from Swansea to Shrewsbury. This scenic railway weaves its way through the lonely hills and valleys of mid-Wales and is popular with walkers who want to do a linear route or those wanting to see the Victorian spa towns of Builth Wells and Llandrindod Wells.

VISIT THE EXHIBITION
The Offa's Dyke Centre
offasdyke.demon.co.uk
West Street, Knighton, Powys
LD7 1EN | 01547 528753
Open summer daily 10–5
This centre holds an interesting interactive exhibition that allows you to explore the dyke, its long-distance footpath and the border area through interesting interactive displays. The free exhibition covers the construction of Offa's Dyke, the Welsh princes of the Anglo-Saxon period, the flora and fauna of the area, the history of Knighton and the maintenance of the Dyke and the National Trail. The Offa's Dyke Centre also houses the local Tourist Information Centre and a shop.

ENTERTAIN THE FAMILY
Spaceguard Centre
spaceguarduk.com

Llanshay Lane, Knighton, LD7 1LW
01547 520247 | Tours: May–Sep Wed–Sun 10.30, 2, 4, Oct–Apr 2, 4; day or evening group tours can be booked for any time
Who doesn't love the thought of seeing an unidentified flying object – UFO? Well, here at the Spaceguard Centre you can learn all about them. Somewhat bizarrely, it's the only organisation in the UK dedicated to addressing the hazard of Near Earth Objects (NEOs); these consist largely of asteroids and comets that come close to, and sometimes collide with, Earth. The centre aims to provide timely information to the public, press and media, as well as an education service about the threat of asteroid and comet impacts, and the ways in which we can predict and deal with them.

PLAY A ROUND
Knighton Golf Club
knightongolfclub.co.uk
Ffrydd Wood, LD7 1DL
01547 528046 | Open Mon–Sat
all year
An upland course with fine
views over the England border
and some hard walking.

EAT AND DRINK
Milebrook House Hotel ❀
milebrookhouse.co.uk
Milebrook, LD7 1LT | 01547 528632
When the legendary explorer
and travel writer Sir Wilfred
Thesiger (1910–2003) took time
out from crossing Arabia, he
returned home to this
handsome 18th-century
Marches mansion in the Teme
Valley. The riotously colourful
gardens must have been balm
to his soul. These now supply
the kitchen with heaps of fresh,
seasonal fruit, vegetables
and herbs. The kitchen
delivers deceptively simple
and well-balanced modern
British dishes cooked with
flair and imagination, which
impress with their light
touch and flavour combos.
Simply delicious.

▶ PLACES NEARBY

Close to Knighton is a restored
Victorian town house, and – for
petrol heads – a car rally
school. Further afield is the
Elan Valley (see page 163) and
Rhayader (see page 280).

The Judge's Lodging
judgeslodging.org.uk
Broad Street, Presteigne, LD8 2AD

5 top long-distance walks

▶ **All Wales Coastal Path**
(walescoastpath.gov.uk):
Opened in May 2012, this
870-mile track is the first
continuous coastal path in
the world. Running from
Chepstow in the south to
Queensferry in the north, it
takes in 18 medieval castles,
12 National Nature
Reserves, 41 blue-flag
beaches and the major
towns of Swansea, Cardiff
and Llandudno. It should
take around 70 days to walk,
start to finish, and is
increasingly becoming a
bucket-list ambition.

▶ **Cambrian Way**
(cambrianway.org.uk): At
275 miles, this is a wild and
challenging trek north to
south over the remote
Cambrian Mountains.

▶ **Glyndŵr's Way** (nationaltrail.
co.uk/offasdyke): Taking in
the sights associated with
the great 15th-century hero
Owain Glyndwr, this
135-mile route crosses the
remote mountains and lakes
of mid-Wales.

▶ **Offa's Dyke Path**
(nationaltrail.co.uk/
offasdyke): This 177-mile
route built by King Offa
traces the line of the
eighth-century earthwork
marking the border between
England and Wales.

▶ **Wye Valley Walk**
(wyevalleywalk.org): A scenic
136-mile sea-to-source trek
following the River Wye from
Chepstow to Plynlimon in
mid-Wales.

01544 260650 | Open Mar–Oct Tue–Sun 10–5, Nov Wed–Sun 10–4, Dec Sat–Sun 10–4, closed Mon A few miles south of Knighton you'll find this restored Victorian town house with integral courtroom, cells and service areas. Be prepared to step back into the 1860s, as it's all accompanied by an 'eavesdropping' audio tour with voices from the past. Explore the fascinating 'upstairs, downstairs' world of the Victorian judges, their servants and criminal guests at this award-winning historic house. Various special events take place throughout the year, so telephone for details.

Phil Price Rally School
philprice.co.uk
Coed Harbour, Llangunllo, LD7 1TD
01547 550300
Here you can try out authentic rally stages with rear-wheel drive and four-wheel drive Subaru Imprezas. The fully qualified instructors will bring out the best of your driving skills, providing hands-on driving and teaching such things as slides, drifts, the Scandinavian flick and the opposite lock, plus much more. If you want to know what it feels like sliding through corners, your heart beating overtime to the roaring sound of the rally car, then this is the place.

▸ **Lampeter** MAP REF 328 C4

Lampeter is a town in Ceredigion, best known for its university. With a population of around 3,000, it's fairly small but busy with an up-beat go-getter vibe. Lampeter evolved as a market town with a strong crafts industry, catering for the nearby rural area. There were several woollen mills, one of which in the mid-18th century was already producing the complex double-woven tapestry cloth later associated with the Welsh woollen industry. There were also carpenters, blacksmiths, saddlers, hatters and bootmakers. The town was one of the main centres on the Welsh drovers' road for the dispatch of cattle and sheep to the markets of southeast England. Today, you can be reminded of the town's former importance by visiting some of its pubs, with names such as the Nag's Head, the Drovers and the Three Horseshoes. Another key delight is Jen Jones' Gallery, with probably the finest collection of vintage Welsh quilts and blankets in Wales.

EAT AND DRINK
The Falcondale Hotel & Restaurant ◉◉
thefalcondale.co.uk
Lampeter, SA48 7RX | 01570 22910
An Italianate mansion built in verdant countryside, Falcondale has 14 acres all to itself. The cooking reveals classical roots, but this is gently modernised stuff, and good use is made of the regional bounty.

▶ **PLACES NEARBY**

Close to Lampeter is a fascinating conservation centre, a shop selling traditional Welsh quilts and blankets and a wonderful country estate.

Denmark Farm Conservation Centre

denmarkfarm.org.uk
Betws Bledrws, SA48 8PB
01570 493358

This conservation centre puts wildlife at the heart of everything they do. Come and learn more about habitat management and species identification, take a workshop in sustainable living or explore some of the nature trails around this 40-acre site.

Jen Jones Welsh Quilts and Blankets

jen-jones.com
Pontbrendu, Llanybydder,
Ceredigion, SA40 9UJ | 01570
480610 | Open Mon–Sat 10–6

This delightful shop is the place to come if you are after Welsh home furnishings. It has a constantly changing stock of over 1,000 quilts and blankets, mostly made between 1820 and 1939. All the pieces were handmade, so each is unique.

Llanerchaeron

nationaltrust.org.uk
Llanerchaeron, Ciliau Aeron,
SA48 8DG | 01545 570200
Opening times vary, call or
check website for details

Llanerchaeron, just inland from Aberaeron on the Cardigan Bay coast, centres on a Regency villa designed by 18th-century architect John Nash. The self-sufficient country estate, villa, service courtyard, grounds, working organic farm and outbuildings remain virtually unaltered. The estate also features a walled garden, ornamental lake, mature woodland and farmland containing Llanwenog sheep and Welsh Black cattle. Produce and plants from the walled gardens are sold in the visitor building. Call for details of annual events.

▶ Laugharne & West Carmarthen coastline

MAP REF 324 A2

Lying on the estuary of the River Taf in Carmarthenshire, Laugharne (pronounced 'Larn') is renowned for being the home of Dylan Thomas from 1949 until his death in 1953. It's also thought to have been the inspiration for the fictional town of Llareggub – just spell it backwards and you'll get an idea of what he was thinking – in *Under Milk Wood*.

Much of this sleepy town, 13 miles from Carmarthen itself and overlooked by a Norman castle, is dedicated to the great man. Fans make pilgrimages to the Boathouse where he lived and the shed where he wrote. Sadly, Brown's Hotel where he drank is closed but the churchyard where he is buried remains.

The town was originally known as Abercorran, but this was changed to Laugharne after the Civil War in honour of Major-General Rowland Laugharne, a local army officer who commanded a parliamentarian army before rebelling in 1648.

Besides Dylan Thomas memorabilia, the most notable feature of the town is the castle, perched on a tree-cloaked cliff looking out across the salt marshes and creeks of the estuary and immortalised by the artist J M W Turner in a vibrant 1830s watercolour.

The main street – lined with Georgian houses, antiquarian shops and bistros – leads to the unusual whitewashed town hall, which has a modest clock tower.

The road from Laugharne to Carmarthen Bay leads to Pendine, with its firm beach of sand and shells, which stretches for seven miles from Gilman Point to Laugharne Sands. In the early 20th century the beach was considered ideal for world land speed record attempts, including Malcolm Campbell's 146.16mph record in 1924. These daring endeavours ended with the fatal accident of Parry Thomas-Jones, whose car *Babs* rolled over in the 1927 attempt for the record. *Babs* can be seen in Pendine's Museum of Speed. Note: The beach is owned by the MoD, which occasionally restricts public access in the area.

TAKE IN SOME HISTORY
Laugharne Castle
cadw.wales.gov.uk
King Street, SA33 4FA
01994 427906 | Open Apr–Oct daily 10–5

The Laugharne Castle of today bears very little resemblance to the building that was erected in the 12th century. The original castle was seized from the English by the Welsh three times before the end of the 13th century; it was then built and extended in several stages. Parts of the ivy-clad building on show today date from the early 14th century, while the gatehouse is thought to be 15th century. The grand entrance arch in the gateway was added later still, probably during the 16th century. In Tudor times Laugharne was leased to Sir John Perrott, said to be the illegitimate son of Henry VIII, who did not find the medieval castle to his courtly taste and set about converting it into a fine Tudor mansion. The castle came under siege during the Civil War, and some of the cannonballs fired at it by the Roundheads have been found deeply embedded in its sturdy stone battlements.

VISIT THE MUSEUM
The Boat House
dylanthomasboathouse.com
Dylans Walk, SA33 4SD
01994 427420 | Open May–Oct & Easter weekend daily 10–5.30, Nov–Apr 10.30–3.30

The celebrated Welsh poet Dylan Thomas spent the last four years of his life living and writing here. His boatshed is now a museum to the life and times of this most troubled writer. The interior is still set up as Dylan left it, with his cluttered desk and discarded papers on the floor. He and his long-suffering wife Caitlin are buried in the nearby churchyard of St Martin's.

HIT THE BEACH

Pendine Sands is an endless beach that once facilitated land speed record attempts by Donald Campbell.

SADDLE UP
Marros Riding Centre

marros-farm.co.uk

Marros, Pendine, SA33 4PN

(Satnav users should use SA33 4PW)

01994 453777

Beach and woodland horse-rides and pony trekking are available.

EAT AND DRINK
The Cors Restaurant ◉◉

thecors.co.uk

Newbridge Road, SA33 4SH

01994 427219

This lovely Victorian rectory has been transformed into a restaurant with rooms. It's just off the main street, and the trees, shrubs, ponds and modern sculptures in the magical bog garden ('cors' is Welsh for bog) are spectacular when lit up at night, while the moody interior has a Gothic edge with its wrought-iron seats and stained-glass windows. It's an atmospheric setting for unaffected, precise cooking that trumpets the virtues of excellent local ingredients. Full-on flavours are more important here than fancy presentation.

▶ **PLACES NEARBY**

Close to Laugharne is the pretty town of Carmarthen (see page 140).

▶ Llanberis   MAP REF 337 D4

OK, Llanberis is never going to win a gong for prettiest town in Wales but there's something about it that sums up north Wales and is nevertheless appealing. It's found at the bottom of Llanberis Pass, which snakes upwards towards Snowdon, flanked by famous climbing crags – you'll often see people moving up and down on ropes.

Llanberis' appeal? It's in the mountains, it's gritty and it's got a great pub, the Heights, where walkers, climbers, kayakers and locals mix. Famously, it's also got Pete's Eats, the heartiest place to dine in these parts. Llanberis has got great history and a stack of B&Bs, campsites and youth hostels, making it a tourist hotspot. Although it's just outside the Snowdonia National Park, it's popular because the Snowdon Mountain Railway (see page 196) leaves from here.

Today, being the closest urban area to Snowdon, the town is largely linked to tourism, but it doesn't take a genius to work out its main reason for being here – Llanberis is all about the slate. Quarrying in the nearby Elidir Fawr Mountain began in the late 18th century and transformed this once-tiny village into the bustling strip it is today. In its prime, the Dinorwic Quarry employed 3,000 men, many of whom travelled from as far afield as Anglesey to work here. Once boasting the largest artificial cave in the world, the quarry closed abruptly in August 1969. It's now become part of Europe's biggest pumped power station but some of the old quarry workshops are still in existence and form part of the National Slate Museum. Here you can get an insight into the life and work of a miner, watch a craftsman split the rock into fine tiles and see the largest waterwheel on mainland Britain. The museum stands on the edge of the Padarn Country Park, where footpaths climb through woodland to reveal splendid views across the town's glacial lakes towards Snowdon. There's also the chance to ride a narrow-gauge steam train – the Llanberis Lake Railway – which chugs along the shores of Llyn Padarn, from the town centre to Penllyn at the lake's northwestern tip.

For more info on Snowdon, see Snowdonia National Park (page 299).

▼ Dolbadarn Castle

GET INDUSTRIAL
National Slate Museum
museumwales.ac.uk
Gilfach Ddu, Padarn Country Park,
LL55 4TY | 0300 111 2333
Open Easter–Oct daily 10–5,
Nov–Easter Sun–Fri 10–4
Set among the towering quarries at Llanberis, the National Slate Museum is a living, working site located in the original workshops of Dinorwic Quarry, which once employed a staggering 3,000 men and boys. You can see the foundry, smithy, workshops and mess room that make up the old quarry, and view original machinery, much of it still in working order. There are fascinating walks, talks and demonstrations all year round.

GET ELECTRIC
The Electric Mountain
fhc.co.uk
Llanberis, LL55 4UR | 01286 870636
Open daily 9.30–5.30
As a bit of background, First Hydro Company manages and operates the pumped storage plants at Dinorwig and Ffestiniog, both of which sell their power to the British electricity market. The Electric Mountain is this company's visitor centre. There's a 60-minute-long tour of the Dinorwig power station, and also a gift shop, cafe and new soft play area for children under 12.

TAKE A TRAIN RIDE
Llanberis Lake Railway
lake-railway.co.uk
Padarn Country Park, LL55 4TY
01286 870549 | Open Apr–Oct Sun–Fri 11–4, Jun–Aug, Nov to mid-Mar limited dates; request a timetable or check website for details
Starting near the foot of Snowdon, these vintage narrow-gauge steam trains, dating from 1889 to 1922, take you on a five-mile return journey along the shore of Lake Padarn, following the route of the old slate railway. You will see spectacular views of Snowdon and nearby mountains. There are Santa Train weekends in December, and an Easter Egg Hunt on Easter weekend. Call for details of these and other events.

Snowdon Mountain Railway
see highlight panel overleaf

5 top industrial heritage sites

▶ **Big Pit National Coal Museum**, page 97

▶ **Blaenavon Ironworks**, page 97

▶ **Llechwedd Slate Cavern**, page 95

▶ **National Slate Museum**, page 194

▶ **National Wool Museum**, page 247

EAT AND DRINK
Pete's Eats
petes-eats.co.uk
40 High Street, Llanberis, LL55 4EU
01286 870117
If you're hungry from a day in the hills, fancy a bit of people watching, or just want to sit and read a book, this is the place to come. The food is hearty and delicious – it's even got fish finger sandwiches on the menu – and the surroundings are super friendly and welcoming. In short, it's the heart of the village and a must-do.

▶ PLACES NEARBY
Dolbadarn Castle lies to the east of Llanberis.

Dolbadarn Castle
cadw.wales.gov.uk
LL55 4UD | 01443 336000
Open all year daily 10–4
Found close to the bottom of Llanberis Pass, Dolbadarn Castle is still standing sentinel to the route it once guarded. Although Dolbadarn was never

▶ Snowdon Mountain Railway

MAP REF 337 D5

snowdonrailway.co.uk
LL55 4TY | 01286 870223
Open mid-Mar to Oct daily (weather permitting)
The journey of just over 4.5 miles takes passengers more than
3,000 feet up to the summit of Snowdon. On a clear day expect to
see the Isle of Man and even the Wicklow Mountains in Ireland. The
round trip to the summit and back takes 2.5 hours, including 30
minutes at the summit.

large, it was of great importance to the Welsh princes. In the late 13th century, when Llywelyn the Last retreated to his mountain stronghold to escape from Edward I, the Llanberis Pass was the main route to the farmlands of Anglesey, from where most of Llywelyn's supplies came. The castle's most striking feature is the single 40-foot round tower, thought by some to be the finest surviving example. Entry was on the first floor, via a flight of wooden steps that could be pulled up inside the castle in the event of an attack. On one side of the castle lie gently undulating hills with the lake twinkling in the distance, while on the other stand the stark Snowdonia Mountains.

▶ Llandeilo   MAP REF 325 D1

Located in Carmarthenshire, at the most westerly point of the Brecon Beacons National Park, Llandeilo is an ancient market town, sitting proudly above the River Tywi. This river – the longest in Wales – begins high in the Cambrian Mountains at 1,601 feet high and flows through the Tywi Forest between Ceredigion and Powys before heading to Carmarthen Bay. The Romans used both it and Llandeilo as a base. Early Christians also made this a main centre; the town, in fact, is named after St Teilo, believed to be a cousin of Wales' patron saint St David. He was a well-travelled man, and at least 45 places of worship are dedicated to him throughout the Celtic world, including churches in Brittany, Cornwall and north Wales. Today, Llandeilo is essentially a rural town, surrounded by woodland, hills and farms, where the Welsh language is still in common use.

TAKE IN SOME HISTORY
Dinefwr Park and Castle
nationaltrust.org.uk
SA19 6RT | 01558 824512
Parkland and castle: open Jan–Apr, Sep–Dec daily 10–4, May–Aug 10–6; Newton House, cafe and shop: open Jan–Apr, Sep–Dec daily 11–4, May–Aug 11–6
This castle has been at the heart of Welsh history and influence for more than 2,000 years and it was here that many important political decisions were made in the 12th century. It was the visionaries George and Cecil Rice, however, who designed the superb 18th-century landscape that you see today. The hands-on exhibition at Newton House gives you an atmospheric experience of the early 20th century. Exhibitions on the first floor tell Dinefwr's story and will inspire you to explore the park further.

EAT AND DRINK

The Angel Hotel

angelbistro.co.uk
Rhosmaen Street, SA19 6EN
01558 822765

This gabled inn commands a position near the crest of the long hill rising from Llandeilo's old bridge across the Towy at the fringe of the Brecon Beacons National Park. Popular as a locals' pub, serving reliable Welsh ales, it also offers an intimate place to dine in Y Capel Bach Bistro, an 18th-century gem tucked away at the rear of the hotel. Most diets are catered for on the ever-changing specials board and fixed price menu.

The Plough Inn ®

ploughrhosmaen.com
Rhosmaen, SA19 6NP
01558 823431

This former pub has morphed into a smartly updated small hotel and restaurant and overlooks the Towy Valley on the edge of the Brecon Beacons, not far from the National Botanic Garden of Wales. Whether you go for the convivial bar or stylish dining room, there's a menu that uses tiptop ingredients sourced from Welsh suppliers. It takes in everything from old favourites to more ambitious, modern ideas.

▶ PLACES NEARBY

To the west of Llandeilo are the wonderful gardens at Aberglasney, while Carreg Cennen Castle (see page 141) is just four miles away.

Aberglasney Gardens

aberglasney.org
SA32 8QH | 01558 668998
Open Apr–Oct 10–6, Nov–Mar 10.30–4

Aberglasney is a 10-acre historic garden and one of the finest in Wales. It contains a host of exotic and unusual plants, a fully restored Elizabethan parapet walk and an award-winning garden, all created within the ruinous courtyard of the mansion. You can also explore the ground floor of the newly renovated mansion. Events such as plant sales, antique exhibitions and craft fairs are regularly held. Call for details.

▶ Llandovery MAP REF 329 E5

Llandovery is a sleepy market town on the northwest side of the Brecon Beacons. Come here on the weekend, however, and you'd be forgiven for thinking you're in the middle of a bikers' convention. Large numbers of motorcyclists congregate here to drink tea and fuel-up at the West End cafe on Broad Street during their spins around the countryside. Tourists come for a different reason – either to access the national park or as a stop-off on their way to Pembrokeshire or west Wales. Those stopping over tend to head for either Llandovery Castle or the

Heritage Centre, though there's also an annual sheep festival if you time it right.

Llandovery is also where a wealthy drover established one of the first independent Welsh banks. Indeed, this town's fortunes have been intertwined with drovers – hired by famers to drive cattle to England and settle accounts when thieves made the roads too dangerous. The fact that they were handling large sums of money led to the introduction of banking systems, some of them even issuing bank notes. One of the most successful of these was David Jones' Black Ox Bank, which was taken over at the turn of the 20th century by Lloyds.

TAKE IN SOME HISTORY
Llandovery Castle
Llandovery

Across the road from The Heritage Centre lie the remains of this castle – basically a battered stump. Built in 1116, it saw many a battle, changing hands between the Welsh and Normans, then falling to the English under Edward I in 1277. Welsh forces, under Llywelyn the Last, briefly retook the castle in 1282 before it was attacked during the Owain Glyndwr rebellion in 1403 and left a partial ruin. It is easily accessible via a short walk from Llandovery town centre.

CHECK OUT THE VISITOR CENTRE
The Heritage Centre
beacons-npa.gov.uk
Llandovery, SA20 0AW
01550 721228 | Open Easter–Sep daily 10–1, 1.45–5

The centre is a gateway for the Western and Central areas of the Brecon Beacons National Park. It stocks a wide range of literature about the park and nearby areas and staff can help you book accommodation. It also sells maps, guides, books and souvenirs, as well as a small range of walking and outdoor equipment. It aims to offer unique insight into the history, culture and the myths and legends in this area.

EAT AND DRINK
The Kings Head
kingsheadcoachinginn.co.uk
1 Market Square, SA20 0AB
01550 720393

Overlooking the cobbled market square, this 17th-century inn was once the home of the Llandovery Bank, known as the Black Ox Bank. Now it's all delightful exposed beams and crooked floors. There are several options for dining, including lunchtime specials (Mon–Fri), light bites, bar, carte, grills, vegetarian choices and children's meals. Representing the principality are real ales from Tomos Watkin's Swansea brewery, alongside Doom Bar.

▸ PLACES NEARBY
Dolaucothi Gold Mines (see page 159) can be found around seven miles from Llandovery.

▶ Llandrindod Wells   MAP REF 330 C3

llandrindod.co.uk

Period shopfronts, frilly wrought-iron canopies and broad avenues lined with villas and hotels mark Llandrindod out as one of the best-preserved Victorian spa towns in Britain. Within Rock Park – one of Wales' earliest public parks dating from the late 1860s – you can visit the original pump rooms and bathhouse, plus bowling green and large lake. Among many period buildings in the town is the Automobile Palace, an early motor showroom housing the National Cycle Collection of some 250 historic bicycles. The town comes to life in late August when it dresses in period costume during Llandrindod's Victorian Week. It's also big on complementary therapies, with several practitioners among the shopfronts.

VISIT THE MUSEUM
National Cycle Collection
cyclemuseum.org.uk
The Automobile Palace, Temple Street, Llandrindod Wells, LD1 5DL
01597 825531 | Open Apr–Oct Mon–Fri 10–4, Nov–Mar Tue, Thu–Fri 10–4 (weekend by arrangement)
This exhibition comprises more than 250 bikes, including 1890s boneshakers, penny-farthings and bamboos, plus slicker modern creations. The people working here are truly inspired and their interest is infectious. Local entrepreneur Tom Norton started the collection and the trike on which he used to ride to work is also here.

INDULGE YOURSELF
Rock Park Complementary Health Centre
actionteam.org.uk
Llandrindod Wells, LD1 6AE
01597 824102 | Call or visit website to make a reservation
Soothe your body at this complementary health centre, offering a range of treatments.

EAT AND DRINK
Metropole Hotel and Spa ◉
metropole.co.uk
Temple Street, Llandrindod Wells, LD1 5DY | 01597 823700
Run by the same family since Queen Victoria's reign, The Metropole has long been a local landmark with its soaring turrets. It opened in the town's heyday as a spa resort and now offers 21st-century spa treatments. It also has a couple of dining options, with an informal brasserie and the Radnor and Miles Restaurant, which takes a slightly more formal approach. There's a regional flavour to the menu, with plenty of game in season, and lamb, beef and chicken cooked on the grill.

The Laughing Dog
thelaughingdog.co.uk
Howey, LD1 5PT | 01597 822406
The oldest part of this reputedly haunted, one-time drovers' pub dates from the 17th century. Here you'll find everything from pub games in

the fire-warmed bar to real ales from respected Welsh microbreweries, such as Rhymney and The Celt Experience. The kitchen makes good use of local sources for its homemade British cooking, with influences from Europe and further afield. It serves a range of interesting dishes.

▶ **PLACES NEARBY**

You can learn how to throw a pot in Newbridge-on-Wye, or enjoy a round of golf in Builth Wells, near Llandrindod Wells.

Alex Allpress Pottery School
alexallpress.co.uk
The Lion House, Main Street,
Newbridge-on-Wye, LD1 6LN
01597 860127
Artist Alex offers day and weekend courses for novices and those with experience.

Builth Wells Golf Club
www.builthwellsgolf.co.uk
Golf Links Road, LD2 3NF
01982 553296 | Open daily all year
This is an 18-hole undulating parkland course with a river running through it.

▼ Llandrindod Wells

▶ Llandudno MAP REF 337 F2

If you are looking for an elegant Victorian seaside resort that has it all, then you should come here. Llandudno is not just Wales' largest seaside resort – don't let the word 'large' put you off, by the way – it's also got a host of attractions. There's the longest pier in Wales, for instance, and Britain's only cable-hauled tramway and award-winning beaches.

If all that is too much, you can just wander around the shops, have a night at the theatre, or spend some money in Mostyn, the foremost contemporary art gallery in Wales. The town's popularity has been helped by a growing amount of boutique accommodation, classy dining and big-name retail outlets such as Parc Llandudno.

No wonder US travel writer Bill Bryson described it as his 'favourite seaside resort'. The main appeal is down the beach – the sweeping sandy northern bay is sheltered by the two great limestone promontories of Great Orme and Little Orme.

GO UNDERGROUND
Great Orme Bronze Age Copper Mines
see highlight panel overleaf

GET OUTDOORS
Great Orme Country Park and Nature Reserve
see highlight panel overleaf

HIT THE BEACH
Two excellent sandy beaches lie either side of the Great Orme. The North Shore has a pier and many family-friendly activities, including a traditional Punch and Judy show.

CATCH A PERFORMANCE
Venue Cymru
venuecymru.co.uk
The Promenade, Llandudno
LL30 1BB | 01492 872000
Open Mon–Sat 10–7
Venue Cymru offers a rich timetable of exhibitions, events and concerts on Llandudno's promenade.

LEARN TO SKI
Llandudno Ski and Snowboard Centre
llandudnoskislope.co.uk
Wyddfyd, Great Orme, Llandudno
LL30 2LR | 01492 874707
This is a great place to learn to ski or to practise your moves on the artifical slopes. It also offers snowboarding, tobogganing and sno-tubing.

PLAY A ROUND
Llandudno Golf Club
maesdugolfclub.co.uk
Hospital Road, LL30 1HU
01492 876450 | Open daily all year
A testing part links, part parkland championship course.

EAT AND DRINK
Badgers Café and Patisserie
badgerstearooms.co.uk
The Victoria Centre, Mostyn Street,
Llandudno LL30 2RP
01492 871649
Waitresses – known as Badgers' Nippies – dressed in

Llandudno

Victorian style, serve delicious teas, coffees and cream cakes. Traditional Welsh treats such as fruity Bara brith and Welsh cakes are on the menu, along with Welsh rarebit, swan meringues and dragon eclairs.

Bodysgallen Hall and Spa ⍟⍟⍟
bodysgallen.com
LL30 1RS | 01492 584466
Set in 200 acres of delightful parkland, rose gardens and geometrically precise parterres the 17th-century hall is the sort of country house for which the word 'stately' was coined. Take in the view, which sweeps across to Snowdonia, Conwy

Castle and the Isle of Anglesey, before pushing on indoors into a bygone era of antiques, oil paintings, dark oak panelling and stone-mullioned windows. The dining room is a refined and elegant space, with grand period character and views over the countryside. The cooking matches the setting with its ambition and refinement, and there is a finely judged inventiveness to the starters.

Characters Old Curiosity Shop & Sandwich House
11 Llewelyn Avenue, Llandudno, LL30 2ER | 01492 872290
This is a lovely little tea room, serving staples from soup to

▶ Great Orme Country Park and Nature Reserve MAP REF 337 E2

conwy.gov.uk

LL30 2XF | 01492 874151

The Great Orme is a limestone headland adjacent to Llandudno. It's an area rich in flora – despite the 200 feral Kashmir goats – and history; in addition to the copper mines, there's an Iron Age fort, Stone Age remains and a sixth-century church. There are several paths to the summit, but it's more fun to take either the tramway, which has been operating since 1902 and is the only cable-hauled tramway left in Britain, or the cable car from Llandudno.

At the summit there is a crazy golf course and kids' play area, as well as a cafe and gift shop, and there's also a warden service. The views are incredible.

▶ Great Orme Bronze Age Copper Mines   MAP REF 337 E2

greatormemines.info
Pyliau Road, Great Orme, LL30 2XG | 01492 870447
Open mid-Mar to Oct daily 10–5
Browse this visitor centre with its quirky model of a Bronze Age village. Take a look at some original 4,000-year-old artefacts and a selection of mining tools. After watching two short films, don a helmet and make your way down to the mines. Walking through tunnels mined nearly 4,000 years ago, you'll get a feel for the conditions our prehistoric ancestors faced in their search for valuable copper ores. Excavation on the surface will continue for decades and one of the team is usually on hand to answer questions.

5 top quirky places to stay

▶ **The Courthouse**, Betws-y-Coed (guesthouse-snowdonia.co.uk): Once a police station and magistrates court for Betws-y-Coed, this guest house is full of memorabilia.

▶ **Graig Wen Campsite**, Arthog, near Dolgellau, Gwynedd (graigwen.co.uk): Sleep in a snug eco-cabin in Snowdonia National Park.

▶ **Llandudno Lighthouse**, Great Orme Country Park (lighthouse-llandudno.co.uk): Perched on the edge of a 328-foot drop into the sea, this is the perfect B&B for a seaside escape.

▶ **Portmeirion** (portmeirion-village.com): Take a trip into fantasyland by staying in this Italianate village – also the filming location for cult TV series *The Prisoner*.

▶ **Tipi Valley**, Cwmdu, LLandeilo, Carmarthenshire (diggersanddreamers.org.uk): This low-impact settlement has a Big Lodge, where visitors can stay.

hot scones with cream and jam. Quirky crockery and cake stands add to the fun atmosphere, while the service is excellent.

The Cottage Loaf
the-cottageloaf.co.uk
Market Street, L30 2SR
01492 870762
For years a bakery, this whitewashed building in the heart of Llandudno only became a pub in 1981 and much of its quirky interior is made up of salvaged materials from a shipwrecked coal schooner. With a log fire for winter and a large garden and sun terrace for summer, this welcoming pub, with its friendly, relaxed atmosphere, attracts visitors all year round. Local Conwy Welsh Pride is one of several ales on offer, alongside a large range of whiskies and wines. There is also an extensive food menu.

Imperial Hotel ☻
theimperial.co.uk
The Promenade, LL30 1AP
01492 877466
Where Snowdonia drops away to the sea Llandudno's promenade basks in the sun, a vision of Victorian leisure in the grand manner. The wedding-cake stucco facade of the Imperial is a landmark on Llandudno's seafront. Chantrey's Restaurant surveys the maritime scene from panoramic windows and there are outdoor tables too. The kitchen turns out menus of classically inflected modern cooking featuring a sound showing of fine Welsh produce.

Indulgence Cafe
10 Clonmel Street, Llandudno, LL30 2LE | 01492 878719
From coffee and cake to full roast dinners, this small, clean cafe shouldn't disappoint. It has a friendly atmosphere and is good value for money.

The Lilly Restaurant with Rooms ◉

thelilly.co.uk

West Parade, LL30 2BD

01492 876513

Located in the sedate West Shore part of Llandudno, and with unrestricted views over the coastline and restless sea, The Lilly is a family-run restaurant with rooms that covers a lot of bases. There's the Madhatters Brasserie, with its grill menu and sandwiches, but the main culinary destination is the flamboyantly decorated restaurant. With only 10 tables and lavish furnishings, the restaurant is the setting for menus that combine creativity with comforting familiarity. It's also the perfect base for taking a day out on the beach or a walk into the town centre.

▶ **PLACES NEARBY**

Close to Llandudno is a golf course at Penryhn Bay, and the towns of Colwyn Bay, with its lively pier (see page 148), and Conwy (see page 149). Stunning Bodnant Garden (see page 100), with its magnificent displays of plants from around the world, are slightly further afield.

Rhos-on-Sea Golf Club

rhosgolf.co.uk

Penryhn Bay, LL30 3PU

01492 548115 | Opening times vary; call or check website for details

This is a parkland-style course with lush fairways beside the sea. Hazards include several lakes and abundant trees. It also has a fine-dining restaurant and a well-stocked golf shop.

▶ # Llanelli MAP REF 324 C3

Llanelli, the largest town in Carmarthenshire, is found on the Loughor Estuary about 10 miles northwest of Swansea. It's not so much a tourist hotspot as a working town, famed for its rugby tradition. Historically a mining town, Llanelli grew rapidly in the 18th and 19th centuries with the mining of coal and later with the tinplate industry and steelworks. These were largely served by the Llanelli and Mynydd Mawr Railway, which opened in 1803.

By the latter half of the 19th century, Llanelli had become such an important tin producer that it was called 'Tinopolis'. The closure of coalmines and competition from steel plants overseas meant that Llanelli, like many other towns in south Wales, experienced sustained economic decline from the late 1970s. In recent years, it has attempted to promote such outlets as the Machynys Golf Club, new retail parks at Trostre and Pemberton, and the Millennium Coastal Park, in a bid to attract tourism and trade. The town is mostly known for its Scarlet Rugby Union team and its local Welsh bitter, Felinfoel. The brewery is just outside the town.

People from Llanelli are sometimes nicknamed 'Turks'. The origin of this name is uncertain, but one theory is that Turkish sailors once called at the port during their voyages.

EAT AND DRINK
Sosban Restaurant ◉◉
sosbanrestaurant.com
The Pumphouse, North Dock,
SA15 2LF | 01554 270020
This may have once had the unglamorous job of providing hydraulic power for Llanelli's docks. Now, though, it's been completely revitalised as an industrial-chic powerhouse on the local gastronomic scene. The 90-foot-high stone tower is a local landmark, which makes it easy enough to find. Inside, the setting is all walls of arched glass, Welsh slate floors and classy bare wooden tables, all beneath the exposed industrial skeleton of the heritage building. There's an open-to-view kitchen where the team turns out a French-accented, brasserie-style repertoire with broad appeal.

▶ **PLACES NEARBY**
Close to Llanelli is the National Wetland Centre Wales (see page 241), and Pembrey Country Park.

Pembrey Country Park
discovercarmarthenshire.com/parks
Pembrey, SA160EJ | 01554 742424
Open daily dawn–dusk
Consisting of 500 acres of parkland and woodland, and running along eight miles of Cefn Sidan beach, this park contains a dry ski slope, several adventure play areas and mountain bike trails. It also has the longest toboggan run in Wales, a manicured parkland for Frisbee or cricket, eight wildlife trails and picnic and barbecue sites. The beach is popular with kitesurfers and bodyboarders. Horse riding and bike hire are available.

▶ **Llanfair PG** MAP REF 336 C3
This village on Anglesey has traded on its name (the full version, that is) to become quite a tourist attraction. Arrive at the railway station, and you'll find it hard to resist snapping a picture of: *Llanfairpwllgwyngyllgogerychwyrndrobwyllllantysilio gogogoch*. At 58 characters, it's the longest place name in Europe and one of the longest in the world. Somewhat understandably, the town is commonly known as Llanfair PG. The tongue-twister was so named in the 1860s as a publicity stunt to attract tourists to the village, following the construction of the North Wales Coast Railway line between Holyhead and London. Never let it be said that the Welsh aren't enterprising souls. There have been attempts to steal the village's record by rival Welsh towns. The Carmarthenshire village of Llanfynydd unofficially adopted the name

*Llanhyfryddawelllehynafolybarcudprindanfygythiadtrienusyrhaf
nauole* in 2004 in protest at plans to erect a wind farm nearby
(the name means 'a quiet beautiful village; a historic place
with rare kite under threat from wretched blades').

A station on the Fairbourne Railway was also named
*Gorsafawddacha'idraigodanheddogleddollônpenrhynareur
draethceredigion* (translated as 'the Mawddach station and its
dragon under the northern peace of the Penrhyn Road on the
golden beach of Cardigan Bay') for promotional purposes.
Neither have stuck or gained any recognition. If you do come
here, feel free to visit the nearby visitor centre to have your
passport stamped.

▶ PLACES NEARBY

Close to Llanfair PG are
Beaumaris (see page 86) and
Plas Newydd country house
on Anglesey, and Bangor (see
page 81) on the mainland.

Plas Newydd

nationaltrust.org.uk
LL61 6DQ | 01248 714795
Open 16 Mar–6 Nov, Sat–Wed;
house 12–5; guided tours 11–12
This grand house is in an idyllic
location on the sheltered east
side of Anglesey, with views
across the Menai Strait to the
mountains of Snowdonia.
There's been a house here since
the 14th century, but nothing
traditional remains. In the early
1800s English architect James
Wyatt redesigned the house
with Gothic and neoclassical
features. Until 1976, it was the
home of the marquesses of
Anglesey. It passed into the care
of the National Trust, but
reminders of the family are
everywhere. There are paintings
of the first marquess, who
commanded Wellington's
cavalry at Waterloo. There's
also a collection of uniforms
and headdresses, which
continue the military theme. In
the 1930s, the sixth marquess
commissioned leading British
artist Rex Whistler to paint a
huge mural in the dining room.
The artist's largest ever work –
some 58 feet long – it was
completed just before the
outbreak of World War II, during
which he lost his life. The
mural, which features Whistler
as a gardener, now forms the
centrepiece of an exhibition of
his work.

▶ Llangefni MAP REF 336 C3

With a population of roughly 5,000, Llangefni is the second
largest settlement on Anglesey after Holyhead. However, the
two towns are very different in outlook. While Holyhead is very
much a port town, Llangefni is the island's main commercial
and farming town. It also has a very high Welsh-speaking
population, with around 80 per cent of people speaking it.

The town is near the centre of the island on the River Cefni, after which it is named, and its attractions include the Oriel Ynys Mon Museum, which details the history of Anglesey. In the north, there's a Victorian parish church, St Cyngar's, set in a wooded riverside location called the Dingle.

VISIT THE MUSEUM
Oriel Ynys Mon Museum
visitanglesey.co.uk
Rhosmeirch, Llangefni, LL77 7TQ
01248 724444 | Open all year daily 10.30–5
This purpose-built museum and arts gallery displays a wide range of craftwork and dynamic exhibitions. The centre's history gallery gives an introduction to the island's past through reconstruction, artefacts, sounds and imagery.

▶ **PLACES NEARBY**
Close to Llangefni is the Cefni Reservoir.

Cefni Reservoir
llyncefni.co.uk
Go freshwater fly-fishing at Cefni Reservoir, a great place for brown and rainbow trout.

▶ **Llangollen** MAP REF 339 D5

This small scenic town sits in the fertile Dee Valley of northeast Wales on the edge of the Berwen Mountains. The river is at the heart of the town and come any fair day you'll see scores of people congregating around the Elizabethan stone bridge, watching the fast waters bursting over the riverbed rocks. The bridge was extended in 1863 for the railway line, which linked Wrexham with Barmouth. Following the railway's closure in the 1960s, a preservation society was formed. Now, the station is a reminder of days gone by, with its historic steam engines and rolling stock lined up on platforms.

It's not just the river and train lines that are the transport hubs here. Of major importance is the Llangollen Canal, running parallel to the railway and road. Pioneered by Thomas Telford, it provides another transport leisure link for horse-drawn narrow boats, which take visitors along the canal and over the spectacular Pontcysyllte Aqueduct, some 120 feet above the River Dee.

Increasingly, Llangollen is becoming a modern tourist attraction, with boutique guest houses, restaurants and cottages springing up. There's also a wealth of independent shops to explore. Llangollen is part of the UNESCO World Heritage Site that runs along 11 miles of the canal from Gledrid to the Horseshoe Falls, taking in the aqueduct. In 2013, the town was awarded Cittaslow status – meaning it is retaining its distinct identity in the face of homogenisation.

▲ Pontcysyllte Aqueduct

TAKE A TRAIN RIDE
Llangollen Railway
llangollen-railway.co.uk
Abbey Road, LL20 8SN | 01978
860979 | Open most weekends,
daily services Apr–Oct, principally
steam-hauled; refer to timetable
for diesel and off-peak
This heritage railway features
steam and classic diesel
services running along the
picturesque Dee Valley. The
journey consists of a 15-mile
round trip between Llangollen
and Carrog. A special coach for
people with disabilities is
available on all services.
Call for more information.

TAKE A BOAT TRIP
Horse Drawn Boats Centre
horsedrawnboats.co.uk
The Wharf, Wharf Hill, LL20 8TA
01978 860702 | Open Easter–Oct
daily 9.30–5; tea room also open
Nov–Mar Sat–Sun 10–4.30

Take a horse-drawn boat trip
along the beautiful Vale of
Llangollen. There is also a
narrowboat trip that crosses
the Pontcysyllte Aqueduct –
the largest navigable aqueduct
in the world. There is a full bar
on board and an informative
commentary throughout.

GET ON THE WATER
JJ Canoeing and Rafting
jjraftcanoe.com
Mile End Mill, Berwyn Road,
Llangollen, LL20 8AD
Check website for details
Offers white-water rapid
experiences and much more.

SADDLE UP
Pont-y-Meibion Trekking
ponytreks.co.uk
Pont-y-Meibion, Glyn Ceiriog,
Llangollen, LL20 7HS
01691 718686
Try a pony or quad trek.

PLAY A ROUND
Vale of Llangollen Golf Club
vlgc.co.uk
Holyhead Road, LL20 7PR
01978 860906 | Open daily all year
A favoured venue for national
and country competitions.

EAT AND DRINK
The Hand at
Llanarmon ◉
thehandhotel.co.uk
Llanarmon Dyffryn Ceiriog, Ceiriog
Valley, LL20 7LD | 01691 600666
This 16th-century free house
was once a stopping place for
drovers and their flocks on the
old drovers' road from London
to Anglesey. Original oak
beams, burnished brass and
large fireplaces set the scene in
the bar, where travellers and
locals mingle over pints of
Weetwood Cheshire Cat. The
pub has established a strong
reputation for no-nonsense
dishes, cooked from scratch
with flair and imagination. The
same menu is served in the bar,
the restaurant and on the sunny
patio garden.

Honey Pots Ceramic Café
honey-pots.com
18 Castle Street, Llangollen,
LL20 8NU | 01978 869008
At Honey Pots you can enjoy
delicious teas or coffees and
tasty cakes and snacks in
smart modern surroundings
while admiring the views of
Dinas Bran's hilltop castle.
When you've had your fill,
you can turn your hand to
designing your own, unique
piece of pottery.

Vintage Rose Tea Room
1 Oak Mews, Llangollen, LL20 8NR
07712 186391
This lovely vintage tea room is a
firm favourite both with locals
and tourists alike. All the decor
(inside and out) is vintage, from
the table cloths to the tea sets
to the walls covered with World
War II land army posters. More
importantly, the food is great.
Scones are fresh, the menu
offers good variety and there's
a tea garden out the back. The
cafe is also dog friendly.
Booking is possible, and
perhaps advisable as there are
only a few tables.

▶ PLACES NEARBY
Close to Llangollen is an
exciting mountain pass, an
aqueduct, the ruins of an abbey
and a country park. Further
afield are the towns of Chirk
(see page 146) and Wrexham
(see page 320).

The Horseshoe Pass
This mountain pass in
Denbighshire, northeast
Wales, separates Llantysilio
Mountain to the west from
Cyrn-y-Brain in the east. The
road – the A542 – from
Llandegla to Llangollen runs
through the pass, reaching a
maximum height of 1,368 feet.
It travels in a horseshoe shape
around the sides of a valley,
giving the pass its name. This
route dates from 1811, when a
turnpike road was constructed
across the area. The road is
frequently closed in winter due
to snowfall or landslides.

Valle Crucis Abbey

cadw.wales.gov.uk

LL20 8DD | 01978 860326 | Open
Apr–Oct daily 10–5, Nov–Mar 10–4

The name of this romantic,
tree-framed ruin – one of the
most beautiful in Wales – is the
'Vale of the Cross'. Founded in
1202, this Cistercian house fits
perfectly the monks' vow to
glory in their poverty. The
slender windows of the western
end are particularly beautiful.

Pontcysyllte Aqueduct

pontcysyllte-aqueduct.co.uk

Station Road, Trevor Basin,
Wrexham, LL20 7TG | 01978
292015

When Thomas Telford built this
aqueduct in 1805, this 'canal in
the clouds' was deemed to be
one of the wonders of Britain.
To be honest, even with our
advancements in engineering
over the past two centuries,
it's still mind-bogglingly
impressive. The challenge
Telford faced was how to carry
the Ellesmere Canal across the
valley of the River Dee near
Wrexham in north Wales. His
design involved using 18 piers,
126 feet high, and 19 arches,
each with a 45-foot span, to
carry it across its 1,000-foot
length. To keep the aqueduct as
light as possible, he used
slender masonry piers that
were partly hollow and tapered
at the summit. Interestingly, the
mortar came from ox blood,
lime and water – with a
consistency not dissimilar to
treacle toffee. Construction
techniques may have come a
long way, but this remains the
tallest navigable aqueduct in
the world and still a breathtaking piece of engineering.

Ty Mawr Country Park

attractionsnorthwales.co.uk

Cae Gwilym Lane, Cefn Mawr,
Wrexham, LL14 3PE | 01978
822780 | Park open all year daily;
visitor centre Easter–Sep daily
10.30–4.30, Oct–Easter Sat–Sun

Like your animals in all shapes
and sizes? Come here – there's
sheep, donkeys, pigs, rabbits,
chickens and more. A kid's
paradise, it's also got a great
adventure playground and cafe.
The River Dee is close by, with
great spots for a picnic.

▼ Valle Crucis Abbey

▶ Llangorse Lake MAP REF 331 D6

Llangorse is a delightful little village, located towards the east end of the Brecon Beacons. You can't miss the main attraction – it's the largest natural lake in south Wales. Stretching for a mile in length and half a mile in width, it covers an area of 327 acres, although to walk around its circumference would be a five-mile trek. The water has drawn settlers since ancient Celtic times. In the 12th century, clergyman and chronicler Gerald of Wales (Giraldus Cambrensis) commented that 'the beautiful lake had plenty of waterfowl'. A main feature is the central crannog or manmade defensive island. It's thought to date back to AD 890 and to have been one of the royal sites of medieval Brycheiniog, one of the kingdoms of medieval Wales.

Today Llangorse is a lively, community village with local cider and music festivals. The lake also draws a crowd of water-sports lovers and anglers, interested in coarse fishing. All types of boating fun takes place here – including sailing, canoeing and water-skiing, and the surrounding countryside and mountains are delightful for walking and hiking. Those interested in horse riding can take to the saddle, while others can get a bird's-eye view of the dramatic landscape by going gliding with the Black Mountains Gliding Club. The excellent Llangorse Rope Centre is the place to practise your climbing skills for adventures in bouldering or pot-holing.

The lake is a Site of Special Scientific Interest mainly because it is naturally eutrophic – meaning that the water is high in nutrients – which tends to make it appear slightly murky. It also means, however, that the habitat is highly productive, which goes a long way to explain why this expanse of water is so popular with wildlife.

GET ACTIVE

Llangorse Multi-activity Centre
activityuk.com
The Gilfach, Llangorse, Brecon, LD3 7UH | 01874 658272
A fantastic indoor climbing and riding centre.

TAKE OFF

Black Mountains Gliding Club
blackmountainsgliding.co.uk
The Airfield, Brecon, Powys, LD3 0EJ
01874 711463
This is one of the best places in Britain to try your hand at ridge and wave gliding.

▶ Llanrwst MAP REF 337 F4

Set on the edge of Snowdonia National Park in north Wales, Llanrwst – pronounced 'lanrust' – is a small town that's often overshadowed by its larger neighbour, Betws-y-Coed (see page 90). It grew up in the 13th century, largely owing to an edict by Edward I who prohibited any Welshman from trading within 10 miles of Conwy Castle. At 13 miles away, Llanrwst became a strategic place for trading, business and crafts. Wool was an important industry here – as was the manufacture of harps.

More recently, of course, its main industry, apart from being a market town, has been tourism. You can admire its narrow three-arch stone bridge – Pont Fawr – said to have been designed by the architect Inigo Jones in the early 17th century. The bridge connects the town with Gwydir, a local fortified manor house dating from 1492, and a 15th-century courthouse known as Tu Hwnt i'r Bont. Originally built to carry horses and carts, the bridge has stood up well to modern traffic, not to mention the regular floods. Other attractions are the two 17th-century chapels and St Grwst's Church, which holds the stone coffin of Llywelyn the Great. The Gwydyr Forest lies to the southwest of the town, beyond the bridge. On the hills above the town is the Moel Maelogan wind farm. The electricity that is generated by these turbines is sent to the sub-station in the town.

TAKE IN SOME HISTORY
Gwydir Castle
gwydircastle.co.uk
LL26 0PN | 01492 641687
Open Apr–Oct Tue–Fri, Sun 10–4.
Limited opening at other times
Set in 10 acres of gardens, this Tudor courtyard house has hosted several royal guests, including King Charles I, and King George V and Queen Mary. The two antiques-filled period rooms feature four-poster beds and garden views, and there's a fully equipped gatehouse. The castle now operates as a B&B and wedding venue, but tours of the building and grounds are also available.

SEE A LOCAL CHAPEL
Gwydir Uchaf Chapel
cadw.wales.gov.uk
01492 640578 | Open all year daily 10–4. To gain access, call 01492 641687, 24hrs in advance

Built in the 17th century, this simple stone chapel is noted for its painted ceiling and wonderfully varied woodwork.

▶ PLACES NEARBY
Close to Llanrwst is a fishery at Llyn Crafnant, and an inn and a woollen mill at Trifriw.

Llyn Crafnant Fishery
crafnant.free-online.co.uk
Llyn Crafnant, above Conwy Valley near Trefriw | 01492 640818
Llyn Crafnant covers over 60 acres and is well stocked with rainbow and brown trout. Fish from a boat or the bank. Boat hire and permits are available.

The Old Ship
the-old-ship.co.uk
High Street, Trefriw, LL27 0JH
01492 640013
A perfect refuelling stop following a tramp in the hills,

this traditional inn is situated in a peaceful village on the wooded eastern edge of the Snowdonia National Park. Sit by the log fire with a pint of Purple Moose Glaslyn ale and peruse the daily chalkboard menu.

Trefriw Woollen Mills

t-w-m.co.uk

Trefriw, LL27 0NQ | 01492 640462

Turbine and shop open Mon–Sat 9.30–5.30 (winter 10–5), Easter–Oct open daily; Weaving open mid-Feb to mid-Dec, Mon–Fri 10–1 & 2–5; additional machinery can be viewed Apr–Oct

The busy clatter of machinery leaves you in no doubt that this is very much a working mill. It's been owned by the same family for more than 140 years and specialises in the manufacture of Welsh double weave, bedspreads and tweeds. You can see the weaving process and the hydroelectric turbines that replaced the waterwheels in the 1930s. Beautiful, hard-to-resist rugs, bedspreads, cushions and skirts are for sale in the shop. You can also tour the mill and see goods being made or buy them from the shop. From small coin purses to knitting kits and travelling rugs, this mill has it all.

▶ Llansteffan Castle MAP REF 324 A2

cadw.wales.gov.uk

01443 336000 | Open all year daily 10–4

As far as location goes, this is simply stunning: this castle stands on a flat green headland overlooking the gorgeous sand flats of the River Tywi in Carmarthenshire. Initially, Norman invaders, recognising the strategic strength of this plot of land, established an earth-and-timber enclosure within the ancient defences of an Iron Age fort. The castle controlled an important river crossing and it changed hands several times during fierce fighting between the Normans and the Welsh. The gradual transformation of the early earth-and-timber stronghold into the powerful masonry castle visible today was undertaken mostly in the 13th century. At the close of the 15th century, King Henry VII granted it to his uncle, Jasper Tudor, who was probably responsible for blocking the great gatehouse passage to create additional accommodation. More recently, it was used as farm buildings before coming under the care of Cadw.

▼ Llansteffan Castle

▲ Llyn Brenig

▶ **Llyn Brenig** MAP REF 338 B4

In the wilderness of north Wales, between Denbigh and
Corwen, lies Llyn Brenig. It's a 920-acre reservoir sited high in
the wilderness of the Denbigh Moors – an upland region in
Conwy. The huge reservoir, formed by the flooding of the Afon
Fechan and Brenig valleys, is very popular for fishing, sailing
and walking. The visitor centre is full of information on the
area, including its archaeological heritage. Unfortunately, some
of that heritage lies beneath the water, but on the northeast
shores you can discover mesolithic camps with artefacts dating
back to 5700 BC.

GET OUTDOORS
Llyn Brenig Visitor Centre
hiraethog.org.uk
Cerrigydrudion, Corwen, LL21 9TT
01490 420463 | Open all year
daily 8–4
Llyn Brenig is one of the largest
areas of inland water in Wales,
surrounded by a stunning
landscape of heather moor and
forestry. Visitors can explore a
network of waymarked trails on
foot or by bike. Bike hire is
available. Enjoy home-cooked
food and homemade cakes in
the cafe, with panoramic views.
There is outstanding fly-fishing
from the bank or boat.

EXPLORE BY BIKE
One Planet Adventure
oneplanetadventure.com
Coed Llandegla Forest, Ruthin Road,
Llandegla, LL11 3AA | 01978
751656
Hire a bike and choose from
over 27 miles of purpose-built
bike trails in Llandegla Forest
and around Llyn Brenig.

GO FISHING
Permits from Llyn Brenig Visitor
Centre | 01490 420463
Day permits for fly-fishing are
available from machines on
site. It's a great place in which
to hook up with a rainbow trout.

▶ Llyn Peninsula MAP REF 332 B2

gwynedd.gov.uk

Sticking 30 miles out into the Irish Sea, the Llyn Peninsula is a sliver of north Wales with a truly distinct identity. Historically it was popular with pilgrims travelling to the nearby island of Bardsey. Now people come to enjoy the excellent beaches and coastline – most of it designated an Area of Outstanding Natural Beauty; its scattering of villages, great wildlife and its very Welsh culture is possibly the most Welsh experience that Wales has to offer.

This perceived remoteness from urban life has lent the area an unspoilt image, which has made it a popular destination for tourists and holiday home owners. These second homes remain a bone of contention among locals, many of whom are forced out of the housing market by incomers.

At the base of the peninsula is Porthmadog (see page 268), a small town linked to Snowdonia by two steam railways – the Welsh Highland Railway and the Ffestiniog Railway. These were voted North Wales' top attraction in the 2013 National Tourism Awards, and for visitors of a certain age, childhood memories of Ivor the Engine are never far away. Other popular places on the southern coast are Criccieth (see page 153), with a castle on its headland overlooking the beach, Pwllheli (see page 275), and Abersoch and the St Tudwal Islands (see page 71). Elsewhere, the peninsula is all about wildlife, tranquillity, and ancient sacred sites. Tre'r Ceiri hill fort is an Iron Age settlement set beside the coastal mountain of Yr Eifl, while Bardsey Island (see page 61), off Aberdaron at the tip of the peninsula, was the site of a fifth-century Celtic monastery.

As for the north coast goes, Nefyn (see page 243) is the largest of the villages, and the peninsula gets more sparsely populated the further westwards you go. The area was largely the preserve of fishermen in days gone by – the locals still fish for crabs and lobsters – but the lonely cliffs, coves and beaches are a real haven for holidaymakers looking for a little elbow room. Porth Oer (see page 63), better known as Whistling Sands owing to the texture of the sand grains that make them whistle underfoot, is a larger beach, backed by steep grassy cliffs, with safe bathing and a cafe.

TAKE IN SOME HISTORY
Plas yn Rhiw
nationaltrust.org.uk
LL53 8AB | 01758 780219
Open 21–27 May & 5–30 Sep

Thu–Mon 12–5, 29 May–2 Sep,
Wed–Mon 12–5, 3 Oct–3
Nov Thu–Sun 12–4
Hell's Mouth Bay (Porth
Neigwl in Welsh), named for

its reputation as a graveyard for sailing ships, is hardly an inviting address for this small manor house which is on the west shore of the bay. Dating from the medieval period, Plas yn Rhiw was extended in the 1630s and again in the 18th and 19th centuries. Later the house stood empty for years, but thankfully this little gem was rescued, and is now in the care of the National Trust. The 50 acres of gardens and grounds, stretching down to the shoreline, are full of rhododendrons, azaleas and some sub-tropical shrubs. Box hedges and grass paths divide the gardens and a stream and waterfall tumble down towards the bay. The house and grounds are at the centre of an estate that extends for a further 416 acres and includes traditional Welsh cottages, an old windmill and the area known as Mynydd y Graig – a remote and dramatic stretch of Llyn Peninsula coastline.

WALK THE COASTAL PATH
There is some of the best coastal path walking in Wales here, with good facilities and plenty of cafe stops en route.

▶ Machynlleth MAP REF 333 F5

It may be only small and in the middle of nowhere but Machynlleth – pronounced 'Ma-hun-khleth' – has a lot going for it. Found in rural west Wales and often known just as Mack, it claims to be the green capital of Wales. This prestigious accolade – for much of Wales is pretty green – stems largely from the Centre for Alternative Technology (CAT, see page 222, located three miles out of town. Although the townspeople were initially sceptical of the eco-warriors who launched the project, they've now embraced not only the tourism that it brings but also the ethos. You won't have to search far to find eco-friendly shops, vegetarian cafes or places to try yoga or herbal remedies.

Machynlleth is also pretty in its own right. A 17th-century, four-arched stone bridge spans the main road leading into the town. Another landmark is the ornately designed Victorian clock tower standing 80-foot tall. It bears witness to the goings on of the main wide Maengwyn Street, where the weekly Wednesday markets are held. Here you'll also find Parliament House, a medieval town house standing on the site of the building where Owain Glyndwr established a parliament in 1404. It now hosts an Owain Glyndwr interpretative centre. All this – and the fact that the town is situated in some beautiful countryside, especially for mountain bikers – makes it well worth a visit.

VISIT THE MUSEUMS AND GALLERIES

Corris Craft Centre

corriscraftcentre.co.uk
Corris, SY20 9RF | 01654 761584
Open 31 Mar–2 Nov daily 10–5;
many workshops also open at other
times, call to check

Ever wondered how to blow glassware? Or make silver jewellery? This is the place to find out. It's a collection of workshops, where visitors can meet the craftworkers and see them at work every day. Crafts includes glassware, leatherwork, traditional wooden toys, candles, rustic furniture, designer cards and sewn household items and gifts. As well as an educational centre, it's also a perfect place to find unusual items for the home and garden. Drop in for pottery painting or candle-dipping, or book a workshop to make a piece of rustic furniture or learn how to sew.

MOMA Wales

momawales.co.uk
The Tabernacle, Penrallt Street,
SY20 8AJ | 01654 703355
Open Mon–Sat 10–4; closed Sun
A fantastic gallery showing the best of modern Welsh art.

GO UNDERGROUND

Corris Mine Explorers

corrismineexplorers.co.uk
Corris Craft Centre, Corris,
SY20 9RF | 01654 761244
Open all year daily 10–5;
pre-booking recommended
Explore the virtually untouched historic workings of an old Welsh slate mine. First worked in 1836 and abandoned by the miners 40 years ago, it captures more than 130 years of mining history. Find old machinery, miner's tools and candles, while listening to tales about the mine.

King Arthur's Labyrinth

kingarthurslabyrinth.co.uk
Corris, SY20 9RF | 01654 761584
Open 31 Mar–Nov daily 10–5
Just occasionally it's been known to rain in Wales. Under those circumstances, it's probably best to be indoors or – even better – underground. Found deep beneath the mountains near Corris, King Arthur's Labyrinth is one of the most exciting and mysterious visitor attractions to be found in mid-Wales. Here, you will sail underground, in the care of a hooded boatman, through a waterfall and back across a thousand years. Submerged in the darkest of the Dark Ages, you will hear tales of the legendary King Arthur and other ancient Welsh figures as you explore the dramatically floodlit underground caverns and winding tunnels.

PLAY A ROUND

Machynlleth Golf Club

machynllethgolf.com
SY20 8UH | 01654 702000
Open daily all year
This heathland course is surrounded by hills; check out the views from the fifth and eighth holes.

EAT AND DRINK

Plas Ynshir Hall Hotel ◉◉◉◉

ynyshir-hall.co.uk
Eglwys Fach, SY20 8TA
01654 781209

We are used to places that Queen Victoria once passed through on her travels through her realm, but this bears rather more of the regal imprint than most. The Queen once owned this tranquil country house, where she oversaw the planting of lots of trees – many of which still survive – and saw its value as a bird paradise. She was right. Now 1,000 acres of the original estate are owned by the RSPB. This place is also a gastronomic magnet. Welsh lamb and Wagyu beef, and fish from Cardigan Bay and the local rivers are combined with herbs from the gardens and foraged wild ingredients to create a delightful menu.

Wynnstay Hotel

wynnstay-hotel.com
Maengwyn Street, SY20 8AE
01654 702941

It was here in 1780 that politician Sir Watcyn Williams-Wynne built his pied-à-terre, later to become the Wynnstay, Herbert Arms and Unicorn Hotel, a mouthful since abandoned. From the balcony of the Wynnstay Hotel in 1932 and 1937 Prime Minister David Lloyd George watched as the Eisteddfod processions passed by. Brothers Paul and Gareth Johns run this child- and dog-friendly hotel, whose bar serves several Welsh real ales and 10 wines by the glass. Committed, as far as he can, to sourcing ingredients from within a 50-mile radius, Gareth ensures local origins are name-checked on the menus.

▶ PLACES NEARBY

Take time to visit the falconry at Forge or the RSPB centre.

Falconry Experience Wales

raptorexperiencewales.co.uk
Forge, SY20 8RR | 01654 700317

Meet birds of prey, fly and handle a bald eagle or white-faced owl. Ring for opening times and flying options.

RSPB Nature Reserve Ynys-hir

rspb.org.uk
Visitor Centre, Cae'r Berllan,
SY20 8TA | 01654 700222
Reserve open all year daily 9–9
(or sunset if earlier); Visitor Centre
open Apr–Oct daily 9–5, Nov–Mar
Wed–Sun 10–4

The mixture of different habitats here is home to an abundance of birds and wildlife. The salt marshes in winter support the only regular wintering flock of Greenland white-fronted geese in England and Wales, in addition to peregrines, hen harriers and merlins. The sessile oak woodland is home to a host of birds. Otters, polecats, 30 types of butterfly and 15 dragonfly species are also present. Guided walks and children's activities are available. Telephone for details of events running throughout the year.

Machynlleth, Centre for Alternative Technology MAP REF 334 A5

cat.org.uk

SY20 9AZ | 01654 705950 | Open summer daily 10–5, call for winter opening hours; closed 23–28 Dec; railway closed in winter

On the outskirts of Machynlleth, overlooking the Snowdonia National Park, this award-winning eco-centre is the place to come to if you want inspiration on how to make the world a better place. It was founded in 1973 by old Etonian businessman-turned-environmentalist Gerard Morgan-Grenville and a handful of helpers.

Now, it has a staff of 90 and many volunteers working on the seven-acre site. Quite early on in your visit to the centre you are told, 'Earth is one big creature working together and, if we don't interfere, it should last forever.' Wishful thinking, perhaps, but this is what the centre is all about – making you think. CAT is dedicated to exploring and demonstrating global sustainability and ecologically sound technologies. Despite its name, it doesn't give undue attention to alternative technology, but focuses instead on general environmentalism. It also avoids the 'doom and gloom' approach and opts for being constructive and positive, demonstrating all kinds of

▼ A wind turbine

environmental technologies in an interesting and informative way. These include solar and hydro-power and a reed-bed sewerage system. Other facilities include a water-balanced funicular railway, a low-energy house, a site-wide electricity grid powered by renewable energy (any excess is sold to the national grid), a hydraulic ram pump and straw-bale buildings. The aim is to give practical visions of how heat, power, water, food and waste can be handled with a minimal eco-footprint.

The centre is also a reliable source of information on almost any aspect of organic gardening and sustainable living, such as how to achieve more with less and how to include nature in our living and working spaces. It also promotes the right of communities to control their immediate environment and can help with practicalities – from changing light bulbs to building a new house. Staff are more than willing to pass on their knowledge in simple, practical ways – it's what they want to do.

Not only is the centre interesting for grown-ups, it's great for kids too. There's plenty of activities and demonstrations explaining solar, wind and wave power. For fun, there's also an adventure playground, a maze, and a smallholding with farm animals. The centre holds residential courses, and publishes information on organic farming, gardening and ecologically friendly living.

▼ Solar panels and wind turbine

▶ Manorbier Castle MAP REF 323 D6

manorbiercastle.co.uk/castle

Manorbier, near Tenby, SA70 7SY | 01834 871394 | Open Mar–Oct daily 10–5

Overlooking the South Pembrokeshire Heritage Coast, five miles west of Tenby, Manorbier Castle draws visitors from all over – a feat, of course, helped by the beautiful sandy Manorbier Beach at its feet. The castle was begun in the 12th century but managed to avoid major attack from both the Welsh and Cromwell's armies. The first stone buildings were a three-storey-high square tower and a long hall. In the 13th century, the curtain walls were raised with flanking towers and a fine gatehouse, while two large barns were added in the 17th century. Manorbier's considerable defences – including the sturdy walls, battlements, portcullises and ditches – were never put to the test.

The castle is, perhaps, most famous as the birthplace of Giraldus Cambrensis, or Gerald of Wales as he is also known. Gerald was a highly respected scholar who travelled extensively before he became an archdeacon. He was also a dedicated chronicler and his sensitive and incisive observations (written in high-quality Latin) provide an extremely valuable record of life in medieval Wales and Ireland. Alongside his analysis of Welsh politics and history, he described the people and their way of life – how they slept on communal beds of rushes wearing all their clothes, and how their feuding and vengeful natures were balanced by their love of music and poetry.

HIT THE BEACH

Manorbier Beach is sandy, dog-friendly and popular with rock poolers and surfers alike.

▼ Manorbier Castle

EAT AND DRINK

Beach Break Tea Rooms, Giftshop and Gardens

beachbreaktearooms.co.uk

Manorbier House, Manorbier, Tenby, SA70 7TD | 01834 871709

Freshly refurbished in 2014, these delightful tea rooms offer a warm welcome and all the staples – from soup to paninis, ice cream sundaes to Eton mess. Be sure to try the cafe's own blend of Pembrokeshire roasted coffee. In sunny weather, the gardens are a treat, while the gift shop offers lovely trinkets, pieces of local art and ceramics.

▲ Sand banks in the Mawddach Estuary

▶ **Mawddach Estuary** MAP REF 333 E4

This beautiful stretch of water is located on the west coast of
Wales between Barmouth (see page 83) and Fairbourne. It's
a walkers' paradise – particularly the route from Dolgellau to
Barmouth – with sensational views of the Snowdonia
Mountains down to sea level. It's not just for walkers, though.
Cyclist and nature lovers all appreciate this stretch of Wales.
It's helped by the fact that the southern bank of the estuary,
along which used to run a section of rail track, has been turned
into the Mawddach Trail – a nine-mile path running from
Dolgellau (see page 159) to Morfa Mawddach on the southern
side of the Barmouth railway bridge. It's managed by the
Snowdonia National Park Authority as a route for walkers and
cyclists, and is part of the Sustrans Cross-Wales Cycling Route.

The good water levels in the Mawddach make for superb
angling – salmon, sea trout and eels abound.

▶ Menai Strait MAP REF 336 C4

The Menai Strait (Afon Menai in Welsh) is a narrow stretch of shallow tidal water about 15.5 miles long, which separates the island of Anglesey from mainland Wales. The industrial era bought the first permanent island–mainland connection with Thomas Telford's iconic 560-foot Menai Suspension Bridge, completed in 1826. Its got a 98-foot-high central span, allowing the passage of tall ships underneath. In 1850, Telford's stunning creation was joined by a second bridge – Robert Stephenson's Britannia Bridge. Originally this carried rail traffic in two wrought-iron rectangular box spans, but after a disastrous fire in 1970, which destroyed everything bar the limestone pillars, it was rebuilt as a steel box girder bridge and now carries both rail and road traffic. Between the two bridge crossings there is a small island in the middle of the strait, Ynys Gorad Goch, on which there's a house and outbuildings and the remains of a fish trap.

As for the water underneath the bridge, the differential tides at the two ends of the strait cause very strong currents to flow in both directions at different times, creating dangerous conditions. One of the most dangerous areas is known as the Swellies, or Swillies, between the two bridges. Here rocks near the surface create local whirlpools, which can cause small boats to founder on the rocks. This was the site of the loss of the training ship HMS *Conway* in 1953. Entering the strait at the Caernarfon end is also hazardous, owing to the frequently shifting sandbanks that make up Caernarfon Bar. On the mainland side at this point is Fort Belan, an 18th-century defensive fort built in the time of the American War of Independence.

MEET THE SEALIFE
Anglesey Sea Zoo
angleseyseazoo.co.uk
LL61 6TQ | 01248 430411
Open all year daily 10–5.30
Nestling by the Menai Straits, this all-weather undercover attraction contains a shipwreck bristling with conger eels, a lobster hatchery, a sea horse nursery, crashing waves and the enchanting fish forest. Visit the invertebrates in the No Bone Zone, and watch out for the submarine wolves.

MEET THE BUGLIFE
Pili Palas Nature World
pilipalas.co.uk
Penmynydd Road, Menai Bridge,
LL59 5RP | 01248 712474
Pili Palas is the Welsh for butterfly – and this is the place to come if you want to see lots of them. Enjoy the lush vegetation, tropical birds, bugs and many snakes and lizards. You can get up close during animal handling sessions. Maybe you can even hold a cockroach.

PLAY A ROUND

Llanfairfechan Golf Club
Llannerch Road, LL33 0ES
01248 680144 | Open Mon–Fri
all year

A hillside 9-hole course enjoying panoramic views of the Strait. The course enjoys good all-year-round conditions due to its situation.

▶ Merthyr Tydfil MAP REF 326 B3

Merthyr Tydfil is a town better known for its industrial and political history than as a traditional tourist destination. Located in a bowl at the head of the south Wales Taff Valley, ringed by slagheaps and quarries, it has enjoyed its fair share of both boom times and economic hardships over the years. While it might not make the itinerary of every visitor to Wales, it does boast attractions such as the Cyfartha Castle Museum and Art Gallery, which are well worth a visit.

Merthyr Tydfil rose to prominence during the Industrial Revolution, thanks to its rich natural resources. In its heyday, 200 years ago, this bowl was on fire with the largest ironworks in the world, due to its close proximity to iron ore. Then, rich coal reserves were discovered and by the early 19th century it was a boom town, with workers coming from all over the world. The smaller towns of Dowlais, Penydarren and Cyfarthfa gradually merged into Merthyr, which, at its peak around 1850, had a population of some 80,000. These people lived and worked in appalling, disease-ridden conditions and the town became famous for its political radicalism.

The Merthyr Rising of 1831 was the violent climax of years of simmering working class unrest. Rebels ripped up debtors' and account books and apparently cried *caws a bara* ('cheese and bread') – they wanted a reduction in the price of them – and *I lawr â'r Brenin* ('Down with the King'). Men working in the pit were persuaded to join the protest. Eventually, around 10,000 workers marched under a red flag – later adopted internationally as the symbol of the working classes. The rioting continued for a month, facing opposition from the army. At one point shots were fired and some of the protestors were killed.

Just 50 years later, however, the scene was very different. The demand for iron and steel dwindled and one by one the ironworks closed. By 1935, the unemployment rate was an astonishing 60 per cent and a Royal Commission even suggested that the town be abandoned. Today, there are shoots of regeneration, such as the nearby BikePark Wales (see page 229), which has managed to bring much-needed revenue and a new lease of life to the town.

VISIT THE MUSEUM
Cyfarthfa Castle Museum and Art Gallery
museums.merthyr.gov.uk
Cyfarthfa Park, CF47 8RE
01685 727371 | Open Apr–Sep daily 10–5.30, Oct–Mar Tue–Fri 10–4, Sat–Sun 12–4

Built by ironwork owner William Crawshay II at the height of its industrial heyday, this is a plush and stylish Gothic mansion. It's set in wooded parkland beside a beautiful lake, and now houses a superb museum and art gallery covering the last 3,000 years. The collections of fine art, social history and objects from around the world are wonderful to behold.

TAKE A TRAIN RIDE
Brecon Mountain Railway
breconmountainrailway.co.uk
Pant Station, Dowlais, CF48 2UP
01685 722988 | Call or check website for scheduled timetable

Opened in 1980, this narrow-gauge railway follows part of an old British Rail route, which closed in 1964. The present route starts at Pant Station and runs for 3.5 miles through the Brecon Beacons National Park, as far as Taf Fechan Reservoir. The train is pulled by a vintage steam locomotive and is one of the most popular railways in Wales. A special Santa train service operates in December.

PLAY A ROUND
Choose from Morlais Castle Golf Club, a moorland course, or Merthyr Tydfil Golf Club, a mountaintop course in the Brecon Beacons.

Merthyr Tydfil Golf Club
merthyrtydfilgolfclub.com
Cilsanws Mountain, Cefn Coed,

▼ The gardens of Cyfarthfa Castle

CF48 2NU | 01685 373131
Open daily all year daily

Morlais Castle Golf Club
morlaiscgolf.com
Pant, CF48 2UY | 01685 722822
Open Sun–Fri all year

▶ **PLACES NEARBY**

Just south of Merthyr, at
Abercanaid, is BikePark Wales,
ideal for the whole family.

BikePark Wales
bikeparkwales.com
Gethin Woodland Centre,
Abercanaid, CF48 1YZ (use CF48
4TT for Satnav but, after leaving
the roundabout turn right, not left)
07730 382501

Opened in 2013, BikePark
Wales is the country's newest
mountain bike park in the heart
of the south Wales valleys, built
by riders for riders. Whatever
your experience of mountain
biking, you'll find something to
enjoy here. Routes are graded
as ski-runs, from green to
black. You can pay to get a lift to
the top or push-up by pedal
power the hard way.

▶ **Milford Haven** MAP REF 322 C5

Milford Haven (Aberdaugleddau in Welsh) is located in
Pembrokeshire on a natural harbour that's been in use since
the Middle Ages. Founded in 1790, it was designed to be a
whaling centre, though by 1800 it was mostly used as a Royal
Navy dockyard. In the 1960s, it became a commercial dock
aiding the logistical shipment of fuel oil and liquid gas for the
local Esso plant. The town now plays an important part in the
UK's energy sector. Tankers fill the sea, a new gas-fired power
station is in place and huge new storage plants send gas across
south Wales and beyond via an underground pipeline.

The port saw action long before the oil refineries moved in,
however. Viking fleets wintered here, and in 1171, Henry II
attacked Ireland from here, as did Cromwell in 1649.

Guarding the entrance to the harbour are the Dale and
Angle peninsulas (both names are Norse). The Dale Peninsula
is the sunniest place in Wales and its sheltered waters have
turned it into a busy sailing and water-sports centre. Some of
the first inhabitants of Milford Haven were Quaker whaling
families from Nantucket in New England. Their meeting house
dates from 1811 and the grid pattern of streets they laid out –
three roads rising parallel to the waterway – is still in place.
Major fishing took hold in the 1880s, helping the town to
prosper. The story of the town is told in the Milford Haven
Museum, housed in one of its oldest buildings, the Old Custom
House, dating from 1797 and formerly used for storing whale
oil. The old town docks have also been redeveloped as a
modern marina with cafes and restaurants.

VISIT THE MUSEUM
Milford Haven Museum
milfordhavenmuseum.org.uk
The Old Custom House, The Docks,
SA73 3AF | 01646 694496
Open Mon–Sat 11–5, Sun 12–6
Housed in one of the oldest
buildings in Milford Haven, the
museum collection reflects the
town's history, especially the
maritime aspect.

CATCH A PERFORMANCE
Milford Haven Torch Theatre
torchtheatre.co.uk
St Peter's Road, SA73 2BU
01646 695267
There's a rich programme of
events at this super theatre.
Check the website for details.

PLAY A ROUND
Milford Haven Golf Club
mhgc.co.uk
Woodbine House, Hubberston,
SA73 3RX | 01646 697762
Open daily all year
A fantastic parkland course
with excellent greens.

▶ PLACES NEARBY
Enjoy a day out at sea on the
Pembokeshire coast.

Celtic Wild Cat
celticwildcat.com
Neyland Yacht Haven, SA73 1PY
01646 600313
Fishing and diving trips, as well
as sightseeing tours on board a
fast catamaran.

▶ Moelfre MAP REF 336 C2
This pretty little village on the east coast of Anglesey is best
known for its dramatic and daring lifeboat rescues. You can find
out all about them at the Moelfre Seawatch Centre, which is
located not far from the harbour. Here you can also watch the
iconic red boats head out from the lifeboat station.

Whitewashed fishermen's cottages are scattered on the
headland overlooking a small harbour. There's also a shingle
beach and the little island Ynys Moelfre. There are wonderful
cliff-top paths to Dulas Bay, and in the opposite direction to
Benllech and Red Wharf Bay. Moelfre is also on the Anglesey
Coastal Path. In English, Moelfre means 'bald or barren hill'
– which described the land behind the village as it was seen
from the sea.

ENTERTAIN THE FAMILY
RNLI Seawatch Centre
Moelfre, LL72 8HY | 01248 410300
Open Easter–Oct daily 10.30–4
The centre is a reminder of the
island's rich maritime history.
Enjoy looking at a real 20th-
century lifeboat and learning
about historic shipwrecks. The
worst was in 1859, when the
Royal Charter sank off the coast
of Anglesey in a fierce storm.
The men of Moelfre formed a
human chain to try and save
those on board but, despite
their valiant efforts and many
lives saved, 454 people died in
the disaster.

HIT THE BEACH

This area has some of the finest beaches in Anglesey, including Traeth Bychan, Porth yr Aber, Moelfre, Porth Helaeth, Traeth Lligwy, Traeth Penrhyn and Traeth yr Ora.

EAT AND DRINK

Ann's Pantry

annspantry.co.uk
The Beach, LL72 8HL
01248 410386

Enjoy a proper Welsh breakfast, simple lunch or hearty dinner in this relaxed cottage set slightly back from the harbour. If you come in summer, make the most of the pretty, lawned garden. Sunday lunch is served in winter. Don't forget to try the cakes.

▶ PLACES NEARBY

The Celtic settlement of Din Lligwy is close to Moelfre.

Din Lligwy

cadw.wales.gov.uk
01443 336000
Open all year daily 10–4

In woodland, a mile or so inland from Moelfre (see opposite) is this wonderfully preserved Celtic settlement. The half-acre site consists of foundations of a number of buildings, with the entire area enclosed by a thick double wall. In a nearby field are the remains of a neolithic burial chamber, the *Lligwy* tomb. A massive capstone weighing about 25 tonnes covers the remains of 15 to 30 people, alongside possessions and pieces of pottery.

▶ Mold MAP REF 339 D3

Located in northeast Wales, six miles south of the coastal town of Flint (see page 167), is Mold, a busy little market town that was once the capital of the old county of Flintshire. The splendid parish Church of St Mary, with its 16th-century aisled nave and magnificent 18th-century tower, dominates the lovely High Street and, indeed, the whole of the Alyn Valley. Look out for the unusual and attractive art deco flooring in the war memorial chapel.

CATCH A PERFORMANCE

Clwyd Theatr Cymru

clwyd-theatr-cymru.co.uk
Raikes Lane, Mold, CH7 1YA
01352 701521

Check out the website for its rich programme of events.

PLAY A ROUND

Watch out for the signature hole on the 18th at Old

Padeswood Golf Club or play at Mold Golf Club, a parkland course with great views of five counties.

Mold Golf Club

moldgolfclub.co.uk
Cilcain Road, Pantymwyn,
CH7 5EH
01352 741513
Open all year daily

Old Padeswood Golf Club
oldpadeswoodgolfclub.co.uk
Station Lane, Padeswood, CH7 4JL
01244 547401 | Open daily all year
Nine holes are flat and nine
are gently undulating at this
challenging course.

EAT AND DRINK
Glasfryn
brunningandprice.co.uk
Raikes Lane, Sychdyn, CH7 6LR
01352 750500
Open Mon–Sat 12–9.30, Sun 12–9
This dining pub was converted
from a judge's country
residence some years ago.
Inside, you'll find quirky prints,
old furnishings and wood
flooring that complements the
Arts and Crafts style of the
original building. The pub has
real ale pumps, and
comprehensive wine and malt
whisky lists. Fine pub grub is on
offer; there's a great range of
starters and mains.

▶ PLACES NEARBY
Ewloe Castle lies to the
northeast of Mold and there are
some great restaurants and a
country park close by.

Ewloe Castle
cadw.wales.gov.uk
Deeside, Flintshire, CH5 3BZ
01443 336000
Open all year daily 10–4
Standing in Ewloe Wood are the
remains of Ewloe Castle. It is a
native Welsh castle and Henry II
was defeated nearby in 1157.
Part of the Welsh Tower in the
upper ward still stands to its
original height, and there is a

well in the lower ward. You can
also see remnants of walls and
another tower.

Loggerheads Country Park
visitclwydianrange.co.uk
Ruthin Road, CH7 5LH
01352 810614 | Open daily 10–5
Set in a beautiful wooded river
valley, with dramatic cliffs and
outcrops, this park is great for a
short stroll or to start exploring
the Clwydian Range. It has a
well-marked Discovery Trail
and easily accessible pathways
around the park and to the hills
and valleys beyond.

Stables Bar Restaurant
soughtonhall.co.uk
Northop, CH7 6AB | 01352 840577
This free house created in
Soughton Hall's stable block
dates from the 18th century.
The magnificent main house
was built as a bishop's palace.
Original cobbled floors and roof
timbers remain intact. The
selection of real ales includes
Stables Bitter, and there's a
wine shop if you prefer a bottle
with your meal.

White Horse Inn
Cilcain, CH7 5NN | 01352 740142
This 400-year-old pub is the
last survivor of the five that
once existed in this village at
the centre of the local gold-
mining industry in the 19th
century. It is popular with
walkers, cyclists and horse
riders. The food is made by the
landlady using best quality local
ingredients and there's a good
range of real ales.

▲ Monnow Bridge

▶ **Monmouth** MAP REF 327 F2

Monmouth may be in Wales – just – but it actually feels more English in nature. This is probably no surprise as it has hopped over the border countless times. It sits at the junction of the River Wye and River Monnow, and is a busy and affluent market town. Famously, King Henry V – victor at the Battle of Agincourt in 1415 – was born here. His statue still stands in the town square, looking down upon a statue of another of the town's favourite sons, Henry Rolls – the aviation pioneer and co-founder of Rolls-Royce.

Today, Monmouth is known for its very good comprehensive and private schools, and the Rockfield Studios. Situated just outside the town, they are where Queen recorded *Bohemian Rhapsody* in 1975, and where, in 1995, Oasis recorded their multimillion selling album *(What's the Story) Morning Glory?* Musicians are frequently spotted in and around the town, so keep your eyes peeled. Each August, Monmouth hosts the Monmouth Show – a large rural show that attracts thousands. Tourism is also big business, largely due to Monmouth being such a great base from which to explore the beautiful Wye Valley – and what a lot there is to see. Tintern Abbey (see page 145) is the main attraction. Founded in the 12th century, it's now roofless, yet this doesn't detract from its beauty. Instead, it simply exposes the graceful arches and vast windows. Handily, it's located in the most stunning wooded valley, and also next to a pub, river and several circular walks.

VISIT THE MUSEUMS
Monmouth Castle and Regimental Museum
monmouthcastlemuseum.org.uk
Castle Hill, NP25 3BS | 01600 772175 | Open Apr–Oct daily 2–5
By the standards of most Welsh castles, Monmouth is really nothing to write home about, largely because all, bar the great tower, was dismantled in the 17th century. The stone was used to build Great Castle House next door, now the headquarters of the Royal Monmouthshire Regiment. Inside, the museum documents the history of the regiment from the 16th century.

The Monmouth Museum and Local History Centre
welcometomonmouth.co.uk
Priory Street, NP25 3XA | 01600 710630 | Open Mar–Oct Mon–Sat 11–1, 2–5, Sun 2–5, Nov–Feb Mon–Sat 11–1, 2–4, Sun 2–4
Admiral Horatio Nelson visited Monmouth in 1802. Although his links with the town run little deeper than that, Lady Llangattock, a more-than-slightly obsssive local aristocrat, began collecting Nelson memorabilia, resulting in this quirky museum. It includes original letters, glass, china, silver, medals, books, models, prints and Nelson's fighting sword. Other displays deal with the more mundane, such as Monmouth's past as a fortress market town, and the development of the Rolls-Royce company. The museum is also known as the Nelson Museum.

CATCH A PERFORMANCE
Savoy Theatre
monmouth-savoy.co.uk
Church Street, NP25 3BU
01600 772467
This is a great little theatre with a rich and varied programme of events and the added bonus that you can enjoy a glass of wine while watching the show of your choice.

GO CANOEING
Monmouth Canoe and Activity Centre
monmouthcanoe.co.uk
Castle Yard, Old Dixton Road, NP25 3DP | 01600 716083
This is just the place to hire two-person canoes for half days, day trips and longer.

PLAY A ROUND
Enjoy the hilly and challenging parkland course with several lakes and ponds surrounded by woodland at The Rolls of Monmouth Golf Club – watch out for the magnificent 17th and 18th holes. Monmouth Golf Club is another superb local course with beautiful views, and its eighth hole, the Cresta Run, is renowned as one of Britain's most challenging.

Monmouth Golf Club
monmouthgolfclub.co.uk
Leasbrook Lane, NP25 3SN
01600 712212 | Open daily all year

The Rolls of Monmouth Golf Club
therollsgolfclub.co.uk
The Hendre, NP25 5HG
01600 715353 | Open daily all year

EAT AND DRINK

Bistro Prego ◉◉

pregomonmouth.co.uk
7 Church Street, NP25 3BX
01600 712600

This welcoming little cafe and bistro is simple in style but big on charm. Prego hums with a constant bustle of local fans won over by its all-day approach, serving everything from light snacks to lunch through to a more sophisticated evening bistro offering. The food here is all about sourcing top-class local ingredients, which are brought together without undue fuss – and, as you may have spotted in the name, a strongly Italian vein courses through it all.

The Inn at Penallt ◉◉

theinnatpenallt.co.uk
Penallt, NP25 4SE | 01600 772765

This 17th-century inn in a tiny village in the Wye Valley is nicely traditional – slate floors, ceiling beams, wooden furniture by the truckload, a fireplace in the bar and a jolly atmosphere throughout. Really, what more could you ask? However, the food is the draw here too; its appeal due to good quality ingredients prepared in a straightforward way. There's a smarter dining room out back.

The Lion Inn

lioninn.co.uk
Trellech, NP25 4PA
01600 860322

Although best known for its food and drink, The Lion Inn once showed true versatility by providing the best-dressed entry in the Monmouth raft race. Built in 1580 as a brewhouse and inn by a former sea captain, it consists of two rooms, both with open fires; one is a traditional bar, the other a restaurant. Debbie Zsigo has run it for the past 20 years and knows instinctively what works. In the bar, the answer is Wye Valley Butty Bach, and a number of local ciders, including Raglan Cider Mill Snowy Owl. In the restaurant, you'll find bar snacks, pizzas, light meals and a good range of main dishes. The garden has a stream and an aviary, and there are beautiful views from the suntrap courtyard. There's a beer festival in June and one for cider-drinkers in August.

The Potting Shed Vintage Garden Teas and Seasonal Plants

1 The Barton, Agincourt Square, Monmouth, NP25 3BT
01600 772299

As the name suggests, this tea room is decorated in a potting shed theme, with plants and flower pots and plant racks, etc. The fun surroundings are enhanced by the lovely food, which may or may not come served on a shovel decorated with small flowers. Try the crab pâté, or any of the fresh quiches or salads. There's also a good range of locally sourced teas and gluten-free options. The food is well-priced and the service excellent.

▶ **PLACES NEARBY**

Close to Monmouth is a castle, manor house, restaurants and the towns of Abergavenny (see page 66) and Usk (see page 315). The three castles of Grosmont, Skenfrith and White (see page 173) are also slightly further afield.

Raglan Castle

cadw.wales.gov.uk
NP15 2BT | 01291 690228
Open Mar–Jun, Sep–Oct daily 9.30–5, Jul–Aug 9.30–6, Nov–Feb Mon–Sat 10–4, Sun 11–4

This castle is an astonishing statement of wealth and power. From the great tower to the great gatehouse, this whole castle was built for show. Mind you, it did hold off Oliver Cromwell's forces for 13 weeks in one of the last sieges of the Civil War. It's hard to believe that the castle was taken and partially destroyed because what remains is so impressive. That, and the fact it is different – owing to being built in the 1430s, much later than most of the other castles – makes it a real treat. The large bay oriel window is one of Raglan's defining features – lighting up the high table at the end of the hall. It was the BBC's film location of choice for *Merlin*.

Fountain Inn

fountaininntrellech.co.uk
Trellech Grange, Tintern, NP16 6QW
01291 689303

This is a fine old inn, dating from 1611 and set in lovely countryside, with a garden overlooking the Wye Valley. The pub menu offers a choice of several curries as well as more traditional fare. The owner's passion for real ales and ciders is evident both in the great bar line-up, and at the September beer festival.

High Glanau Manor

ngs.org.uk
Lydart, Monmouth, NP25 4AD
01600 860005 | Opening times vary; check website for details

Four miles southwest of Monmouth is this Arts and Crafts manor house. Found high up on a hillside, with breathtaking views over the Vale of Usk to Sugar Loaf and the Brecon Beacons, it was designed in the 1920s by H Avray Tipping, a garden designer and editor of *Country Life*. Original features include impressive stone terraces, a pergola, herbaceous borders, an Edwardian glasshouse, rhododendrons, azaleas and woodland walks.

The Stonemill and Steppes Farm Cottages ❀❀

thestonemill.co.uk
Rockfield, NP25 5SW
01600 716273

Just a few miles from Monmouth, and close to the Wye Valley and the Forest of Dean, this beautifully converted barn in a 16th-century mill complex with self-catering bed and breakfast cottages provides an impressive setting for accomplished ingredients-lead cooking. Inside it's a riot of oak beams and vaulted ceilings, with chunky rustic tables around an ancient stone cider press. The kitchen's modern approach makes sound use of fresh regional and Welsh produce to deliver accurately cooked and simply presented modern European dishes.

The Whitebrook ◎◎◎
thewhitebrook.co.uk
Whitebrook, NP25 4TX
01600 860254

Situated in the Wye Valley, the Whitebrook, a one-time drovers' inn dating from the 17th century, offers classy accommodation in eight rooms, but first-and-foremost it's a cracking restaurant. A la carte and tasting menus are available, including vegetarian versions. The lunchtime menu is particularly excellent value. The cooking may well be pin-sharp and modern, but flavour certainly leads the way.

▼ Raglan Castle

▶ Montgomery MAP REF 335 E5

Six miles south of Welshpool in the border country of mid-Wales lies Montgomery, named after William the Conqueror's friend, Roger de Montgomery, who built the castle here. Although it is perfectly pleasant, there's not that much to do or see. If you do happen to stroll through, you'll see a fine clock tower adjoined to the red-brick town hall. The 16th-century houses are half-timbered and there are a few places to sup a pint and get a decent night's rest. Walkers of the nearby Offa's Dyke Path often stop off here.

TAKE IN SOME HISTORY

Montgomery Castle
cadw.wales.gov.uk
01443 336000 | Open all year
daily 10–4
Initially an earth-and-timber structure guarding an important ford in the River Severn, Montgomery, one of many Norman castles on the border between Wales and England, was considered a suitable spot for the building of an 'impregnable castle' in the 1220s. Building continued for another 30 or so years, but the final conquest of Wales by Edward I meant the castle lost much of its importance, gradually becoming more of a military backwater and prison than a frontline fortress.

EAT AND DRINK

Castle Kitchen
8 Broad Street, SY15 6PH
01686 668795
A lively cafe with old-world rustic charm and winding stair cases, where staff go out of their way to accommodate specific diets. Often you can see fresh cakes and other food being prepared in the kitchen. The only downside is that it can sometimes get so busy, it's a struggle to find a table.

Ivy House Cafe
Church Bank, SY15 6PU
01686 668746
This small cafe serves the staples. It's dog friendly and upstairs there are second-hand books for sale.

▶ The Mumbles MAP REF 325 D4

The Mumbles (Y Mwmbwls) is the southernmost headland of the beautiful, curving Swansea Bay and Swansea's most upmarket suburb. It must be posh – actress Catherine Zeta-Jones built a £2 million pad here and singer Bonnie Tyler has a home here too. It's not known where the name Mumbles came from, although some do hazard that it's from the word *mamucium* – thought to derive from the Celtic for breast-shaped hill – or maybe that's just fantasy. Either way, the description is quite accurate. The headland is hilly in shape and contains a lighthouse, built during the 1790s.

It's also home to a mile-long strip of pastel-painted houses and a few trendy bars, and ends with Mumbles Pier, which overlooks a sandy beach and has the usual amusements. Opened in 1898, the pier was built at the end of Mumbles Railway, which was one of the longest-running railway passenger services in the world. It opened in 1807 and operated horse-drawn engines between here and Swansea until 1906. The area, historically known as Mumbles, has swallowed up Oystermouth, a pretty fishing village with a 13th-century castle.

TAKE IN SOME HISTORY
Oystermouth Castle
Newton Road, SA3 4BE | 01792 369233 | Open Mar–Sep daily 11–5
In 2013, a serious load of cash was spent to help restore this castle. Now, you can explore parts of the castle that have been hidden away for centuries. Check out graffiti from the 14th century (Banksy would approve, no doubt) and the maze of deep vaults and secret staircases, then be sure to marvel at the views from the 30-foot-high glass bridge. Events are held throughout the year.

HIT THE BEACH
Caswell Bay is an excellent small beach, popular with surfers. It also has a good cafe. No dogs allowed May–Sep.

▶ Narberth MAP REF 323 E4

For the cool and the crafty, Narberth is the place to come. Located inland in Pembrokeshire, this small town has recently developed a style all its own. The shops are individual and sell boutique goods, ranging from fine art to fine food – a must-do stop is the Spanish deli. There are galleries, cool cafes and great pubs bursting with honky-tonk pianos. If you're into fashion, you'll find everything from sheepskin boots to lingerie and couture dresses.

The centre of town has the Old Town Hall, an impressive structure with a double staircase leading to the entrance. Then there's the Queen's Hall on High Street, where jazz, blues and comedy are performed throughout the year. The town also has three major events. The big plant sale in the spring is a perfect place for stocking up on garden plants. Narberth Civic Week, which culminates in the renowned Narberth Carnival, takes place in July. Finally, the Narberth Food Festival, at the end of September, brings thousands of food-lovers to the town for tasty treats and an impressive line-up of international culinary talent. The town also runs a Greenway scheme, encouraging people to visit and travel around by bike.

TAKE IN SOME HISTORY
Narberth Castle
visitpembrokeshire.com
Narberth SA67 7BD
Open all year daily
Believed to be on the site once occupied by the palace of Pwll, home to the Prince of Dyfed, as recounted in the collection of ancient tales known as the *Mabinogion*, Narberth Castle is all about myths and legends. The rectangular castle is now in ruins, but these have been renovated and were opened to the public in 2006.

EXPLORE BY BIKE
Pembrokeshire Bikes
pembrokeshirebikes.co.uk
1 Rushacre Enterprise Park, Redstone Road, Narberth
SA67 7ET | 01834 862755
Based in Narberth, this company also offers a bike delivery service to Fishguard.

EAT AND DRINK
The Grove ⊚⊚⊚
thegrove-narberth.co.uk
Molleston, SA67 8BX
01834 860915
There's quite a history to this house, whose architectural changes took place well in the 1870s. Now it's truly beautiful, surrounded by 24 acres of lush rolling countryside and flower gardens. It makes an impression on the inside too, with a touch of individuality and character to the period features of the house. The restaurant has plenty of traditional charm, with local artworks on the walls and tables dressed up for what

lies ahead, and it delivers too, with smart, clearly focused contemporary cooking. The kitchen garden delivers its bounty, but what can't be grown in situ is sourced locally and with care.

The New Inn
newinnamroth.co.uk
Amroth, SA67 8NW | 01834 812368
Originally a farmhouse, this 16th-century inn belongs to Amroth Castle Estate and has been family run for nearly 40 years. The pub has considerable old-world charm with beamed ceilings, a Flemish chimney, a flagstone floor and inglenook fireplace. It is situated conveniently close to the beach, with views towards Saundersfoot and Tenby from the dining room upstairs. Enjoy food or drink outside on the large lawn complete with picnic benches. There is even a toddlers' menu in addition to the children's menu.

▶ PLACES NEARBY
Close to Narbeth is the Blue Lagoon Water Park and Oakwood Park (see page 256).

Blue Lagoon Water Park
bluelagoonwales.com
Bluestone, SA67 8DE | 01834 862410
With tropical temperatures, slides and flumes, a lazy river and water pools for all ages, the Blue Lagoon is one of the great Pembrokeshire attractions for all ages and swimming abilities.

▶ National Botanic Garden of Wales   MAP REF 324 C2

gardenofwales.org.uk

SA32 8HN | 01558 667149 | Open Apr–Sep daily 10–6, Oct–Mar 10–4.30

Roll over Kew Gardens – this bountiful creation is twice the size and equally impressive, though admittedly not as mature. Located 10 miles east of Carmarthen, the National Botanic Garden of Wales only opened in 2000 but it's achieved a lot in that time. Although essentially a teaching and research facility, the garden is laid out with the visitor in mind. There's a Japanese garden, a double-walled garden and a marsh linking the lake and pond. The centrepiece is a great glasshouse – an amazing tinted glass dome with a 19-foot ravine – designed by Norman Foster.

Meanwhile, there are also plants from Mediterranean-style landscapes around the world, enabling you to experience the aftermath of an Australian bush fire, pause in an olive grove or wander through fuchsia collections from Chile. The Tropical House features orchids and palms, while a herbaceous broadwalk forms the spine of the garden and leads to the children's play area and cinema. Land train tours will take you around the necklace of lakes surrounding the central garden.

▶ National Wetland Centre Wales   MAP REF 324 C3

wwt.org.uk

Llanelli Centre, Penclacwydd Llwynhendy, Llanelli, SA14 9SH

01554 741087 | Reserve open all year daily 9.30–5; grounds open Mar–Oct until 6pm

For bird-lovers and wildlife enthusiasts, this place is a must-do. Located near Llanelli (see page 207), it's a 450-acre mosaic of pools, streams and lagoons adjoining the salt marshes of Burry Inlet. The variety of habitats means it's a haven for many different plants and animals. Year-round, birds make their home here, but seasonal flocks can boost numbers by 50,000. If you're lucky you'll catch a glimpse of a bittern – these rare birds are becoming more frequent – black-tailed godwits, hawks and owls and little egrets, virtually unknown in Wales 20 years ago but now thriving.

Other wildlife is also abundant here. Some 20 species of dragonfly have been recorded, alongside water voles, otters and many types of fish. Several rare moths make it their home, including the scarlet tiger moth and rosy wave moth. Plant-wise, there are wild orchids, rock sea lavender, marshmallow and eel-grass; spring and summer are the best times to visit if you want to see them in their true multicolour glory. It's not all watching though – you can get interactive by hand-feeding some of the tamer swans and flamingoes. There are also hides for birding, as well as a Millennium Discovery Centre and a play area with tunnels and a maze.

▶ Neath   MAP REF 325 E3

Seven miles northeast of Swansea (see page 306) lies Neath, a close-knit town where 'everyone knows everyone'. That's the impression classical singer Katherine Jenkins gives anyway. She describes the people as having 'massive hearts', but also describes the town as being in 'pretty bad shape' – that's why she spent a significant amount of her time raising money for renovations at St David's Church, where she sang as a child and continues to sing at Christmas. Indeed, the town is quite run-down, and not really on the tourist map at all. Instead, it's a busy market and industrial town, with most visitors going to Trade Centre Wales, a huge car supermarket close to the town. If you're not car shopping, highlights of the town include the 12th-century Benedictine Neath Abbey and a Norman castle.

Nearby, Briton Ferry, with its small dockyard, is now part of the borough, although largely overshadowed by the massive viaduct carrying the M4 motorway round the south Wales coast.

TAKE IN SOME HISTORY
Neath Abbey
cadw.wales.gov.uk
SA10 7DW | 01443 336000
Open all year daily 10–4
The ruins of Neath Abbey, founded around 1130 by Richard de Granville as a Cistercian abbey and gatehouse, are substantial and pretty impressive. Exceptionally heavy rainfall in recent years has damaged much of the abbey's stonework and repairs are currently under way, restricting access in certain parts. Call or check the website for more information before visiting.

VISIT THE MUSEUM
Cefn Coed Colliery Museum
see Aberdulais, page 63

GET OUTDOORS
Gnoll Estate Country Park
visitnpt.gov.uk/gnollcountrypark
SA11 3BS | 01639 635808
Open summer daily 8–8, winter 8–5
Once owned by a wealthy industrial family, the Mackworths, the extensively landscaped Gnoll Estate offers tranquil woodland walks, lovely picnic areas and stunning views. The country park was recently voted Best Picnic Spot in Wales – quite an accolade. There's also a nine-hole golf course and coarse fishing. For children, there are play areas and an adventure playground. Activities run throughout the year, particularly during school holidays.

▲ Morfa Nefyn

PLAY A ROUND
Neath Golf Club
neathgolfclub.co.uk
Cadoxton, SA10 8AH

01639 632759 | Open all year daily
This is an historic 18-hole
heathland course suitable for
golfers of all levels.

▶ **Nefyn** MAP REF 332 B2

Located on the northwest coast of the Llyn Peninsula, Nefyn is
a small town of just 2,000 inhabitants. Having said this, it's still
the largest of the surrounding villages and its tempting sandy
beaches are certainly a draw. With a harbour at one end, Nefyn
Beach lies in a beautiful spot below the main village, sheltered
by bushy cliffs. Nearby is the beach of Morfa Nefyn – again
mainly sand – and further along to the west is the small
picturesque fishing hamlet of Porthdinllaen. It's got a rocky

promontory with an Iron Age hill fort on top and is home to the local lifeboat station. More famous is its pub, the Ty Coch, which lies – somewhat amazingly – right on the sands at the top of the beach.

East of Nefyn, the road turns inland to climb over the shoulders of the neighbouring granite mountains, Yr Eifl. Perched on the east summit is Tre'r Ceiri, one of the best-preserved ancient forts in Wales. A gigantic Bronze Age burial cairn lies in the centre of an elaborate ancient settlement, where shattered stone walls enclose the circular foundations of dozens of huts. It's well worth taking the zig-zag roadside path through the heather to see them.

HIT THE BEACH

Nefyn is a sweeping bay with two miles of sand, excellent for water sports, sunbathing and swimming.

▶ PLACES NEARBY

Close to Nefyn is Porthdinllaen, one of Wales' most scenic and sandy beaches, with a pub right on the beach.

▶ Nevern   MAP REF 323 E2

This stunning village is a collection of cottages located on the slopes overlooking the River Nyfer in Pembrokeshire, west Wales, nine miles from Newport and close to the Preseli Hills. A firm candidate for the title of most beautiful village in Wales, it's most famous for its intricately carved Celtic cross of St Brynach, standing more than 12 feet high in the churchyard. There are other carved stones nearby, and the churchyard also has a famous 'bleeding' yew, which secretes blood-red sap.

SEE A LOCAL CHURCH
St Brynach Church

On the south side of the church is the Nevern Cross, dating mainly from the 15th century. It consists of two sections of local dolerite stone, cut and fitted together.

▶ PLACES NEARBY

Close to Nevern is a great coaching inn-cum-restaurant. The pretty town of Newport (see page 253) is slightly further afield

Salutation Inn

salutationcountryhotel.co.uk
Felindre Farchog, Crymych,
SA41 3UY | 01239 820564
This tastefully modernised, 16th-century coaching inn stands on the River Nevern. The owner has 20 years' experience of North African and Middle Eastern restaurants but prefers to cook local delights, such as ham and chips or chicken breast. Felinfoel, Brains and local guest ales are on tap in the well-stocked bar.

▸ New Quay
see **Aberaeron & New Quay,** page 58

▸ Newborough Warren & Forest   MAP REF 336 B4

Near the village of Newborough on Anglesey, this warren and forest covers some 5,607 acres. Comprising a large dune and beach system, this special habitat was created in the 13th century when storms buried farmland beneath sand dunes. Rabbits soon moved in and, in a bid to protect it, forward-thinking Queen Elizabeth I made it an offence to cut down the dunes' natural vegetation, marram grass, which was used for making mats. Later on, a pine forest was planted to offer further protection. Now a National Nature Reserve and SSSI, the dunes of the area host many species of wild flowers, including the marsh orchid and grass of Parnassus. There are red squirrels, too. The site includes Llanddwyn Bay and Malltraeth Bay, and forms part of the Anglesey Coastal Path.

▼ View from Newborough Warren over Caernarfon Bay

ENTERTAIN THE FAMILY
Anglesey Model Village and Gardens
angleseymodelvillage.co.uk
Newborough, LL61 6RS | 01248
440477 | Open Easter–Sep 10.30–5
This is Wales' most popular
model village. Follow the path
through an array of Anglesey
landmarks, all built on a scale
of one-twelfth the full size. It's
even got a working model
railway stopping at the very
famous *Llanfairpwllgwyn
gyllgogerychwyrndrobwllllanty
siliogogogoch* (see page 208).

SADDLE UP
Tal-y-Foel Riding Centre
tal-y-foel.co.uk
Dwyran, Anglesey, LL61 6LQ
01248 430377
A fantastic riding school
offering treks and rides.
Accommodation is available.

▶ PLACES NEARBY

Close to Newborough is an
island, and also the town of
Llanfair PG (see page 208).

Llanddwyn Island
Isle of Anglesey
Llanddwyn Island, off the
southwest coast of Anglesey,
is named after St Dwyn, or
Dwynwen, a misty female
figure from the Dark Ages. Her
saint's day, 25 January, has
seen a revival in recent years
as the Welsh equivalent of
St Valentine's Day. She was one
of the many children of the
legendary King Brychan. The
main legend goes that she loved
a man named Maelon Dafodrill,
and fled to the woods after her
father determined she should
marry someone else. She
begged God to make her forget
Maelon, and had a vision of an
angel with a potion that would
erase her memory of Maelon
and turn him into a block of ice.
God then gave her three wishes.
First she prayed for Maelon to
be thawed, next that all true
lovers should either achieve
their desires or be freed of
love's fever, and last that she
would never marry. She became
the unofficial patron saint of
lovers in Wales and her church
at Llanddwyn attracted
numerous pilgrims. Today, you
can come and consult the fish
in the saint's holy well; their
movements will reveal your
future. The ruins of a chapel
still exist.

▶ Newcastle Emlyn MAP REF 328 A5
Stop for a cuppa in any of this town's coffee shops and friendly
Welsh-speaking locals will greet you, and you'll hear the odd
toot from a passing tractor. Situated a 30-minute drive from
Llandysul and 20 minutes from Cenarth in Carmarthenshire, it
is a stop-off town for those heading to Cardigan Bay on holiday.
   Its name may have come about after the rebuilding of the
castle in the 15th century, its creators wanting to distinguish
it from the older Cilgerran Castle further downstream. In

addition to being on a main transport route to the west coast, the town has got a fair amount going for it in its own right. Several antiques shops have popped up in recent years, and it's not far from the Teifi Valley Railway (see page 139), which operates a steam train service. It's also got a local mozzarella-making factory, which employs many of the town's workforce.

The town was the site of the first printing press in Wales, set up in 1718, and was also a centre of the mid-19th-century Rebecca Riots, in which men dressed as women to protest against the toll roads.

VISIT THE GALLERY
Helen Elliott's Studio
elliottart.net
Toll Gate House Studio, Carmarthen Road, Newcastle Emlyn, SA38 9DA
01239 711735 | Open all year Wed–Sat 11–6; other times by appointment
Helen is one of the country's best-known and best-loved painters – her works are aptly described as 'happy art for happy people'. She paints in a colourful, vivid, naive style with an instantly recognisable approach. Her work has been exhibited in France, Germany, Poland and New York. Her studio and gallery opened by the banks of the River Teifi in 2008 and has been welcoming visitors ever since.

▶ PLACES NEARBY
Close to Newcastle Emlyn is a wool museum and coracle centre. Further afield is the town of Cardigan (see page 137).

National Wool Museum
museumwales.ac.uk
Drefach Felindre, SA44 5UP
02920 573070 | Open Apr–Sep daily 10–5, Oct–Mar Tue–Sat 10–5

The whole history of Wales' wool industry is explored at this museum, a former mill, in the tiny village of Drefach Felindre in the Teifi Valley between Llandysul and Newcastle Emlyn. Once nicknamed the 'Huddersfield of Wales', this town historically turned out shirts and shawls, blankets and bedcovers, woollen stockings and socks – all sold locally and globally. The museum explores this story, and also gives demonstrations on 19th-century textile machinery of the fleece-to-fabric process.

The National Coracle Centre
coracle-centre.co.uk
Cenarth Falls, SA38 9JL
01239 710980 | Open Easter–Oct daily 10.30–5.30; other times by appointment.
Situated by the beautiful Cenarth Falls, this fascinating museum has a unique collection from all over the world, including Tibet, India, Iraq, Vietnam and North America. Cenarth is a centre for coracle fishing, and coracle rides are available in summer. Look out for the salmon leaping by the flour mill.

▲ The Transporter Bridge

▶ **Newport (Monmouthshire)**   MAP REF 327 D4

In answer to the 2009 hit *Empire State of Mind*, the Jay-Z song about New York that featured Alicia Keys, some locals created *Newport (Ymerodraeth State of Mind)* ('Ymerodraeth = empire'). Although legal pressures caused YouTube to withdraw the video, the millions who watched it got the point. It's a self-mocking skit that sums up this gritty young town and Newport's rich seam of down-to-earth humour – in the noughties, local comedy rap band Goldie Lookin' Chain also achieved national success with their acerbic take on life in south Wales.

Situated 12 miles from Cardiff (see page 122), on the mouth of the River Usk, the Normans built a castle here, but Newport really grew up in the 19th century when its port became the place from which to export coal around the world – until Cardiff took over in the 1850s. It was also the site of the last large-scale armed insurrection in Britain, the Newport Rising of 1839. Led by the Chartists, a parliamentary reform movement

Newport

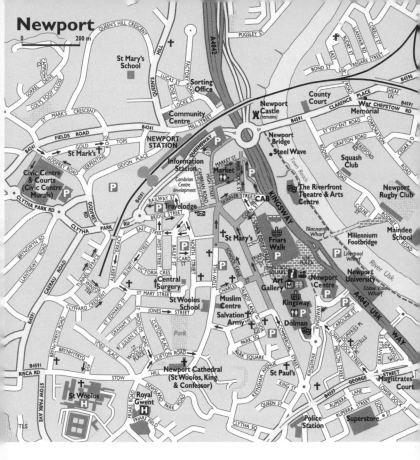

that grew in strength during Queen Victoria's early reign, some 5,000 men from the south Wales valleys converged on Newport on 4 November 1839, intent on taking the town and starting a national uprising. They tried to storm the Westgate Hotel where a violent stand-off with police resulted in 20 people being killed. In the end, it wasn't successful – the leaders were arrested and deported to Australia. The town still remembers and commemorates the uprising with plaques, monuments and the bullet-scarred entrance pillars to the Westgate.

The docks may have declined in importance but Newport survived, building on manufacturing, engineering and service industries – some government departments are located here too, such as the passport office.

Newport is also trying very hard to reinvent itself. First off, it was granted city status in 2002, beating off competition from five other Welsh rivals, including Aberystwyth and Wrexham. It also opened the Usk footbridge in 2006, which won a number of awards, and attracted some big-name discount retail outlets. More recently, it hosted the prestigious 2010 Ryder Cup at the nearby Celtic Manor Resort.

TAKE IN SOME HISTORY
The Newport Ship
newportship.org
Newport Medieval Ship Centre, Newport City Council, Unit 20, Estuary Road, Queensway Meadows, NP19 4SP | 01633 274167 | Check website for open days

It's amazing what you can find stuck in the mud. In 2002, the remains of a 15th-century ship, buried in the River Usk, were discovered during the construction of the new Rover Arts Centre. Extensive research has uncovered that the ship was probably built around 1447 and spent 20 years at sea. It was being dismantled in Newport when something – probably an accident of some sort – caused it to sink instead. Amazingly, it still has onboard pieces of uncut cork – possibly the remnants of cargo; pieces of beeswax – used when sewing sails; fish bones – the crew were probably eating fish; and some balls of shot – suggesting the ship could defend itself against pirates. The ship is now the most complete surviving example of a European vessel intended to trade along the Atlantic seaboard in the 15th century. Lots more work needs to be done to find out more about its incredible history.

GET INDUSTRIAL
The Transporter Bridge
newport.gov.uk/transporterbridge
West side: NP20 2JG | East side: NP19 0RB | 01633 656656
Open Mar–Sep Wed–Sun 10–5

This is a must-see in Newport. Opened in 1906 to avoid a four-mile detour around the river, it has dominated the skyline ever since. Until it was built a ferry used to take passengers across the water, but the extreme rise and fall of the tide meant this wasn't very practical for those needing to cross for work. The bridge cost £98,000 to complete and was opened in September 1906 by Lord Tredegar of Tredegar House. Twenty such bridges were created around the world – today, it is one of only six that remain.

PLAY A ROUND
Tredegar Park Golf Course is a rolling open course with good views, while The Celtic Manor Resort is a world-renowned golf venue boasting three championship courses.

The Celtic Manor Resort
celtic-manor.com
Coldra Woods, NP18 1HQ
01633 413000 | Contact resort for details

Tredegar Park Golf Club
tredegarparkgolfclub.co.uk
Parc-y-Brain Road, Rogerstone, NP10 9TG | 01633 894433
Open daily all year

EAT AND DRINK
Le Patio at the Manor House ⍟
celtic-manor.com
The Celtic Manor Resort, The Manor House, Coldra Woods, NP18 1HQ
01633 413000

If you're splashing out on a golfing week at the sprawling Celtic Manor Resort, you can ring the changes by eating in a different venue every day you're there. Tucked away in the historic part of the old manor house, Le Patio is the place to head for when you need a hit of hearty French country cooking, served in an informal glass-roofed extension done out with blonde-wood tables and wicker seats.

Rafters ◉

celtic-manor.com
The Celtic Manor Resort,
Coldra Woods, NP18 1HQ
01633 413000
The upmarket golf-centric Celtic Manor Resort offers a huge spread of dining options, but golfers who fancy eating without having to miss the action can get the best of both worlds in Rafters grill, where the Ryder Cup Course fills the view outside the window. The restaurant is striking, with cedar wood beams climbing high to the ceiling, and a smart contemporary look. The kitchen's main culinary building blocks come from Welsh suppliers.

Terry M at The Celtic Manor Resort ◉◉◉

celtic-manor.com
Coldra Woods, NP18 1HQ
01633 413000
The Celtic Manor is a vast hotel complex with spacious public rooms off a soaring atrium, tournament-level

5 top spots to play a round

▶ **Aberdovey**, page 65: This stunning links course offers a wild and windswept experience.

▶ **The Celtic Manor Resort**, Newport, page 250: A perfect championship course and site of the 2010 Ryder Cup.

▶ **Nefyn and District**, page 277: The perfect holiday golf course, set on a narrow strip of land with sheer cliffs on either side.

▶ **Royal Porthcawl**, page 268: Probably Wales' most famous links course; the wind whips in off the Bristol Channel.

▶ **Royal St David's**, Harlech, page 176: The brooding presence of Harlech Castle adds to the thrill of playing these undulating fairways.

golfing, a spa, fitness centre and even a kiddies' club. It has its fair share of eating options too, with the jewel in the crown being Terry M. The flagship fine-dining venue is a truly elegant space with a contemporary gloss – pristine white walls, darkwood flooring, slinky gold lighting, shimmering crystal bead chandeliers, and high-backed ivory leather chairs at linen-clad tables. It's the kind of space that promises a memorable experience, and such hopes are borne out by scrupulously professional yet unstuffy service and the kitchen's high-flying culinary output. Carefully sourced, seasonal produce – meat from selected Welsh farms, fish delivered daily from Cornwall – are given upfront modern treatments, resulting in dishes with fresh, powerful flavours. The menu holds plenty of interest and variety, and dishes are notable for their judicious combinations. Vegetarians are also well catered for here.

▶ PLACES NEARBY

Close to Newport are two wonderful attractions – Cwmcarn Forest and Tredegar House. Newport is also near the town of Caerleon (see page 110), with its impressive Roman ruins.

Cwmcarn Forest
Cwmcarn, Crosskeys, NP11 7FA
01495 272001

Just 20 minutes' drive from Newport is one of south Wales' highlights – Cwmcarn Forest. Large and hilly, with views over the Severn Estuary and the Black Mountains, it offers the chance of a forest drive experience or – better yet – great walking and mountain biking. For bikers, there are 10 miles of almost pure singletrack, with a cross country trail and a downhill trail. For walkers, there's the choice of the 12-mile circular Raven Walk, encompassing Cwmcarn Forest and the Sirhowy and Ebbw valleys, or the 'Coal, Celts and Contrasts', which takes in the impressive Twmbarlwm mountain.

Tredegar House
newport.gov.uk
NP10 8YW | 01633 815880
House open Easter–Oct Wed–Sun;
park open all year daily 9–dusk

▼ Tredegar House

This 17th-century mansion is an architectural wonder of Wales, and the most significant building from this period in the whole of Britain. Set a few miles from Newport, in 90 acres of beautiful gardens and parkland, it's a red-brick house in fantastic condition.

For more than 500 years, the house was home to one of the greatest Welsh families, the Morgans – later lords of Tredegar. Their lives impacted on the population of southeast Wales socially, economically and politically, and influenced the heritage of the area. They were also great benefactors to the community; they gave land for the construction of the Royal Gwent Hospital and encouraged the building of recreation and educational facilities. After its eventual sale, and more than 20 years as a school, the estate was purchased by Newport Borough Council. Visiting today, you get a real sense of how this great house worked as you wander through its well-appointed rooms. The kitchen, with its roasting range and spit, is fascinating.

▶ Newport (Pembrokeshire)   MAP REF 323 D2

While its next-door neighbour Fishguard (see page 165) is bustling with cars and lorries rushing to make the ferry to Ireland on time, life in little Newport – tucked away in the far northwest corner of Pembrokeshire – chugs along at a more relaxed pace.

Here the distinctive Carn Ingli (Angel Mountain) rises from the back gardens of the villagers' cottages, while small boats bob from their moorings or lean against the sandbars of the Nevern Estuary. Despite being only 1,138 feet (347m) high, Carn Ingli is distinctively rugged and cloaked in heather and gorse. On top are the remains of an Iron Age fort, boasting the foundations of early settlers' circular huts.

Newport Castle is part fortress, part manor house, and has been lived in as a private dwelling for the past 150 years. Built in the 13th century, it was held for centuries by the powerful lords of Cemaes. It was often involved in bloody conflict – first in 1215 when captured by Llywelyn the Great, then later by Owain Glyndwr. The River Nevern divides Newport's two beaches. On the north side there's an excellent sandy beach with safe bathing away from the currents. Parrog Beach on the south side is for walkers who can stroll along the cliff tops, past thickets of colourful gorse. Coastal walking is big business here, both for those out on short day trips and for those trekking the Pembrokeshire coastal paths. The views are nothing short of stunning, stretching out over Dinas Island, Morfa Head, Carningli Mountain and Newport Bay.

SADDLE UP
Harvard Stables
havardstables.co.uk
Trewyddig Fawr, Dinas Cross,
Newport, SA42 0SR | 01348 811452
Pony-trekking and horse-
rides with sea, country and
mountain views.

GO WALKING
Newport sands are the perfect
place for a stroll. This mile-
long beach has a safe
swimming zone manned by
lifeguards in the summer.
Check out the remains of a
petrified forest, visible at
low tide.

PLAY A ROUND
Newport Links Golf Club
newportlinks.co.uk
SA42 0NR | 01239 820244
Open daily all year
A lovely seaside links with easy
walking and great views.

EAT AND DRINK
Llys Meddyg ◉◉
llysmeddyg.com
East Street, Newport, SA42 0SY
01239 820008
Llys Meddyg used to be a
coaching inn but is now a
comfortable, smartly done-out
restaurant with rooms. There's
a cosy stone-walled cellar bar
with flagstones and a wood-
burner, an elegant restaurant
hung with art and a lovely
kitchen garden for pre-dinner
drinks. The kitchen takes great
pains to buy local produce from
sustainable sources whenever
possible. Or it goes foraging
for ingredients such as
pennywort, wild sorrel or
beetroot. A seasonal theme
runs through the dishes – even
down to the puddings.

Morawelon Café Bar and Restaurant
Parrog, Newport, SA42 0RW
01239 820565
Set on the Parrog beachfront,
you can indulge yourself with
cake, tea and coffee or a main
meal, such as freshly caught
crab. The menu is fairly short
but well priced, and the food is
high quality and comes in
good-sized portions. In short,
everything you could wish for.

▶ PLACES NEARBY
Close to Newport is one of
Wales' finest examples of a
neolithic burial chamber. The
town of Cardigan (see page
137) is a 20-minute drive away.

Pentre Ifan Burial Chamber
cadw.wales.gov.uk
Follow the signs from the A487
east of Newport and the B4329 at
Brynberian to Preseli | 01443
336000 | Open all year daily 10–4
As one of the finest megalithic
monuments in Britain – and
certainly the largest in Wales
– this neolithic burial chamber
or dolmen occupies a
spectacular site on
Pembrokeshire's Preseli Hills
(see page 273). It's located
about three miles south of
Newport and 10 miles from
Cardigan, and boasts a
capstone more than 16.5 feet
in length and thought to weigh
some 16 tonnes, delicately

▲ Pentre Ifan

balanced eight feet above ground by three pointed uprights that have supported it for the last 5,000 years. The stones are of the same bluestone that was transported from here and used to construct Stonehenge in Wiltshire. Nearby is Castell Henllys Iron Age Fort (see page 142).

▶ Newtown (Powys) MAP REF 335 D6

Newtown may be the largest town in Powys, but that doesn't mean there's much going on here. It's best known as the birthplace of Robert Owen, the 18th-century founder of the Cooperative movement and so-called father of socialism – long before Karl Marx. He was born in 1771 over a saddler's shop in Broad Street and, at the tender age of 10, began work in the town's flourishing textiles industry. He went on to become a self-made man, running and owning some of the largest textile factories in Britain. His former house is now a museum and there are several statues of him dotted around town. It was this textile and flannel industry that enabled the town to grow in the 18th and 19th centuries, fuelled by the completion of the Montgomeryshire Canal. At one time, it was known as the 'Leeds of Wales' but the industry fell into decline after Chartist demonstrations rocked the town in 1838. After this, agriculture became the main focus of the town – which was given the status 'new town' in 1967.

Today, a main attraction for visitors is Oriel Davies, one of Wales' major public galleries, which shows contemporary arts and crafts from around the world. The town also holds a food and drink festival each year, usually September, with a recent theme being 'Farm to Fork', promoting locally sourced food.

VISIT THE MUSEUM
Robert Owen Museum
robert-owen-museum.org.uk
The Cross, Broad Street, SY16 2BB
01686 625544 | Open Tue–Thu
11–3; times vary on other days, so
call for details

Robert Owen may only have lived in Newtown for the first 10 years of his life – returning just before his death in 1858 – but the town has every right to claim him as their own. By the age of 20, this go-getter was a successful manager in the mills of Manchester, but the working conditions, particularly of children, appalled him. When he became a manager of a large cotton mill at New Lanark, outside Glasgow, he created a model environment – with a village, school and shop selling goods at a fair price. He went on to campaign for better living and working conditions for all.

CATCH A PERFORMANCE
Theatr Hafren
theatrhafren.co.uk
Llanidloes Road, Newtown,
SY16 4HU | 01686 614555
A lively centre showcasing local talent and big names. In recent years, international star Cerys Matthews has sung here. Comedienne Lucy Porter and the Birmingham Stage Company have also performed.

SADDLE UP
Mill Pony Trekking
midwalesoffrd.co.uk
Bwlch-y-Ffridd, Newtown, SY16 3JE
01686 688440
Open Easter–Oct daily
This centre takes riders for scenic jaunts over moorland and by lakes. Children and nervous riders welcome.

▶ Oakwood Park MAP REF 323 D4
oakwoodthemepark.co.uk
Canaston Bridge, Narberth, SA67 8DE | 01834 815170 | Open Easter–Oct;
times vary, call or check website for details

This Pembrokeshire theme park, located five miles south of Narberth, is known as Wales' biggest family adventure. If you're feeling fearless, check out 'Megaphobia', a wild wooden roller coaster voted the best ride in Britain. If that's not enough, try 'The Bounce', Wales' only shoot-and-drop tower, which shoots riders into the air at high speed then lets them drop. And if *that's* still not enough, try 'Drenched', the steepest and wettest ride in Europe. In all, there are more than 30 spine-tingling rides and attractions. Playtown is aimed at younger children, while Techniquest is an indoor science and discovery centre. In August, there are fireworks displays and later opening hours.

For nearby attractions and places to eat, see Narberth, page 239.

▶ Offa's Dyke Path MAP REF 335 E5

The Offa's Dyke long-distance footpath winds 177 miles from Chepstow (see page 144) on the Severn Estuary to sunny Prestatyn (see page 274) in north Wales. It's based on Offa's Dyke, a monument built by King Offa in the eighth century to mark his boundary from that of the Welsh princes. Today, only 80 miles of the dyke remains – it's partly built on and partly overgrown – but the path follows it as closely as it can, forging its way through a range of scenery from river valleys to hills, ancient oak forest to heathland, and high moors to green fields.

In total, the walk spans eight different counties and crosses the Anglo–Welsh border more than 20 times. It explores the tranquil Marches border region, then passes through the Brecon Beacons National Park (see page 105) on the spectacular Hatterall Ridge. It also links three Areas of Outstanding Natural Beauty – the Wye Valley, the Shropshire Hills and the Clwydian Hills. Although it feels like it's always been here, the path is actually pretty recent. The brainchild of both the Offa's Dyke Association and the Ramblers' Association, it took years of patient campaigning to bring it to fruition. In July 1971, the path was officially opened by Lord Hunt, of Everest fame, at Knighton.

Today, it's a very popular trail with both independent trekkers and guided groups. Most people take 12 days to complete it, often adding two rest days to make a fortnight. Some (mad) people have been rumoured to complete it in four days. Doing short day trips or completing sections at a time is also popular. There are many places to stay, eat and drink near the trail, and public transport is available to key points. Towns en route provide welcoming stop-offs.

▼ Offa's Dyke Path

▶ Parkmill (Melin y Parc) MAP REF 324 C4

In medieval times this village, found at the bottom of a valley on the Gower Peninsula (see page 170) between the villages of Penmaen and Ilston, lay within a deer park. Today, that's not difficult to imagine as the area is still so heavily wooded.

There's really not much to see in terms of buildings. A former school is now a Girl Guides' activity centre and there's just one small chapel, erected in 1822 and rebuilt in 1890. Visitors mainly flock here for the 12th-century watermill, which powered cloth manufacturing and gave the village its name.

In 1990, Parkmill was renovated and a group of crafts people moved on to the site. They subsequently set up the Gower Heritage Centre, a vibrant crafts and rural life museum. The area is also ideal for walkers – it's only 15 minutes to Three Cliffs Bay, or you can take a stroll through the woods of Green Cwm to visit the Giant's Grave, a megalithic tomb dating back to 3500 BC.

VISIT THE MUSEUM
The Gower Heritage Centre
gowerheritagecentre.co.uk
Y Felin Ddwr, SA3 2EH
01792 371206 | Open all year
daily 10–5
Themed around a 12th-century, water-powered corn mill is this countryside crafts centre. You can explore the sawmill, wheelwright's shop, miller's cottage, agricultural museum and craft shop, then tuck into tea and cake in the tea room. There's a children's play area with numerous small animals. The centre makes the most of weekends – with themes such as cider or Vikings.

TAKE A BOAT TRIP
Gower Coast Adventures
gowercoastadventures.co.uk
07866 250440
Ride the waves by taking a RHIB (rigid hulled inflatable boat) out to explore the coast and wildlife.

SADDLE UP
Parc-Le-Breos Riding Centre
parc-le-breos.co.uk
Penmaen, Gower, SA3 2HA
01792 371636
Half- and full-day pony treks through the beautiful Gower Peninsula.

PLAY A ROUND
Pennard Golf Club
pennardgolfclub.com
2 Southgate Road, Southgate,
SA3 2BT | 01792 233131
Open daily all year
A magnificent links course with an old-fashioned charm and good coastal views.

▶ PLACES NEARBY
Nearby is a hotel, and the sweeping Gower Peninsula (see page 170).

King Arthur Hotel
kingarthurhotel.co.uk
Higher Green, Reynoldston,
Gower, SA3 1AD | 01792 390775

Set back from the large village green, the charming King Arthur Hotel is well known for its menu of pub favourites. Choose from the restaurant, the main bar or the family room. There's a cosy atmosphere with real log fires for those cold winter days, and a pleasant garden in summer.

▶ Pembroke Castle MAP REF 323 D5

pembroke-castle.co.uk

Pembroke, SA71 4LA | 01646 684585 | Open Apr–Aug daily 9.30–6, Mar, Sep–Oct 10–5, Nov–Feb 10–4

It may be the county town of Pembrokeshire, but in reality Pembroke is all about its breathtaking and atmospheric castle. Built by the Earls of Pembroke, it stands on a crag overlooking the town, surrounded by water on three sides. In its heyday it was one of the biggest and most powerful castles in Wales. The walls are 7 feet thick and 75 feet high, widening to an astonishing 16 feet on the great tower, where they're capped by an unusual stone dome. The castle has the distinction of being the only one in Britain that is built over a natural cavern, a large cave known as the Wogan.

In 1457, Henry Tudor – a descendant of Llywelyn the Great – was born here. In his late 20s, he and his army defeated Richard III at Bosworth Field, after which he was crowned King Henry VII, the first Tudor king and the last monarch to win the throne on the battlefield. The castle is a great place for kids to explore, especially the Dungeon Tower, where they can peer into a smelly old prison cell. There are 100 steps leading to the top and many watchtowers to walk along. Other interesting points include the view from the basement, looking straight up at the dome, the medieval graffiti scored into the plaster wall of the Monkton Tower, and the secret underground passageway leading from the great hall to the harbour – a much-needed escape route when the castle was under siege.

Guided tours are available all year, while in summer there are often battle re-enactments, craft shows, dragon days and falconry displays. Shakespeare's plays are regularly performed here, with the castle providing a fitting historical backdrop to the Bard's most popular works.

As for the town below, it's largely a pretty strip of Georgian and Tudor houses and bustling shops, with the dock a couple of miles away, busy with ferries. In 1977, Pembroke was designated an Outstanding Conservation Area. If it's peace and quiet you are after, there are also gentle walks along the Mill Pond (look out for kingfishers and otters) and to the remains of Monkton's Benedictine priory.

VISIT THE MUSEUM
Pembroke Dock Heritage Centre
sunderlandtrust.com
Royal Dockyard Chapel, Meyrick Owen Way, SA72 6WS | 01646 684220 | Open Apr–Oct daily 10–4, Nov–Mar closed Sun

This informative heritage centre covers the military and maritime history of Pembroke Dock. It is divided into two sections, one highlighting the historical development of Pembroke Dock over 200 years and the second focusing on the history of the Sunderland flying boat T9044 and the key role it played in World War II. Both topics reflect the national and international importance of Pembroke Dock and its military legacy. Packed full of displays and interactive exhibits, it's of great interest to all ages.

PLAY A ROUND
South Pembrokeshire Golf Club
southpembrokeshiregolfclub.co.uk
Military Road, SA72 6SE
01646 621453 | Open daily all year
A hillside course on an elevated site overlooking the Cleddau and Haven waterway on the outskirts of Pembroke Dock.

EAT AND DRINK
BEST WESTERN Lamphey Court Hotel and Spa ◉
lampheycourt.co.uk
Lamphey, SA71 5NT | 01646 672273
Lamphey Court is a great white whale of an edifice with massive columns fronting a portico entrance. Built in 1823, it is now equipped with a very 21st-century spa and gym. If you're looking to get even more exercise while you're here, the Pembrokeshire Coastal Path isn't far away, while the national park is all around. The kitchen turns out homely food with one or two flourishes of modern British.

▶ PLACES NEARBY
At Lamphey, near Pembroke, are the ruins of a palace.

Lamphey Bishop's Palace
cadw.wales.gov.uk
Lamphey, SA71 5NT | 01646 672224
Open all year daily 10–4
This ruined 13th-century palace once belonged to the Bishops of St Davids, who used it as a place of retreat. The great hall is a particularly fine architectural achievement, so too the western hall and inner gatehouse – both still standing.

▶ Pembrokeshire Coast National Park
MAP REF 322 C6
pcnpa.org.uk
Pembrokeshire SA72 6DY | 0845 3457275
Geologists love this place, with its rocky outcrops, blowholes and glacial meltwaters. But here, in Britain's only truly coastal park, there's something for everyone. Most important, for those seeking to get away from it all, the park offers acres of

▲ Whitesands Bay

breathing space, with fresh air whipping in off the Irish Sea. Established in 1952, the park takes up a third – roughly 240 square miles – of the county, stretching from Preseli (see page 273) in the north, where Stonehenge's bluestones came from, down to Tenby (see page 311) in the south. If you like beaches, this park is ideal. It incorporates Barafundle (see page 99), Marloes, Porthgain and Dinas – some of the best not just in Wales or Britain but the world. Then there's the tiny gem of St Davids (see page 288), named after Wales' patron saint. It's also got the magical islands of Skomer and Skokholm (see page 297), Caldey (see page 314), and Ramsey (see page 290). The action isn't all on the coast. Two inland areas are also in the national park, namely the Preseli Mountains, and the upper reaches of the Daugleddau Estuary, often called 'the secret waterway' and containing Picton and Carew castles (see page 314). For wildlife lovers, this place is also teeming with huge populations of seabirds, seals, dolphins, porpoises and whales. Even leatherback turtles have been seen here.

The entire park is astonishingly attractive, but a highlight is Whitesands Bay – a long beach with St Davids Head a short walk away. At the very tip of the cliffs is Strumble Head (see page 304), with great views to the south from the Iron Age hill fort site of Garn Fawr. Fishguard (see page 165) is a harbour town with ferries over to Rosslare in Ireland. Another outstanding viewpoint is Wooltack Point near Marloes, which overlooks Skomer and Skokholm. Bosherston's lily ponds (see page 99) is another huge attraction, as is the Green Bridge of Wales, a stunning natural arch. Close to there is the climbing hotspot of St Govan (see page 293), and a tiny chapel wedged incongruously in the rocks.

The park also runs an extensive programme of activities and events for both adults and children. These include rockpool safaris, crab catching, bat-spotting walks, themed tours, canoe trips and minibus tours. To find out more information, and get advice on where to go walking or climbing, ask in one of the three national park centres in Tenby (see page 311), St Davids (see page 288) and Newport (see page 253). Most towns have a local tourist information centre too; they're all listed in the free annual *Coast to Coast* newspaper, so pick one up when you get here. It might also be an idea to get a tide timetable – it's an essential for many sections of this coast.

The park is obviously known for its 186-mile coastal path – perhaps the most famous in Britain, now incorporated into the whole Wales coastal path. It weaves around the coast from the more rugged north to the level cliffs in the south. It's one of the most spectacular long-distance walks in Britain and can easily be split into smaller more manageable chunks. If you are trying to decide when to walk, remember that spring and summer are good times for migratory birds and wild flowers. Walk in late summer and you're likely to see migrating whales in the waters below and lots of butterflies. In autumn you'll be sharing the rocks with seals that come ashore to give birth. Winter isn't an ideal time to trek, as lots of the hostels and campsites are closed between October and Easter and buses are less frequent. Be warned: although it might sound tempting to walk alone without having to share the path with hoards of tourists, these are precipitous cliffs and probably aren't best tackled in wild, wet weather.

Penarth   MAP REF 326 C6

Penarth may be just over the headland from Cardiff – overlooking Cardiff Bay (see page 132) – but it seems a million miles away from the bustling, diverse capital. It's your classic traditional seaside town, complete with pier, ice-cream stands, terrace houses and lots of wooden benches to sit on, eat your 99 and gaze out at the muddy waters.

Always a fishing port, Penarth couldn't help but be affected by Cardiff's huge rise during the Industrial Revolution. Back then, the wealthy coal and iron merchants quite fancied the shingle beach, seaside air and views across Bristol Channel, so built fine villas here. Houses do still come with a high price tag, even if the area is slightly old-fashioned.

The Victorians introduced tourism to the area, when first a long esplanade was constructed on the south shore and then a pier. Flower-decked gardens gave it its nickname – the 'gardens by the sea'. Now those running the waterbuses from Cardiff barrage jokingly refer to it as 'Costa del Penarth, where the palm trees grow'. This new development has brought a bit more life to the area. The boats bring tourists here to see the working part of the barrage – the sea locks, sluices and fish pass – and a chance to watch boats go through the locks. In another regeneration, the old harbour has been replaced by an attractive yacht marina.

VISIT THE GALLERY
Ffotogallery
ffotogallery.org
Turner House, Plymouth Road, CF64 3DH | 029 2070 8870
Open Tue–Sat 11–5
Ffotogallery is the national centre for lens-based media in Wales. A programme of changing photography and print exhibitions encourages and supports photographers in Wales in their mission to create an ongoing record of the country's culture. In the school holidays, children are encouraged to participate in fun stuff – such as making and using pin-hole cameras.

GO BACK IN TIME
Cosmeston Lakes Country Park and Medieval Village
valeofglamorgan.gov.uk
Lavernock Road, CF64 5UY
029 2070 1678 | Open all year daily 11–5 summer, 11–4 winter; country park open all year daily

Deserted during the devastating plagues and famines of the 14th century, the original medieval village at Cosmeston Lakes was rediscovered through archaeological excavations. The buildings you see today have been faithfully reconstructed on top of the excavated remains, creating a living museum dedicated to medieval village life. Special events throughout the year include lively re-enactments, and it's an obvious film set. Many scenes from the popular BBC television series *Merlin* were filmed here.

PLAY A ROUND
Glamorganshire Golf Club
glamorganshiregolfclub.co.uk
Lavernock Road, CF64 5UP
029 2070 1185 | Open Mon, Wed–Sun
A fantastic parkland course overlooking the Bristol Channel.

▶ Pistyll Rhaeadr   MAP REF 334 D3

pistyllrhaeadr.co.uk

Near Llanrhaeadr-ym-Mochnant, Powys, SY10 0BZ | 01691 780392

OK, so it's not quite Victoria Falls but, at 230 feet, it is Wales' highest single-drop waterfall and somewhat enchanting. Located in the Berwyn Mountains, just west of Oswestry, it's found in a long, sparsely populated valley, which just adds to the peaceful setting. It comprises a narrow ribbon of water dropping into a wooded rock basin, broken in mid-flight by a manmade rock arch placed there to enhance the whole effect.

The falls are open all year round. You can walk to the top of the rocky outcrop on a path, which takes about 20 minutes, but you'll need to wear proper walking shoes – or watch the spectacle from the picnic area at ground level. Other walks can be accessed over an iron bridge that crosses the river, leading to a woodland and public footpath.

EAT AND DRINK
Tan-y-Pistyll Café
pistyllrhaeadr.co.uk
Waterfall Lane,
Llanrhaeadr-ym-Mochnant,
SY10 0BZ
01691 780392

At the base of the falls is this cafe – its name means 'little house under the waterfall'. It serves tea, snacks or light meals – all accompanied by splendid views of the cascading water.

▶ Port Eynon   MAP REF 324 B5

Port Eynon is a bustling beach resort with a regular stream of summer visitors. It's a 0.75-mile stretch of beach and dunes found at the Gower's (see page 170) most southerly point, with several well-located campsites and caravan parks nearby. While it's not quite at the no-space-for-your beach-towel levels of Devon and Cornwall, it does pack them in when the sun shines. The fact that the village streets are so narrow that there is rarely room for two cars to pass adds to the sense of congestion. Once on the beach, however, there's a real old-fashioned seaside atmosphere, with bucket-and-spade shops, a couple of fish and chip shops and a surfboard outlet. The sands turn into dunes, then rugged cliffs dotted with a line of whitewashed cottages.

If you're too much of an adventurer to want to loll about on a deckchair, then the seven-mile coastal walk to Rhossili Bay (see page 283) is one of the finest on the Gower. Be sure to check out the Paviland Cave.

Historically, Port Eynon got its name from the 11th-century Welsh prince Einon ap Owain, who more than likely built the long-gone port. In its heyday during the 19th century more than 40 oyster skiffs operated from the port, and limestone from a nearby quarry was exported too. The blue-green stones you'll see scattered on the shoreline are not part of Gower geology, but ballast from cargo ships.

Tales of smuggling are common and it is said that the old salt house – the ruin beneath the cliffs of the western promontory – was used as a storehouse for contraband. At one time there were eight customs and excise officers based here. Next to the salt house is the youth hostel. Formerly a lifeboat station, it was closed following a disastrous rescue attempt in 1916 in which three of the crew died.

HIT THE BEACH
Port Eynon Bay is a commercialised beach with cafes, campsites and gift shops. No dogs May–Sep. Round the point is Oxwich Bay and Rhossili (see page 283).

▶ PLACES NEARBY
At Oxwich, just east of Port Enyon, you will find an impressive nature reserve.

Oxwich National Nature Reserve
As an Area of Outstanding Natural Beauty, Oxwich Bay combines an impressive range of wildlife with a superb beach resort. It is an excellent location for swimming and surfing. The beach is easily accessible and the reserve supports several diverse wildlife habitats, including freshwater lakes and marshes, swamps, salt marshes, dunes, cliffs and woodland. It is home to more than 600 species of flowering plants and a wide range of birds feed on the wet sands at low tide, and on the marshes. At the western end is the charming little village of Oxwich.

▶ Port Talbot MAP REF 325 E4
Drive along the M4 from Cardiff to Swansea and you see a different side of Wales from the 'green green grass of home' that Tom Jones once sang about. With a cityscape dominated by its steelworks – Europe's largest – Port Talbot is a town which might not make for a natural tourist destination, but is essential to the local economy.

Blast furnaces billowing out water vapour dominate the skyline. There's also a chemical plant and a deep-water harbour capable of discharging iron-ore vessels. All of this industry renders it the most polluted town in Wales and the second most polluted in the UK, after London.

Looking down on it from the M4, it's hard to believe anything other than the works exist here, such is their dominance. Yet, it does. Towards the sea, you'll find Margam Castle, a Grade I-listed building built in Gothic Victorian style and set in the beautiful 850-acre Margam Country Park, which includes an orangery, deer herd, sculpture trail and kids' attractions such as Go Ape!, Visitors to this area rave about the ghost walk too.

For such an industrial town, it has produced a good number of famous people. Actors Richard Burton and Anthony Hopkins came from here. Michael Sheen also grew up here and has come back to perform works – most notably a modern retelling of *The Passion* in 2011, which he performed on Aberavon beach with the National Theatre Wales. The play began at 5.30am on Good Friday with a seafront scene watched by a few hundred, but as the play progressed around 6,000 spectators gathered, hearing about the performance through word of mouth. The play carried on through the weekend, with scenes acted throughout the town, returning to the beach on Easter Sunday. Funnyman Rob Brydon was also born in Baglan, a village just outside the town.

TAKE IN SOME HISTORY
Margam Castle
margamcountrypark.co.uk
Margam, Port Talbot, SA13 2TJ
01639 881635 | Open in summer months; call for details
Located in Margam Country Park, this castle is actually more of a large manor house than a castle as we know it. Check out the spectacular stone staircase and lavishly decorated library and dining room.

WALK THE HIGH ROPES
Go Ape! Margam
goape.co.uk/sites/margam
Margam Country Park, Port Talbot, SA13 2TJ | 0845 643 9215
See website for availability (pre-booking advised)
Get up to some full-scale monkey business in this treetop adventure playground. Traverse bridges, zip down wires and pretend you are Tarzan on a rope course set high above the forest floor.

▶ **Porthcawl** MAP REF 325 E5
Head west from Cardiff (see page 122) for 25 miles and Porthcawl is the first real beach you hit. It's not stunningly breathtaking like the beaches further west, but it's got sand nevertheless, and has decent enough waves for surfing and kite surfing. For those not up for some board action, the town has plenty of other things for visitors to do. There's a promenade and funfair, and each September it hosts an Elvis Festival,

where the whole town dons blue suede shoes and greased-up quiffs in honour of the star – lashings of cider help the cause.

The town developed as a coal port during the 19th century, but its trade was soon taken over by more rapidly developing ports such as Barry (see page 84). Northwest lies an impressive array of sand dunes, known as Kenfig Burrows. Hidden in it are the last remnants of the town and Kenfig Castle, which were overwhelmed by sand in about 1400.

GO BACK IN TIME
Kenfig Burrows
kenfig.org.uk
Kenfig National Nature Reserve, Ton Kenfig, Bridgend, CF33 4PT
01656 743386
Open all year daily
A medieval castle and village were buried under sand here in about 1400. All that can be seen is the top of the castle's 50-foot keep, which was uncovered in the early 20th century. The sand network on this Glamorgan coast is the largest in Europe, rising to a height of over 200 feet.

GO WALKING
The Glamorgan Heritage Coast
see page 168

PLAY A ROUND
Royal Porthcawl Golf Club
royalporthcawl.com
Rest Bay, CF36 3UW | 01656 782251

Open Tue, Thu and Fri all day, Wed am, Mon and weekends pm
This is one of Britain's greatest links courses.

EAT AND DRINK
Finnegans Fish and Chips
16 New Road, Porthcawl, CF36 5DN | 01656 782883
If anyone knows how to do fish and chips, the Welsh do. This is a multiple award-winning chippie selling a range of freshly cooked fish with hand-cut chips. Served in a box with a wedge of lemon, it's the perfect seaside tea.

Pietro's
32 Esplanade, CF36 3YR
01656 771492
With a superb seafront location, Pietro's serves good coffee and whopping ice-cream sundaes. There are 25 flavours, served by genuine Welsh-Italians.

▸ **Porthmadog** MAP REF 333 E2
Centred on a small harbour, Porthmadog is the most popular holiday resort on the Llyn Peninsula (see page 218), and whichever way you approach the town, you'll find mind-blowing views. The mountain, Moel y Gest, dominates the town and also the Glaslyn Estuary, renowned as a haven for migrating birds and wildlife. The town itself isn't that pretty, but it's got a decent number of independent shops and places to eat. Most

▲ Porthmadog harbour

people speak Welsh here and are very friendly. It's an ideal base for a few days if you want to explore Snowdonia National Park (see page 299).

The Italianate town of Portmerion (see page 271) is nearby, and Porthmadog is a great place for steam railway buffs, boasting both the Ffestiniog and the Welsh Highlands railways. Jump on a train at either end of town to enjoy the mountain scenery and talk endlessly of Fat Controllers, Thomas the Tank Engine and everything there is to know about steam. Be sure to look out for the Cob, too – a sea wall across the Glaslyn Estuary that carries the Ffestiniog Railway. Built in 1811 by slate magnate William Alexander Maddocks – after whom the town is named – it effectively flooded the wetland habitat behind it, creating a deep harbour and granting access to great sailing ships, which carried slate mined from Blaenau Ffestiniog (see page 94) around the world. In the late 19th century it's estimated that around 1,000 vessels a year departed from this harbour.

TAKE A TRAIN RIDE
Ffestiniog Railway
festrail.co.uk
Harbour Station, LL49 9NF
01766 516024 | Open late Mar–Oct daily; limited winter service; Santa specials in Dec; open Xmas week and Feb half term; call or check website for a timetable

One of the Great Little Trains of Wales, this railway runs for 13.5 miles through Snowdonia. Originally built to carry slate from the quarries at Blaenau

Ffestiniog to the harbour at Porthmadog, it now carries passengers through the beautiful scenery of the national park. A licensed at-your-seat refreshment service is available on all main trains. Day rover tickets allow you to break your journey to make the most of your day.

The Welsh Highland Railway

festrail.co.uk
Harbour Station, LL49 9NF
01766 516024 | Call or check website for a timetable

Originally completed as a slate railway linking Caernarfon and Porthmadog, this ambitious line lasted only 18 years before closure in 1941. However, following years of dedicated work, the line fully reopened in 2010 to offer passengers a mouth-watering journey through the beautiful mountainous countryside around the outskirts of Snowdon to pretty Beddgelert (see page 88) and through the spectacular Aberglaslyn Pass. At Porthmadog, the line links with the Ffestiniog Railway (see previous page), creating one of Europe's most extensive narrow-gauge railway systems.

HIT THE BEACH

Morfa Bychan is a long, sandy beach ideal for bathing and water sports, while Borth-y-Guest is a beautiful sandy bay, with a horseshoe-shaped promenade of colourfully painted houses.

PLAY A ROUND

Porthmadog Golf Club

porthmadog-golf-club-co.uk
Morfa Bychan, LL49 9UU
01766 514124 | Open daily all year

This fantastic course offers a challenging but playable mixture of heathland and links, with some beautiful scenery.

EAT AND DRINK

The Big Rock Cafe

71 High Street, LL49 9EU
01766 512098

This cool church-run cafe is something of a hub in Porthmadog. The menu stretches to cooked breakfasts, soups, sandwiches and sweets, and there are plenty of newspapers to peruse. It's child-friendly, and everything from the hash browns to the bread is homemade. The cinnamon buns are a real treat. Be warned – cash, no cards.

Royal Sportsman Hotel ◉◉

royalsportsman.co.uk
131 High Street, LL49 9HB
01766 512015

Built as a coaching inn in 1862, this unpretentious family-run hotel has been thoroughly updated. The stone and slate fireplaces are still in place in the lounge and bar, while the kitchen is committed to using fresh Welsh produce.

▶ PLACES NEARBY

Close to Porthmadog are Criccieth (see page 153) and Portmeirion (see page 271). It's also the gateway to the Llyn Peninsula (see page 218).

▶ **Portmeirion** MAP REF 333 E2

portmeirion-village.com
LL48 6ER | 01766 770000 | Open Oct–Mar daily 9.30–5.30, Apr–Sep
9.30–7.30

Two miles from Porthmadog on the Llyn Peninsula is Portmeirion, a weird, intriguing yet magical seaside utopia of heavy Italianate influence. You'll either love or hate this Disneyesque village that's completely artificial with no inhabitants. Designed by Sir Clough Williams-Ellis in the 1920s, it took more than 50 years to create out of material from abandoned stately homes. Clough liked to call it the 'home for fallen buildings'. It was subsequently deemed a conservation area and all the buildings were listed.

In reality, Clough's vision wasn't bad. With a strong passion for merging beautiful architecture with nature, he wanted to create a site that didn't defile the surrounding environment. There's no getting away from the fact, however, that it's basically a whimsy – a vision of towers and domes, courtyards and arches. There's multi-coloured houses, many of which are now used as holiday lets, and lots of statues and fountains.

Peacocks have the run of the streets. Portmeirion pottery, made by Clough's daughter Susan, can also be bought, though these days it's made in Stoke-on-Trent. The village stands in more than 70 acres of woodlands, and there is even a cemetery for the estate's dogs, started around 1900 by the reclusive old lady from whom Sir Clough bought the estate. It's a touching place, as some of the stories on the headstones can attest, and the tradition of burying much-loved pets here has been continued to this day.

There's nothing real about this place – and that's probably why it's so often used as a film and TV location. In the 1960s, the classic television series *The Prisoner* was filmed here, and its devotees still make pilgrimages. More recently it was the setting for the closing scenes of the final episode of the TV series *Cold Feet*.

▼ Traeth Bach Beach

EAT AND DRINK
The Hotel Portmeirion ◎◎
portmeirion-village.com
Minffordd, LL48 6ET
01766 770000

The fantasy Italianate village on the north Wales coast, created by Sir Clough Williams-Ellis over half a century ago, was conceived around the ruin of what is now the hotel. When the whole place began to take shape in 1926, the hotel, then unlicensed, was its focal point. It's still a gem, with views over the Dwyryd estuary and the hills beyond. A gracefully curving dining room was added in 1931. It's a striking place, filled with antiques and artwork. Fresh, lively, modern Welsh cooking enhances the whole experience no end and the dishes are well executed and nicely presented without being too flashy.

▼ Chantry House

▶ Preseli Hills MAP REF 323 D3

These hills may not have the height of Snowdon (see page 299), but what they may lack in stature they more than make up for in mystery and intrigue. Found inland from Fishguard (see page 165) and Newport (see page 253), they comprise the only upland area of the Pembrokeshire Coast National Park (see page 260). At their highest point of Foel Cwmcerwyn, they only reach 1,758 feet (536m) above sea level but are great for walking and fell running. A popular race, the Ras Beca, takes place here each August to commemorate the Rebecca Riots of the 1840s, when men dressed up as women to smash down tollbooths.

These hills are also at the centre of a rich prehistoric landscape. Neolithic tribes lived here long before the 'true' Welsh, the Celts, came from across the sea. Stone tombs lie across the hills, as do hill forts and standing stones. An ancient track called the Golden Road runs along the hill ridge, passing the stone circle of Bedd Arthur, a site of 13 standing stones in an oval shape.

Most intriguingly of all is the link the Preselis have with Stonehenge in Wiltshire. The rock from which the 31 famous monoliths were carved is an igneous dolerite, exclusive to this region. In fact, it's been pinpointed as coming from the outcrops around Carnmenyn and Carn Goedog at the eastern end of the Preselis. It's thought that the bluestone must have held religious significance for the builders of Stonehenge. How they transported these four-tonne weights the 240 miles to Wiltshire is not known.

A re-enactment in 2000 by a group of volunteers failed to move a single stone – it slipped from its raft and sank just a few miles into its watery journey down the River Cleddau. Some believe the stones may have been transported by ice age glaciers and dumped in Wiltshire some 12,000 years ago.

EAT AND DRINK

Tafarn Sinc

tafarnsinc.co.uk
Rosebush, Maenclochog, Clynderwen, SA66 7QU
01437 532214

It's quirky, it's painted red, and has sawdust on the floor. This delightful pub is one of Wales' best. It's the highest licensed pub in Pembrokeshire, set in stunning hilly scenery. Its success today is largely due to the fact it's a Welsh-language pub, albeit a very friendly and welcoming one. It refuses to bow to the 'whims of modernisation' and steadfastly maintains its nostalgic originality. It's full of charm, with old-fashioned furniture and photos. It's also got its own beer – Cwrw Tafarn Sinc – and the food is hearty and delicious.

▶ Prestatyn MAP REF 338 C1

This small seaside town, situated on Wales' northeast coast close to the mouth of the River Dee, claims to have a sunny micro-climate all of its own due to being shielded by the mountains. It's famous for its sunny sands and coastline with rolling dunes but it's also very handy for walking. Depending which way you look at it, Prestatyn marks the start or end of the Offa's Dyke Path (see page 257). Not only this, but it features the North Wales Path, Clwydian Way and the recently launched Dee Way. The area is rich in history and the surrounding countryside offers walks in Areas of Outstanding Natural Beauty, nature reserves and a Site of Special Scientific Interest (SSSI). The town has also been awarded the 'Walkers are Welcome' accreditation – meaning it's an attractive destination, offering top-quality information on local walks with well-maintained footpaths.

The town itself grew up largely as a fishing village before booming in the 19th and 20th centuries with the arrival of the railways and holidaymakers. It became a hotspot to visit when city-dwelling Victorians decided that there was nothing healthier than a swim in Prestatyn's clean waters, followed by a brisk stroll along the promenade. This sunny reputation was so strong that it even attracted the attention of poet Philip Larkin. In the 1960s, he penned a poem called *Sunny Prestatyn*, about a poster that gradually gets vandalized.

In 2003, the town saw the launching of Britain's first major offshore wind farm, five miles off the coast. It now comprises around 30 wind turbines, with a maximum capacity of 60 megawatts – enough to power 40,000 homes if it was sustained. The town has also produced a few famous people – notably John Prescott and maths brainbox Carol Vorderman.

TAKE IN SOME HISTORY
The Roman Bath House
Melyd Avenue, Prestatyn,
LL19 8RN
On the outskirts of Prestatyn lie the ruins of a Roman bathhouse, thought to have been in use from about AD 120 to AD 150. You can clearly make out the caldarium (hot room), tepidarium (tepid room), frigidarium (cold room) and cold plunge bath. The floors and roof were made with tiles from the workshops of the 20th Legion at Holt near Wrexham. Some of these tiles, stamped with the legend LEG XX VV and their symbol of a wild boar, may be seen in situ to this day .

HIT THE BEACH
Enjoy Prestatyn Beach's four-mile stretch of sand.

SADDLE UP
Bridlewood Riding Centre
bridlewood.co.uk

Ty'n-y-Morfa, CH8 9JN
01745 888922
This riding centre allows visitors to relax and take in the beautiful scenery and surroundings from the saddle of a horse.

PLAY A ROUND
St Melyd Golf Club and Prestatyn Golf Club offer great courses and superb views.

St Melyd Golf Club
stmelydgolf.co.uk
The Paddock, Meliden Road,
LL19 8NB | 01745 854405
Open Mon–Wed, Fri and Sun

Prestatyn Golf Club
prestatyngolfclub.co.uk
Marine Road East, LL19 7HS
01745 854320 | Open daily all year

EAT AND DRINK
The Pendre Coffee Shop
214a High Street, Prestatyn,
LL19 9BP | 01745 853365
Found near the top of the High Street, this cafe does a mean hot chocolate complete with marshmallows and lashings of cream. It also serves toasted sandwiches with small salads and jacket potatoes, just right for a weekday lunch. It's closed on Wednesday.

Pumlumon Fawr   MAP REF 329 E1
One of the three great mountains of Wales, Pumlumon Fawr, at 2,467 feet (752m), lacks the imposing appearance of Snowdon and Cadair Idris only because it rises from almost uniformly high ground. But, as the source of three great Welsh rivers – the Severn, the Wye and the Rheidol – its importance shouldn't be ignored.

Its boggy and mainly featureless slopes show signs of previous industry, such as the remains of lead and silver mines. The easiest approach up to the undistinguished summit is from Eisteddfa Gurig Farm on the A44, between Ponterwyd and Llangurig.

Pwllheli   MAP REF 332 C2
Situated 13 miles from Porthmadog (see page 268) and 21 miles from Caernarfon (see page 111), this is the Llyn Peninsula's largest town and official capital. It grew up around its harbour, through which wines from the Continent were imported, but swiftly became a haven for smugglers and pirates. Pwllheli also developed as one of the main fishing and shipbuilding centres in north Wales, often having 30 ships in production at the same time. The arrival of the railways in the town allowed it to develop further.

Now Pwllheli is bustling and cheery, its narrow streets boasting many independent shops, boutiques, traditional pubs, award-winning chippies and tacky souvenir shops selling seaside rock. There's an open-air market in the main square every Wednesday and Sunday in summer, and a cinema and leisure centre for when the weather is bad. With some 400 berths, Pwllheli Marina is considered one of the best in Britain and is designated a European Centre of Excellence for sailing.

Then, of course, there are the beaches. Handily, they are mainly south facing. They've also been awarded the prestigious European Blue Flag Award. Closest to the marina is Glan y Mor, which is sandy and sheltered, while further away is South Beach – mainly shingle and pebble with a play area and skate park nearby.

Owing to the town's location at the entrance to the peninsula, it's an ideal base from which to explore this northwest corner of Wales. If you're into walking, try the Llyn Coastal Path, some 91 miles long, extending from nearby Porthmadog to Caernarfon on the north coast of the peninsula. Now it forms part of the new Wales Coastal Path, which runs 870 miles around the whole Welsh coast.

▼ The promenade of Pwllheli

WALK THE HIGH ROPES
Ropeworks
ropeworks.co.uk
Hafan y Môr, Chwilog, Pwllheli,
LL53 6HX | 01766 819187
Go climbing on high wires,
aerial crossings and giant
swings; there's even a climbing
wall for the under-eights.

THROW A POT
Biscuit Ceramic Art Studio and Cafe
LL53 7AP | 01758 712077
Check website for opening times
Have family fun stencilling and
sponging paints onto mugs,
plates or tiles. Leave the
pottery for a few days to be
glazed and fired, then pick it up.
There's food and refreshments.

PLAY A ROUND
Nefyn and District Golf Club
nefyn-golf-club.co.uk
L53 6DA | 01758 720966
Open daily all year
Play golf in a truly spectacular
clifftop setting on the Llyn
Peninsula. There's a choice of
two courses – The Old and The
New. The Old Course includes
the world famous Point with 'a
view of the sea from every tee'.

Pwllheli Golf Club
clwbgolffpwllheli.com
Golf Road, LL53 5PS | 01758
701644 | Open daily all year
This flat seaside course, with
easy walking, has outstanding
views of Snowdon, Cadair Idris
and Cardigan Bay.

EAT AND DRINK
Lion Hotel
lionhoteltudweiliog.co.uk
Tudweiliog, LL53 8ND
01758 770244
Standing at a tangent to the road, beyond a garden with tables and chairs, the 300-year-old Lion Hotel is a real treat. The bar features an extensive list of whiskies, alongside real ales from Big Bog, Cwrw Llyn and Purple Moose breweries, all Welsh of course. The menu comprises typical pub grub.

Plas Bodegroes ⑳⑳
bodegroes.co.uk
Nefyn Road, LL53 5TH
01758 612363
This white-painted Georgian manor is full of charm and surrounded by stunning gardens. A picture of pastoral contentment greets the eye, especially in spring and summer, when lavender scents the air, lambs bleat in the meadows, and jays chase each other amid the rhododendrons. Add to that some luxuriously furnished accommodation, a friendly vibe and top-notch cooking in the modern but elegant restaurant and all the bases are covered. The dining room is no dour oak-panelled retreat, but a fresh, airy space with mint-green walls hung with small artworks, and a bare wood floor. For the modern British menu, ingredients are sourced locally, with many of the herbs, fruits and vegetables picked fresh from the manor's kitchen garden.

Ty Coch Inn
tycoch.co.uk
Porthdinllaen, Morfa Nefyn, LL53 6DB | 01758 720498
One of Wales' most famous pubs, and arguably one of the best beachside bars in the world, Ty Coch Inn (Red House) has a great atmosphere and a truly wonderful position, with views across the Irish Sea. The pub was featured in the 2006 Demi Moore film *Half Light*. Check the website to view its popular webcam.

▶ PLACES NEARBY
Close to Pwllheli is a beach, a medieval house and a gallery.

Llanbedrog Beach
Owned by the National Trust, this is a long sandy beach west of Pwllheli – sheltered and beautiful.

Penarth Fawr Medieval House
cadw.wales.gov.uk
Chwilog, LL53 6PR | 01443 336000
Open all year daily 10–5
A picturesque 15th-century hall-house with an impressive timber roof and aisle-truss. It may have been built by Madoc of Penarth in 1416.

Plas Glyn y Weddw Gallery
oriel.org.uk
Llanbedrog, LL53 7TT
01443 336000 | Open daily 10–5, closed Tue outside school holidays
Just outside Pwllheli, this modern art gallery housed in a Gothic mansion has a vaulted wood-beamed roof, plus a shop and cafe. Each July, the gallery

launches its annual summer exhibition, including 50 regular artists and a handful of invited guests. Works range from traditional landscapes and seascapes to modern simplistic abstracts. There's also a collection of sculptural works from bronzes to slate. All works are for sale.

▶ Red Wharf Bay MAP REF 337 D3

On the east coast of Anglesey, north of Beaumaris and lying between the villages of Pentraeth and Benllech, is this wide and sandy bay. It may be simply a bay and nothing else but as an Area of Outstanding Natural Beauty, it draws the crowds.

Each year its sailing club races in a competition from Beaumaris in the south to Traeth Bychan in the north. The race, over 14 miles up the Menai Strait and down the Anglesey coast, is an exhilarating sail that all the locals turn out to watch.

HIT THE BEACH

Red Wharf Bay is a sand, mud and cobble beach that is ideal for walks.

GET ON THE WATER

Red Wharf Bay Sailing and Watersports Club
redwharfbaysc.co.uk
Traeth Bychan, Marianglas, LL73 8PN | 01248 853754

EAT AND DRINK

The Boathouse Cafe
LL75 8RJ | 01248 852731
This family-friendly cafe, with alfresco dining, overlooks Red Wharf Bay. Food is locally sourced, fresh and flavoursome. The cafe serves breakfast through to evening meals, and all dietary requirements are catered for. There's also a good selection of continental beers, and a daily specials board.

The Ship Inn
shipinnredwharfbay.co.uk
LL75 8RJ | 01248 852568
Wading birds flock here to feed on the extensive sands of Red Wharf Bay, making the inn's waterside beer garden a birder's paradise on warm days. Before the age of steam, sailing ships landed cargoes from all over the world on its wharf. Now the boats bring fresh Conwy Bay fish and seafood to the kitchens of this traditional free house. Local fish and seafood feature strongly on the menu.

▶ Rhandirmwyn MAP REF 329 E4

Once an important lead-mining village, Rhandirmwyn lies in the valley of the Upper Tywi, nine miles north of Llandovery in Carmarthenshire. Indeed, its name makes reference to its historic industry – *rhandir* means an area of land and *mwyn* means mineral. For those who like to play on words, however, *mwyn* has another meaning – that of 'gentle'. In reality, it could mean either – mineral land or gentle land for both are true.

This is a real haven for those who like riverside walks, angling and bird-spotting. Two bird reserves are set scenically among the riverside crags. A short distance upstream, where the River Doethie meets the River Pysgotwr, is one of the wildest gorges in mid-Wales. Just a few miles north of Rhandirmwyn, along winding country lanes, is Llyn Brianne Reservoir, surrounded by plantations of spruce and larch.

GET OUTDOORS
RSPB Nature Reserve Gwenffrwd-Dinas
rspb.org.uk

10 miles north of Llandovery on the minor road to Llyn Brianne | 01654 700222 | Open dawn to dusk. Allow 2hrs to complete the trail circuit

This RSPB reserve consists of a nature trail leading through a large wetland area, oak woodland and then the steep slopes of Dinas. There's a cave in the crags here, where Twm Sion Catti, the Welsh Robin Hood, used to hide from his enemies. Red kites can often be seen soaring above the trees, and in summer you might also see dippers, pied flycatchers, common sandpipers and grey wagtails.

▶ Rhayader MAP REF 330 C2

Rhayader's full Welsh name is Rhaeadr Gwy, meaning 'waterfall on the Wye'. Unfortunately – as is the way things go at times – that particular waterfall was blown up in 1780 to make way for the bridge over the river. Situated at a natural crossroads between east and west, north and south, Rhayader has long been a stop-off for travellers. The Romans had a camp nearby in the Elan Valley. Monks travelling between Strata Florida Abbey – an ancient sacred spot near Aberystwyth (see page 304) – and Abbeycwmhir Monastery in Powys also used it as a resting place. So, too, did drovers taking their livestock to far off markets and returning with goods and news.

Today, the historic market town is fairly small and uneventful – the action revolves around a large war memorial clock, standing above a central crossroads – but it is set among dramatic mid-Wales scenery. Agriculture still plays an important role, as witnessed by the busy weekly livestock markets. Walkers tackling the 136-mile Wye Valley Walk or the hills in the Elan Valley may find reason to stop here. It's also close to some great pony trekking and red kite feeding stations. Road biking and mountain biking are popular, and it is frequently the host of races and enduros (offroad motorcycling).

VISIT THE MUSEUM
CARAD (Rhayader's Community Arts and Heritage Centre)
carad.org.uk
East Street, LD6 5ER
01597 810561 | Open Easter–Oct Tue–Sun 10–6, Nov–Easter 2–4
Half gallery, half museum, this centre aims to showcase the best of Rhayader and its surrounding environment. In addition to staging revolving exhibitions, it hosts an array of activities, from circus skills and shadow puppetry to sewing and willow weaving. It is also the venue for live events such as jazz evenings. There's a gallery shop too, selling the eminently collectable creations of many local artists and craftworkers.

MEET THE BIRDS
Gigrin Farm Red Kite Feeding Station
gigrin.co.uk
South Street, LD6 5BL
01597 810243 | Open all year daily 9–6
Gigrin Farm, an upland sheep farm on the A470 nearly a mile south of Rhayader, is an official RSPB feeding station for red kites. Thankfully, these creatures have been brought back from the brink of extinction and are now flourishing in this area. Feeding time is a spectacle, with kites and buzzards swooping down at breakneck speed to foil smaller birds, such as crows. The number of kites visiting the feeding station can vary from a dozen to around 400 or more. Feeding the birds is quite a spectacle; it takes place every afternoon, at 3pm.

GET OUTDOORS
Gilfach Nature Discovery Centre and Reserve
rwtwales.org
St Harmon, LD6 5LF
01597 823298 | Reserve open all year daily; Visitor Centre and Nature; Discovery Centre open Easter–Sep Sat–Sun, and school holidays
Situated in the Cambrian Mountains, Gilfach is special due to its wide variety of habitats, ranging from high moorland to enclosed meadow, and oak woodland to rocky upland river. The reserve supports an abundance of plants and animals within a relatively small area. You can take a number of signposted walks – including the Nature Trail, the Monks Trod Trail and the Oakwood Path. The Nature Discovery Centre offers the opportunity to learn about the various habitats and wildlife. It also shows footage from cameras hidden in nestboxes, and has games and quizzes.

PLAY A ROUND
St Idloes Golf Club
stidloesgolfclub.co.uk
Trefeglwys Road, Llanidloes, SY18 6LG | 01686 412559
Open Mon–Sat and Sun pm
Located 14 miles north of Rhayader, St Idloes is slightly undulating but walking is easy.

▶ Rhondda Heritage Park MAP REF 326 B4

rhonddaheritagepark.com

Coed Cae Road, Trehafod, near Pontypridd, CF37 2NP | 01443 682036

Open all year daily 9–4.30, closed Mon in winter

Northwest of Cardiff lie the valleys associated with south Wales' coal-mining industry. Among them, Rhondda is probably the most famous. Its last pit closed in 1990, changing the face of the area forever. This award-winning heritage park pays homage to Rhondda's history and workforce. Based at the former Lewis Merthyr Colliery, which closed in 1983, it evokes the sounds, smells and sights of what life was like in a working coal mine.

The underground tour, led by ex-miners, vividly recreates working conditions on a shift – there is even a simulated explosion. The multimedia exhibition Black Gold uses the lives of a real miner and his predecessors to illustrate the Rhondda's coal industry from the 1850s, and there are displays about the mining valley communities. A multimedia display explores the daily life for miners and their families. There's also a contemporary art gallery and cafe, with views over the Rhondda Valleys. It houses an ever-changing programme of exhibitions, exclusive artworks, ceramics and jewellery.

For children of all ages there is the Energy Zone play area (Easter–Sep).

▶ Rhosneigr MAP REF 336 B3

Located on Anglesey, seven miles southeast of Holyhead (see page 184), lies the lovely little village of Rhosneigr. There's no doubt about it, it's a popular holiday spot. The village contains four caravan sites, three campsites and lots of holiday homes. In fact, this is the most expensive place to purchase a house on Anglesey, the prices being driven up by second homes.

The village itself is tiny – just a handful of shops and pubs, and Anglesey Golf Club. Beyond this are the beaches that make this village so attractive. They're ideal for swimming, surfing, windsurfing, kite surfing, wakeboarding, shore and boat fishing and water skiing.

HIT THE BEACH

Town Beach is safe, sandy and close to the shops, restaurants and amenities of the village. Broad Beach is a regular Green Coast Award winner, ideal for canoeing, surfing and walking.

GO FISHING

Llyn Maelog

01407 810136

Go freshwater fishing in this SSSI lake of around 65 acres, with good stocks, including perch, bream and pike.

PLAY A ROUND
Anglesey Golf Club
theangleseygolfclub.co.uk
Station Road, LL64 5QX
01407 811127 | Contact club for
opening times
An interesting 18-hole links
course set among sand dunes
and heather, renowned for its
excellent greens, numerous
streams and wildlife

EAT AND DRINK
Mojo's Creperie
7 Marine Terrace, LL64 5UQ
01407 810598

Some say that this is the best
place for a pancake this side of
the Big Pond. It's a small,
trendy place with plenty of
people coming and going.
There's a choice of sweet and
savoury pancakes, plus a range
of other dishes on offer. One
quirky dish is the full English
breakfast wrapped in a large
crepe. Part of the appeal for
kids is that the kitchen is
open, so they can see their
pancake being prepared while
they wait. Booking is advised in
the evenings.

▶ Rhossili   MAP REF 324 B4

Pick up any tourist information brochure of the Gower (see
page 170), and chances are there will be a photo of Rhossili
on the front. At the western end of the peninsula facing
Carmarthen Bay, this beach is the pride of the Gower – a
perfect, gently arching sandy bay flanked by the 250-foot
sandstone cliffs and steep grassy flanks of Rhossili Down. On
top, there's a bridleway, while the updraughts make it popular
with hang-gliders and paragliders. On the summit are the
Sweyne's Howes burial chambers and Iron Age earthworks.

On the beach, as the breeze is often up, the waves are
usually ideal for surfers and bodyboarders. Rhossili also has,
like most of the coast, huge tidal ranges. Each day the high tide
makes islands out of the tiny outcrop of Burry Holms in the
north and the one-mile long rocky spit of Worm's Head in the
south. This most westerly extremity takes its name from the
Old English 'orme' meaning 'dragon' or 'serpent'.

The long ridge is a treacherous route across slippery rocks,
which should only be attempted by the sure-footed, and then
only at low tide. There's basically a four-hour window of
opportunity to get across and back. Make sure you don't get
too distracted by the seals lying around the rocks, or the
puffins during their nesting season of April to July. You
don't want to be rescued – although a young Dylan Thomas
was once, writing about it in the story *Who Do You Wish Was
With Us?* from *Portrait of the Artist as a Young Dog*. More
information is available from the National Trust Visitor
Centre at Rhossili.

At low tide you can see the ghostly wooden skeleton of the *Helvetia*, a Norwegian barque driven ashore by gales in 1887 and now lodged in the middle of the beach. Rhossili village has just one large hotel and a National Trust information centre. A car park gives access to the beach and Worms Head.

LEARN TO SURF
Sam's Surf Shack
samssurfshack.com
SA3 1PL | 01792 390519
Open all year daily from 10am
Just a short walk from the beach you'll find everything you need to hit the beach in style, as well as surf lessons and equipment hire.

EAT AND DRINK
Kings Head
kingsheadgower.co.uk

▼ Worms Head, Rhossili

Llangenith, SA3 1HX
01792 386212
A lane to Rhossili Bay's beach starts just along from this 17th-century village inn. The bar serves a weekly rotating schedule of real ales from the Gower Brewery. Expect much praised homemade food using local produce.

▶ **PLACES NEARBY**
Gower Peninsula
see page 170

5 top beaches

▶ **Barafundle Bay**,
Pembrokeshire
page 99

▶ **Barmouth Beach**, Gwynedd
page 83

▶ **Rhossili Bay**, Swansea
page 283

▶ **Three Cliffs Bay**, Swansea
page 170

▶ **Tywyn Beach**, Gwynedd
page 65

▶ Rhyl MAP REF 338 B2

The seaside resort of Rhyl, four miles west of sunny Prestatyn (see page 274) on Wales' north coast, was made popular by the Victorians. Found at the mouth of the River Clwyd, it's quite substantial in size, having a population of roughly 25,000, many originally from Liverpool and Manchester who came during and after World War II to escape the bombs. It has several well-located caravan parks, a pleasure beach, and a water park for rainy days.

While it still has the feel of an old-school seaside resort, Rhyl is also looking to the future with several regeneration projects under way, largely funded by the European Union. These include an £85 million Ocean Plaza complex, an overhaul of the promenade and the reopening of the town's miniature railway around the Marine Lake.

ENTERTAIN THE FAMILY
Sun Centre
www.rhylsuncentre.co.uk
East Parade, LL18 3AQ
01745 344433 | Opening times vary; call or check website for timetable
An indoor tropical water park, designed to keep kids of all ages happy for hours – a great standby for rainy days.

MEET THE SEALIFE
SeaQuarium
seaquarium.co.uk
East Parade, LL18 3AF
01745 344660 | Open all year daily 10–6
With its open seafront location, this aquarium feels like it's actually part of the ocean. Its nine different zones feature species from around the world. There's the wonderful world of jellyfish, plus an outdoor SeaLion Cove where you can meet and greet delightful harbour seals. A superb glass exhibit gives great underwater views of their acrobatics in their 33,000-gallon pool.

HIT THE BEACH
The beach at Rhyl has three miles of sand that are great for families.

PLAY A ROUND
Rhyl Golf Club
rhylgolfclub.co.uk
Coast Road, LL18 3RE
01745 353171 | Open daily all year
A flat links course with challenging holes at this 125-year-old club.

▶ PLACES NEARBY
You can visit Rhuddlan Castle, Bodrhyddan Hall or play a round of golf close to Rhyl.

Rhuddlan Castle
cadw.wales.gov.uk
LL18 5AD | 01745 590777
Open Apr–Oct daily 10–5; Nov–Mar times vary; call or check website for details
This concentric castle built by Edward I now stands uncomfortably next to a modern housing development. Its once-powerful round towers

are crumbling, as time has eaten away at their roofless tops. Yet Rhuddlan was a vital part of Edward I's campaign in Wales and was designed by master castle-builder James of St George. Indeed, it was here that the Statute of Rhuddlan, also known as the Statute of Wales, was issued in March 1284, proclaiming Edward's dominance over the defeated country. This statute lasted until the Act of Union in 1536.

Rhuddlan Castle is diamond-shaped, with towers at each corner, and has two sets of outer walls. It also has its own dock tower. The building of the castle in its present location necessitated a great feal of military engineering. The site was already historically important owing to it being on a ford over the River Clwyd. Edward wanted his new castle to have access to the sea, so that boats might supply it with vital provisions, but the Clwyd was too shallow. Edward cut a new channel – deeper and straighter than the natural one – and 700 years later it still follows this course.

The castle was badly damaged by Parliamentarian forces in 1646, during the English Civil War, and has been in ruins ever since those days.

Bodrhyddan Hall
bodrhyddan.co.uk
Clwyd, LL18 5SB | 01745 590414
Open Jun–Sep afternoons;
call or check website for details
Only a few miles from the north Wales coast, near Abergele, is Bodrhyddan Hall, the home of Lord Langford and his family. Set in its own parkland, it was built by Sir Henry Conwy in 1700, although the house contains remnants of a previous 15th-century building that stood on the same spot. The new house has two storeys and a great hall as its central feature. Towards the end of the 18th century, a lavish dining room was added, then the house was extended still further with the addition of picturesque wings at each end, making the new main entrance, designed in Queen Anne revival style, face west, with a mile-long drive running down towards Rhuddlan.

The Plough Inn
ploughsa.com
The Roe, St Asaph, LL17 0LU
01745 585080
The bar here is a quirky blend of modern and traditional, with open fires, blackboard menus, an unusual trompe l'oeil bar and real ales from north Wales The restaurant, though modern, retains a vaulted ceiling from its days as a ballroom.

Rhuddlan Golf Club
rhuddlangolfclub.co.uk
Meliden Road, LL18 6LB
01745 590217
Open daily all year
An attractive, undulating parkland course with good views. Well bunkered with trees and water hazards, it is a testing course.

▶ St Brides Bay
see **Haverfordwest & St Brides Bay,** page 178

▶ St Davids   MAP REF 322 B3

Set on a windswept plateau, St Davids is Britain's smallest city – granted the status due to its holy stature based around its magnificent 12th-century cathedral. St David, Wales' patron saint, is buried here and the site has been a place of pilgrimage for more than 1,500 years. In the 12th century, it was believed that two visits to St Davids were the equivalent of one to Rome, and pilgrims have been pouring in ever since then.

You don't have to be religious to enjoy this place though. Today, thousands come for the pretty town with its buzzing but laidback vibe, and great links to coastal areas.

TAKE IN SOME HISTORY
St Davids Bishop's Palace
cadw.wales.gov.uk
SA62 6PE | 01437 720517
Open Mar–Jun, Sep–Oct daily
9.30–5, Jul–Aug daily 9.30–6,
Nov–Feb Mon–Sat 10–4, Sun 11–4
These extensive and impressive ruins are all that remain of the principal residence of the Bishops of St Davids. The palace shares a quiet valley with the cathedral, which was almost certainly built on the site of a monastery founded in the sixth century by St David. There are two permanent exhibitions: the Lords of the Palace and Life in the Palace of a Prince of the Church.

St Davids Cathedral
stdavidscathedral.org.uk
The Close, SA62 6PE
01437 720202 | Open all year
Mon–Sat 8.30–5, Sun 1–5
Begun in 1181 on the reputed site of St Davids sixth-century monastic settlement, the present building was altered between the 12th to the 14th centuries and again in the 16th. The ceilings of oak, painted wood and stone vaulting are of considerable interest. The medieval Shrine of St David, a focus for pilgrimage since the 12th century, was restored in 2012 and now contains five new icons depicting local saints, together with a painted canopy. Guided tours of the catherdral are available. For around nine days in May and June each year, St Davids Cathedral holds a festival of classical music. St Davids' three cathedral choirs attend, as well as many top musicians from around the world.

HIT THE BEACH
Whitesands Bay is one of the best surfing beaches in Pembrokeshire and one of the best tourist beaches in the world.

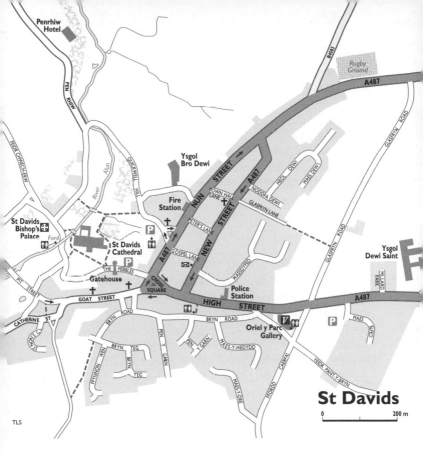

St Davids

0   200 m

TLS

GET ACTIVE
TYF
tyf.com
High Street, SA62 6SA
01437 721611
A great operation offering coasteering, climbing and kayaking for those looking to add a little excitement and adventure to their lives.

TAKE A BOAT TRIP
Thousand Island Expeditions
thousandislands.co.uk
Cross Square, SA62 6SL
01437 721721
Thousand Island Expeditions offers family adventure boat trips across to the RSPB reserve at Ramsey Island.

EAT AND DRINK
Cwtch 🏮
cwtchrestaurant.co.uk
22 High Street, SA62 6SD
01437 720491
Pronounced 'cutsh', this evocative Welsh word means 'snug' and 'cosy'. The restaurant lives up to its name too, with three small dining rooms with whitewashed stone walls, sturdy cross beams and a mini-library of foodie books for diners to leaf through. The cooking takes a similarly restrained approach, leaving Pembrokeshire produce to do the talking without unwelcome interference from trendy ideas.

It's clearly a formula that works, as the local following is loyal and keen for more: the place now opens for lunch.

▶ PLACES NEARBY

Near St Davids is the village of Solva (see page 302), Ramsey Island, with its stunning wildlife, and a few lovely pubs.

Ramsey Island
rspb.org.uk
07836 535733
Open Apr–Oct daily 10–4
Located a mile off the coast, this island is an RSPB reserve and SAC (Special Area of Conservation) surrounded by nutrient rich waters which provide a sanctuary to a wide range of wildlife. Whether your passion is whales and dolphins, sea birds, rocks and gorges or just stunning scenery, this is a good place to visit. The cliffs are up to 394 feet high, the perfect place for breeding seabirds in spring and early summer. The island is awash with colour from May to September, with bluebells, then pink thrift and purple heather. You might see choughs and peregrines nesting on the cliffs. Chances are that if you visit in the autumn, you'll see a colony of breeding grey seals. There is a small shop on the island and refreshments are available.

Get here by one of these companies:
ramseyisland.co.uk
thousandislands.co.uk
aquaphobia-ramseyisland.co.uk

The Shed ❀
theshedporthgain.co.uk
Porthgain, SA62 5BN
01348 831518
The Shed is situated right on the harbourside of this tiny village, tucked away within the

▼ Looking towards Ramsey Island

confines of the Pembrokeshire Coast National Park. It's a friendly, relaxed and informal place and, as its name implies, simply decorated and furnished. Indoors, gingham tablecloths, whitewashed walls and fish-related art create a laid-back setting for dishes that let the sheer quality and freshness of the raw materials do the talking. The daily deliveries of super-fresh fish and shellfish are the main attraction for diners, alongside the self-assured cooking. Timings are spot on, whatever the cooking medium, and the sauces and seasonings are always a well-considered match for the main component, with nothing too over the top. This is a delightful place for a special evening meal.

The Sloop Inn
sloop.co.uk
Porthgain, SA62 5BN
01348 831449
Possibly the most famous pub on the north Pembrokeshire coast, The Sloop Inn is located in the quarrying village of Porthgain. It's particularly enticing on a cold winter's day. The walls and ceilings are covered with pictures and memorabilia from nearby shipwrecks. The harbour is less than 300 feet from the door and there is a village green to the front and a large south-facing patio. The bar is well equipped – with ales such as Felinfoel and The Rev James on the pump – and a varied menu includes breakfasts, snacks, pub favourites, steaks and freshly caught fish.

▶ St Dogmaels   MAP REF 323 E1

Just across the River Teifi from Cardigan, on Wales' west coast, this delightful village runs steeply up a hill, offering wonderful views of the Teifi Estuary. It's extremely pretty and well kept, with colourful terrace houses, upmarket B&Bs, a great chip shop and riverside pub. It's also where the Pembrokeshire Coast Path ends, and where the Ceredigion Coast Path begins. Tucked away are the most stunning Benedictine abbey and stylish new visitor centre.

This spiritual and cultural powerhouse was built and founded in the early 12th century for a prior and 12 monks. The building is mostly in ruins, but extensive walls and arches remain. Among the most important remains that can be seen in the adjoining 19th-century parish church is the Sagranus Stone, a seven-foot pillar inscribed in both Latin and Ogham lettering, which helped scholars to decipher this mysterious script from the Dark Ages.

Just beyond the village are the beautiful and extensive Poppit Sands, which lead up to the wild cliffscape of Cemaes Head.

TAKE IN SOME HISTORY
St Dogmaels Abbey and Coach House Visitor Centre
welshabbey.org.uk
Shingrig, SA43 3DX | 01239 615389
Open Mon–Sat 10–4, Sun 11–3
Learn about the abbey at the coach house next door, now converted into a delightful visitor centre. It tells the story of the medieval Tironensian (Benedictine) abbey, holds craft fairs and medieval fun days and a local produce market on Tuesdays. There's also a small cafe and gallery showcasing local art. It has helped regenerate this lively, friendly community and is a great place to visit.

VISIT THE GALLERY
The Lemon Tree Tea Rooms and Gallery
Norwood, High Street, SA43 3EJ
01239 615321 | Opening times vary; call for details
This is a lovely small gallery showcasing the art and crafts of local artisans. The cafe is on the small and simple side but serves and delicious snacks and light meals. The homemade soups are particularly hearty on a cold winter's day.

ENTERTAIN THE FAMILY
Go crabbing off the jetty – it's a great way to entertain kids and grown-ups.

HIT THE BEACH
Charmingly named Poppit Sands is a marvellous beach banked by low dunes; there's lots of sand exposed even at high tide and lifeguards in the summer. The local RNLI is stationed here.

EAT AND DRINK
Bowen's Fish and Chip Shop
2 High Street, SA43 3ED
01239 613814
This chip shop does wonderful fish and chips. Be warned, though – the portions aren't off the scale as they are in most chip shops, so don't share – have your own.

Teifi Netpool Inn
teifinetpoolinn.com
SA43 3ET | 01239 612680
With gardens right on the estuary and a play park where you can keep an eye on the kids from a distance, this is a perfect family-friendly holiday pub where you can all relax. Serving good homemade meals, it's slightly off the beaten track and popular with ramblers, cyclists and colourful locals. Known locally as the Teifi, it has an array of draught beers, ciders and real ales.

▶ **PLACES NEARBY**
Close to St Dogmaels is a beach, and the hip town of Cardigan (see page 137) .

Poppit Beach
Thirty years ago, Poppit Beach was just a few sand dunes and a thin stretch of sand, with the bulk of the beach being across the estuary over on Gwbert. Since then, the changing tide has shifted all the sand onto

Poppit, transforming it into a glorious and wide beach, great for running, strolling, paddling or swimming. The RNLI station for the area is here, and life guards operate in the summer.

It never really gets too wavy here, and there's a great cafe in the car park, selling buckets and spades, wetsuits and postcards as well as a good range of fresh food.

▷ St Fagans National History Museum
see highlight panel overleaf

▷ St Govan's Chapel   MAP REF 323 D6
This is one of the real gems of the Pembrokeshire Coast, wedged on sheer cliffs just a stone's throw from crashing waves and camouflaged by rock. Approached by a steep flight of steps down through the cliffs near Bosherston, this tiny chapel is believed to date from the 13th century.

The story goes that it is named after St Govan, an Irish priest who lived in a cave in the cliffs following an incident when he was set upon by thieves. He was saved by the cliffs themselves, which opened up just enough for him to hide in a tiny cave, where he stayed until he was out of danger. The chapel was built on the site where his cave once stood.

The waters from St Govan's well, built just below the chapel but now dried up, were reportedly good for treating a host of ailments – from sore skin to poor eyesight. A legend says St Govan's body is buried under the chapel's altar. Nearby there's The Bell rock, which is supposed to contain St Govan's silver bell, encased in rock by angels to stop pirates stealing it.

Also worth a look are the 50-foot cliffs, which make up the area known as St Govan's Head. They are formidably harsh, dropping into a ferocious sea, and are popular with experienced climbers. Unfortunately, much of the area is under the control of the army's Castlemartin range, so when the roads are closed, the area is out of bounds.

Ten minutes' walk to the west of the chapel lies Huntsman's Leap, also known as Penny's or Adam's Leap, a spectacular gash in the cliffs that a huntsman is said to have leaped across on horseback during a chase. Further along is the Green Bridge of Wales or Pen-y-Holt (see page 99), the biggest natural rock arch in the county.

▷ St Tudwal Islands
see **Abersoch & St Tudwal Islands,** page 71

▶ St Fagans National History Museum MAP REF 326 B5

www.museumwales.ac.uk
CF5 6XB | 0300 111 2333 | Open daily 10–5

Located a few miles from the centre of Cardiff, St Fagans is Wales' leading open-air museum and its most popular heritage attraction. It stands in the 100-acre grounds of the magnificent St Fagans Castle, a late 16th-century manor house donated to the people of Wales by the Earl of Plymouth – and recreates many lost aspects of Welsh life and culture. Here you'll find a chapel, a farmhouse of timber and stone, a school and a workmen's institute, as well as more than 40 other buildings, which were moved from their original sites and reconstructed here as museum pieces. It's a beast of a site, and you'll need most of a day to enjoy it properly. Highlights include a row of six miners' cottages from Merthyr Tydfil, each one restored and furnished to represent a different period in Welsh history. There's also St Teilos Church, which took 20 years to move and reconstruct here. You can see craftspeople at work, making blankets, tools and even cider. There are also native breeds of farm animals – be careful of the donkeys, they'll nibble your clothes – and a series of galleries with displays of everyday items on home life, work, festivals and music. The Welsh language is also celebrated and explained in detail. Be warned – renovations are currently under way, with plans for an improved entrance hall and gallery space, and a reconstruction of a medieval court.

▶ Saundersfoot MAP REF 323 E5

Along with neighbouring Tenby (see page 311), this seaside resort is one of the most popular and visited in Wales. Lying on Pembrokeshire's south coast in a wooded valley, it grew up as a fishing village, then boomed as an export port when anthracite coal was discovered in the area and mines were built. When the industry faded away in the early 20th century, the village took advantage of the nearby railway station to attract tourists from England and eastern Wales.

Today, it has an attractive harbour alongside wonderful golden sands, with the beach being popular for fishing, sailing and water sports. It's also making a name for itself as a gourmet resort, largely due to the high-quality restaurants and cafes and the local Pembrokeshire produce.

HIT THE BEACH

Saundersfoot Beach is super accessible, wide and sandy with blue-flag waters, while Glen and Monkstone beaches are just a short walk away; watch out for the razor clams that spit at you.

EAT AND DRINK

Coast Restaurant ◉◉

coastsaundersfoot.co.uk
Coppet Hall Beach, SA69 9AJ
01834 810800

If you were looking for an emblematic 21st-century restaurant venue, you couldn't go far wrong with Coast. It stands on the Pembrokeshire shore, with just the sea and sky before it. Huge picture windows allow for relaxed contemplation, and the interior scene is all simple bare tables, banquettes strewn with cushions, and an atmosphere of serenely informal professionalism. The seafood-strong menu uses local produce.

St Brides Spa Hotel ◉

stbridesspahotel.com
St Brides Hill, SA69 9NH
01834 812304

Built to make the best of the views out across Saundersfoot harbour and Carmarthen Bay, this spa hotel is a good option in fair weather or foul. Obviously, there's the spa to soothe the mind and body, and in terms of food there's the Cliff Restaurant, a dining option that's delivering classic dishes based on high-quality regional produce. There's also a bar (the Gallery) with its own menu, and a terrace that is popular in warmer months.

Shoreline Coffee Shop
2A The Strand, SA69 9ET
01834 813112
This is a busy little cafe in a great location, overlooking the beach with a small terrace to the rear. Be warned – during busy times staff can often be overwhelmed and orders take a long time to arrive. But if you aren't in a hurry, it's a great spot to relax.

▶ **PLACES NEARBY**
Enjoy a walk in glorious gardens or a family day out at a very special park and zoo.

5 top quirky events

▶ **Man versus Horse Marathon**, Llanwrtyd Wells – green-events.co.uk

▶ **The Porthcawl Elvis Festival**, Porthcawl – elvies.co.uk

▶ **The Really Wild Cawl Eating Competition**, Saundersfoot – reallywildfestival.co.uk/ year-round-events

▶ **Welsh Open Stoneskimming Championships**, Llanwrtyd Wells – green-events.co.uk

▶ **World MTB Chariot Racing Championship**, Llanwrtyd Wells – green-events.co.uk

Colby Woodland Garden
nationaltrust.org.uk
SA67 8PP | 01834 811885
Open Feb–Oct daily 10–5
From early spring to the end of June the garden is ablaze with colour, from the masses of golden daffodils to the rich hues of rhododendrons, azaleas and bluebells. Later, hydrangeas line the shaded woodland walks through the bright colours of summer to the glorious shades of autumn. It's also the perfect place for a family picnic.

Folly Farm Adventure Park and Zoo
folly-farm.co.uk
Begelly, SA68 0XA | 01834 812731
Open all year Mon–Fri 9–5,
Sat–Sun 10–5
Folly Farm started as a humble dairy farm but then inspiration struck. After noticing families stopping by the roadside to pet and watch their cattle, the owners decided to diversify, and in 1988 Folly Farm was born. The former dairy farm was converted to receive visitors and now guests can stop to visit the cows and see them being milked. Over the last 24 years, 400,000 visitors have enjoyed the exciting and varied attractions each year. From exotic creatures to vintage funfair rides and adventure playgrounds, Folly Farm has something for everyone.

▶ **Skenfrith**
see **Grosmont, Skenfrith & White Castle,** page 173

▶ Skomer & Skokholm Islands

MAP REF 322 A5/B5

welshwildlife.org

These two rocky island reserves off the western tip of the Pembrokeshire mainland form one of the richest wildlife sanctuaries in Britain. First and foremost, they are breeding sites for seabirds. With its dark, volcanic cliffs, Skomer – the larger and more famous island – becomes home to 500,000 birds in nesting season, including some 14,000 guillemots, 6,000 breeding pairs of puffins and the world's largest colony of Manx shearwaters – more than 150,000 breeding pairs. Porpoises and dolphins are regular visitors. It's also a site of historical importance due to being isolated and uncultivated, and so archaeological traces from farming in the Bronze and Iron Ages have survived on Skomer for thousands of years. On the cliff tops are the remnants of Bronze and Iron Age farms – small huts, animal pounds, farmsteads and elaborate systems of fields – as well as a standing stone and burial cairns. In the Middle Ages the island was used for grazing cattle, sheep and oxen.

Skokholm, meanwhile, has the first bird observatory built in Britain, founded here in 1933 by naturalist Ronald Lockley, who lived on the island and studied its wildlife. Puffins and the rare Manx shearwaters nest on the island, together with colonies of guillemots, razorbills, storm petrels and about 160 grey seal pups, which are born here each year. It also has a large population of rabbits introduced, it is believed, by the Normans after 1066. Its vegetation is an example of long-term rabbit-managed grassland. Visitors can use accommodation for overnight stays on the island in the summer months; visit the website for more information.

▼ Skomer Island

▲ Sunset over Skomer Island from the mainland

TAKE A BOAT TRIP
Dale Sailing Company
pembrokeshire-islands.co.uk
01646 603110

To get here, catch the summer ferry (not Mondays) from Martin's Haven on the headland west of Marloes. Visitor numbers are limited, so go a little out of the main season to avoid disappointment.

▶ **PLACES NEARBY**

Take a tour round Grassholm.

Grassholm
Grassholm is the place to view gannets – there are 39,000 breeding pairs here. The RSPB, which owns Grassholm, does not permit landing, although the Dale Sailing Company runs boat tours around the island.

▶ Snowdonia National Park

MAP REF 334 A3, 337 E3

www.eryri-npa.gov.uk
National Park Office, Penrhyndeudraeth, LL48 6LF | 01766 770274

This park may be home to the wettest spot in Britain – with the knife-edge arête running up to Snowdon's summit boasting an average annual rainfall of 4,473mm – but that simply seems to add to the appeal. With its mighty peaks – the highest south of Scotland – rivers and strong Welsh heritage, it's always been an extremely popular place to visit and live. Indeed, some 26,000 people live in the park (Parc Cenedlaethol Eryri in Welsh) in towns such as Dolgellau (see page 159), Bala (see page 80) and Betws-y-Coed (see page 90), 62 per cent of whom can speak at least some of the native language.

With this popularity in mind, large swathes of the park were granted National Park protection in 1951, making it the third such park in Britain and the first in Wales. Covering 827 square miles, it has 37 miles of coastline, stretching from the north coast near Bangor (see page 81) down to Machynlleth (see page 219) in the south. Unusually, it has a hole in the middle around the town of Blaenau Ffestiniog (see page 94), a slate quarrying centre – it was deliberately excluded from the park in order to allow the development of new light industry to replace the decimated slate industry, which had scarred its cliffs.

This national park status increased Snowdonia's appeal further. The park attracts more than six million visitors annually, making it the third most visited park in England and Wales. The busiest part is around Snowdon – the highest peak at 3,560 feet (1,085m). Around 750,000 people climb, walk or ride the train to the summit each year, enjoying the sleek new summit station, visitor centre and cafeteria – Hafod Eryri – which opened in 2009.

It's worth noting that the railway – Britain's only rack-and-pinion railway, which opened in 1896, unfortunately killing one passenger on its first descent – is very popular, taking people up and down the mountain each year and providing an interesting running commentary en route.

Yet the park is so much more than this one mountain, as it also encompasses coastal areas, complex dune systems, rivers, forests, Wales' biggest natural lake and Coed-y-Brenin, Britain's first mountain bike trail centre.

The northernmost area is the most popular with tourists, and includes (from west to east) Moel Hebog, Mynydd Mawr, the Snowdon Massif, the Glyderau – also known as the Glyders

– and the Carneddau – also known as the Carnedds. These last three groups are the highest mountains in Wales, and include all Wales' 3,000-foot mountains. Many people undertake the challenge of running all three peaks in a single day, starting extremely early in the day from the summit of Snowdon.

The second area includes peaks such as Moel Siabod, Cnicht, the Moelwynion and the mountains around Blaenau Ffestiniog. The third area includes the Rhinogydd in the west, as well as the Arenig and the Migneint – a large area of bog. This is not as popular with tourists as the other areas, due to its remoteness.

The southernmost area includes Cadair Idris, the Tarren range, the Dyfi Hills, and the Aran group, including Aran Fawddwy (2,969 feet/905m), the highest mountain in Britain south of Snowdon. This is, of course, a walker's paradise. But there are also summits that require the use of hands as well as feet – the most famous being Tryfan.

There are also wonderful walks at relatively low levels, and although a significant amount of the park is in private ownership, the right to roam is in full swing here. In fact, the park has 1,479 miles of public footpaths, 164 miles of public bridleways and 46 miles of other public rights of way. The coastline runs from the Llyn Peninsula (see page 218) down

the mid-Wales coast, covering a sand dune network that's been designated a Special Area of Conservation. Rare plants in the park include the Snowdon lily, an Arctic-Alpine plant, and the rainbow-coloured Snowdon beetle. It's also got its own species of fish – the *gwyniad* – found exclusively in Bala Lake (see page 80). Water sports and angling are also big business in the park – you can try anything from kayaking to coasteering. Courses run at the famous Plas y Brenin.

The park publishes a free annual visitor paper detailing highlights, events and how to get around. The Met Office also keeps its website updated. Remember, if you are walking, this isn't a theme park but an area of proper mountains that need to be treated with respect. Low cloud and mist can descend in just moments, requiring substantial layers of clothing. Never head out without carrying food, drink, warm clothing and waterproofs. Also take a 1:25,000 Ordnance Survey map and carry a compass – you may well need it to guide you off a summit. Remember, even-well trodden and popular paths are very exposed and potentially dangerous. The Pyg Track leading up Snowdon is a prime example, having several casualties each year. Be sure to wear good walking boots, and take proper care.

▼ Snowdon Horseshoe from Llyn-y-Mymbyr

▶ Solva MAP REF 322 B3

Three miles east of St Davids (see page 288) on the
Pembrokeshire coast lies Solva. Effectively a village in two
parts, the more modern upper village lines the A487 coast
road, while the lower part – consisting of attractive cottages,
small shops and restaurants – clusters around the harbour,
sheltered at the head of a long winding tidal inlet.

These days Solva is a busy little tourist trap, but it was
founded on maritime traditions. A thriving port until the arrival
of the railways, it had several warehouses and a dozen or so
limekilns, used for lime burning. The rocks at the entrance to
its harbour made it one of the most sheltered anchorages
between Fishguard (see page 165) and Milford Haven (see
page 229). Solva once boasted a passenger service to New
York. It wasn't glamorous though – passengers had to bring
their own food for a voyage that could last up to four months.

Although it's a fine place for pottering about and having a
spot of lunch, Solva is also one of the best bases for a coastal
walk, maybe to St Davids (get the bus back), or just a stroll
along the rocky headland, the Gribin, where there's an Iron Age
settlement and a perfect view back to the village. Solva, despite
its small size, has produced a famous musician. David Gray
– known for his 1998 album *White Ladder* – moved here with his
parents as a child and went to Solva Community School.

TAKE IN SOME HISTORY
Solva Woollen Mill
solvawoollenmill.co.uk
Middle Mill, SA62 6XD
01437 721112 | Open all year
Mon–Sat 9.30–5.30, Sun 2–5.30
The oldest working woollen
mill in Pembrokeshire, Solva
is now the only mill in Wales
specialising in flat-weave
carpets, rugs and runners.
Workers use traditional skills
and 19th-century looms to
create beautiful floor coverings.
Recent commissions include
rugs for Llwynywormwood,
Prince Charles' Welsh
residence. Visitors can watch
the looms at work and browse
in the mill shop. There's also a
good coffee shop.

▶ PLACES NEARBY
Close to Solva, at Abereiddy, is
a fine country house.

Crug Glâs Country House ◉
crug-glas.co.uk
Abereiddy, SA62 6XX
01348 831302
Five plush bedrooms and 600
acres of rolling farmland make
Crug Glâs an inviting prospect.
The owners have renovated the
interiors using local materials
to achieve a balance of smart
modernity without spoiling the
house's history – the place
dates from the 12th century.
Traditional country-house
cooking forms the backbone of
menus that aim to comfort
rather than challenge.

▶ Stackpole   MAP REF 323 D6

Four miles south of Pembroke, Stackpole is a tiny village with a population of around 200. It's basically encompassed within the 2,000-acre Stackpole Estate. Under the care of the National Trust, the estate includes a beautiful stretch of coastline, two sandy beaches – including the world-renowned Barafundle Bay – wooded valleys and a network of artificial ponds famous for their lilies. In terms of the eight-mile stretch of coastline, it covers cliffs, sand dunes and tiny coves. Sites include Barafundle Bay, a jewel of a beach set between limestone cliffs and backed by dunes and woods; Stackpole Quay, a tiny harbour used by local fishermen and small pleasure boats; Bosherston Lakes, famed for their lilies and otters; and Broad Haven South, a safe family bathing beach.

A few miles west of the main estate is Freshwater West, Wales' premier surfing beach.

HIT THE BEACH

Broad Haven South, Freshwater West and Barafundle Bay are all fantastic beaches – try to make time to visit them all.

EAT AND DRINK

The Boathouse Tea Room

Stable Yard, Stackpole, SA71 5DE
01646 672672
Situated close to the old stone jetty, this popular licensed cafe has a large outdoor area for al fresco dining in the summer months. The quiches are delicious, while tasty sandwiches include fresh crab. The cream teas come with tempting cakes.

The Stackpole Inn

stackpoleinn.co.uk
SA71 5DF | 01646 672324
This traditional inn is a walker's delight, set in pristine gardens at the heart of the National Trust's Stackpole Estate and close enough to the spectacular Pembrokeshire Coastal Path to provide a welcome break. There's a rare George V post box in the mellow stone wall outside, a survival from the time when one of the two original stone cottages was a Post Office. Nowadays, the pub offers facilities for walkers, cyclists, fishermen and climbers, as well as those who simply prefer to relax and do nothing. Once inside you'll find a slate bar, ceiling beams made from ash trees grown on the estate, and a wood-burning stove set within the stone fireplace. The pub's free house status means that there's always a guest beer to accompany the three Welsh ales, a couple of real ciders and a varied wine list. Local produce from the surrounding countryside and fish from the coast play a major part in the home-cooked menu.

▶ Strata Florida Abbey MAP REF 329 E3

cadw.wales.gov.uk

Abbey Road, Ystrad Fflur, SY25 6ES | 01974 831261 | Open Apr–Oct daily
10–5; winter opening hours vary, call for details

Now reduced to romantic ruins, this abbey was once one of the
major cultural centres of Wales, governing large parts of the
mid-region. Set in an isolated spot near Tregaron, southeast of
Aberystwyth (see page 72), it was founded in 1184 by a group
of Cistercian monks with roots in France under the patronage
of Prince Rhys ap Gruffydd. The community that built up was
known as Strata Florida (*Ystrad Fflur* or Valley of the Flowers).
From here, administration took place over huge sheep farms
on the surrounding the Cambrian Mountains. The abbey also
became a centre for literary activity and influence.

It is thought that 11 princes from south Wales were buried
here in the 12th and 13th centuries, as well the great 14th-
century poet Dafydd ap Gwilym. A memorial to him is found
under a yew tree on the site, once famously hit by lightning.

Today, all that remains of the abbey is the soaring western
arching doorway and some foundations laid out in the grass.
A modern roof protects an area of medieval floor tiles, where
some of the designs are still visible. Some of these tiles have
been preserved and put on display inside the small onsite
museum. One of them – the 'Man with the Mirror' – depicts a
medieval gentleman admiring himself in a mirror.

▶ PLACES NEARBY

Nearby is a nature reserve, and
further afield lies Aberystwyth
(see page 72).

Cors Caron National Nature Reserve

Off the B4343 Lampeter to
Aberystwyth road between Tregaron
and Pontrhydfendigaid

The nature reserve covers 2,000
acres of the stuff – mainly three
raised bogs built up from deep
layers of peat that have taken
around 12,000 years to form. It
is a wild landscape, made
accessible by a network of
boardwalks that enable visitors
to get right into the heart of
varied habitats and enjoy seeing
the wildlife at close quarters.
Look out for rare wetland birds
such as the golden plover and
the curlew.

▶ Strumble Head MAP REF 322 C2

Take a walk on the wild side at Strumble Head. This rocky
headland – the nearest point to Ireland – towers over the
pounding Atlantic surf, while the coastal path cuts an airy, at
times precarious, line across the top. The lighthouse stands
guard over the peninsula and treacherous waters below,

▲ Strumble Head lighthouse

beaming out its warning – four flashes every 15 seconds – to the huge ferries travelling between Fishguard and Rosslare.

It's not a warning to be taken lightly. At least 60 ships capsized in the area in the 19th century alone. The revolving lights were originally controlled by a massive clockwork system that needed winding every 12 hours. This was replaced in 1965 by an electrically powered system, and the lighthouse was converted to unstaffed operation in 1980.

The jagged rocks and waves below the lighthouse are among the best places in Wales to spot grey seals. The sky is also alive with the screech of seabirds, while porpoises and dolphins are regularly spotted in the turbulent waters. Volunteers from the Sea Trust have monitored these waters for years and estimate that there are around 100 porpoises at peak season, falling to about 50 mid-winter. There have also been sightings of basking sharks, sunfish and four types of whales – fin, humpback, minke and orca. Below the parking area is a World War II area that now serves as a wildlife lookout.

▶ PLACES NEARBY

Close to Strumble Head is Fishguard (see page 165) and a burial chamber.

Carreg Sampson
Signposted off the minor road between Trefin and Abercastle

This prehistoric burial chamber, sometimes known as Samson's Stone and the Longhouse, is set in the midde of a farmer's field – with terrific views of Strumble Head. The dolmen itself is astonishing, with a capstone of monstrous proportions.

▲ Dylan Thomas Theatre and statue

▶ Swansea   MAP REF 325 D4

There's no getting away from it – when it comes to image, Swansea is a bit of a mixed bag. During its heyday in the 19th century, as king of the copper industry, it was known as 'Copperopolis'. Dylan Thomas then called it – probably the most accurately – an 'ugly, lovely town.' Home-grown megastar Catherine Zeta-Jones raves about it. Surveys have concluded it's the best place to live in Britain. Its football team is on the up: in 2011, Swansea City became the first Welsh team to be promoted to the English Premier League, and in 2013 it won the Capitol One Cup by beating Bradford 5-0 at Wembley. Also in 2013, Swansea hosted a BBC Three series: *The Call Centre*.

What can't be disputed is that it is trying. Yes, it has become somewhat rundown, but regeneration is afoot. Like Cardiff (see page 122), its dock area has been redeveloped into an opulent Maritime Quarter, where refurbished old buildings mingle with modern architecture, such as the National Waterfront Museum. There's an elegant Sail Bridge – albeit slightly wobbly – across

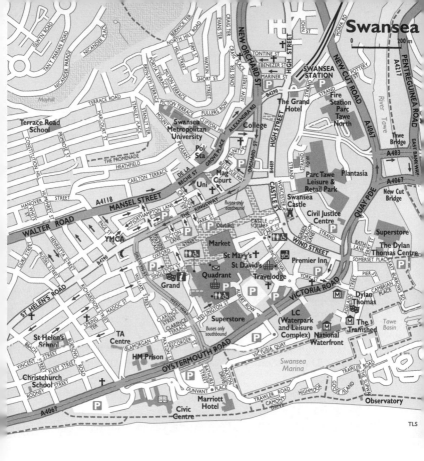

the Tawe, and, of course, The Dylan Thomas Centre, which chronicles his work and links with the city. Around the castle there are some decent shops, and music fans can catch international artists at Brangwyn Hall or the Grand Theatre.

For those interested in nightlife, it's also a city that – when the lights are dimmed – is buzzing with glammed-up young ladies and muscled lads in tight shirts socialising on the 'Swansea mile' – a stretch of pubs along the seafront.

Perhaps it's not so surprising that Swansea has so many images, given that it's Wales' second-largest city and home to a whole raft of people, from university students to locals to immigrants and outdoor lovers.

Little is recorded of Swansea until the Norman conquerors saw its potential as a port. In 1106, Henry de Beaumont, first earl of Warwick, built a motte-and-bailey castle on a cliff overlooking the mouth of the Tawe. After the Welsh sacked the castle in the 13th century, the old structure was rebuilt. The current building dates back to the 14th century, though it didn't have much of a strategic role following the defeat of the Welsh by Edward I. In 1306, Swansea was given the Royal

Charter to build and repair ships, a tradition that continued into the 20th century.

During the 19th century large-scale anthracite mining and the metal industry changed this small village into the metropolis it is today. By the 1850s, the railways had arrived, the first dockyard had been completed and Swansea was supplying 60 per cent of the world's copper requirements. Swansea's other face was of that of a seaside resort – railway adverts compared Swansea Bay with the Bay of Naples and well-to-do Victorians came to take the sea air.

World War II bombing and the mid-20th-century decline in manufacturing saw the city having to reinvent itself. And this is still going on. Of course, you may argue that none of that matters because Swansea isn't about the town but the location on the Gower, with all its natural beauty and easy access to the great outdoors. That is, of course, the real reason why so many people come here.

VISIT THE MUSEUMS
The Dylan Thomas Centre
dylanthomas.com
Somerset Place, SA1 1RR
01792 463980 | Open daily 10–4.30
If you love this old Welsh rogue of a poet, you'll also love this centre. It's the focal point for studies and events based on his life, with a permanent exhibition about his work and home. It also boasts a literature programme, which runs many events throughout the year, including the annual Dylan Thomas Festival during October and November. The year 2014 marked the centenary of his birth (see page 53).

National Waterfront Museum
www.museumwales.ac.uk
Oystermouth Road, Maritime Quarter, SA1 3RD | 0300 111 2333
Open daily 10–5
This museum tells the story of the industrialisation of Wales, with exhibits including working engines. It shows how the Industrial Revolution had such a tremendous impact upon people and communities in the local area and around the world. Check out the stunning glass-fronted building that houses the museum.

Swansea Museum
swanseamuseum.co.uk
Victoria Road, Maritime Quarter, SA1 1SN | 01792 653763
Open Tue–Sun 10–5;
closed 24 Dec–2 Jan
This is the oldest museum in Wales, showing the history of Swansea from the earliest times until today. The museum has an old tram shed and floating boats to explore (summer only). There is a continuous programme of temporary exhibitions and events all year around. The collection's centre is nearby and is open to the public every Wednesday.

GO ROUND THE RAINFOREST
Plantasia
plantasia.org
Parc Tawe, SA1 2AL | 01792 474555
Open daily 10–5; closed Mon in Dec
and first 2 weeks Jan
Plantasia is a unique tropical
haven of exotic plants and
animals. Within the impressive
glass pyramid is a luscious
rainforest filled with more than
500 tropical plants and a
terraced waterfall flowing into a
fish-filled lagoon. There is also
a mini-zoo with monkeys,
reptiles and birds. Check out
the Amazonian Rainforest Hut,
a chance to see how the tribal
people of the Amazon live.

CATCH A PERFORMANCE
Grand Theatre Swansea
Singleton Street, SA1 3QJ
01792 475715
Opened in the late 19th century,
the theatre is home to a
number of theatrical, dance
and music groups.

PLAY A ROUND
Morriston Golf Club
morristongolfclub.co.uk
160 Clasemont Road, Morriston,
SA6 6AJ | 01792 796528
Open daily all year
This is a great course for
golfers of all abilities. The 17th
is aptly nicknamed the Temple
of Doom.

EAT AND DRINK
Cafe at the National Waterfront Museum
museumwales.ac.uk
Oystermouth Road, Maritime
Quarter, SA1 3RD | 0300 111 2333
At the heart of the ultra-
modern museum buildings in
Swansea's Maritime Quarter,
the cafe offers a good choice of
excellent cakes, sandwiches,
quiches, various savouries
and appetising hot meals.
Everything is made onsite using
fresh produce sourced locally
wherever possible.

The Dragon Hotel ◉
dragon-hotel.co.uk
The Kingsway Circle, SA1 5LS
01792 657100
The Dragon is breathing fire
after a megabucks renovation
has brought everything up to
full contemporary spec, making
the most of its location in the
thick of Swansea's town centre
action. Built on a bedrock of
local produce, the modern
European cooking is in tune
with the setting. Keenly priced
two- or three-course dinner
menus, bolstered by a carte,
are served in the contemporary
Piano Restaurant. If you're here
for lunch, similar fare is served
in the buzzy Dragon Brasserie,
a breezy modern venue with
exposed industrial ducting and
spotlights above bare darkwood
tables and ringside seats
looking through full-length
windows onto the busy street.

Hanson at the Chelsea Restaurant ◉◉
hansonatthechelsea.co.uk
17 St Mary Street, SA1 3LH
01792 464068
Lemon-coloured walls give a
fresh feel to this small
restaurant found on a narrow

city-centre side street. It looks like a classic modern bistro inside, with banquettes and high-backed wooden chairs with padded seats, clothed tables and a board listing seafood specials. The service is relaxed and friendly, and the weekly-changing menu is an appealing mix of local produce and French influences, with the emphasis on fish and seafood, not forgetting fine Welsh lamb.

▶ **PLACES NEARBY**

Close to Swansea is a lovely garden and woods, both great for family fun.

Penllergare Valley Woods
SA4 9GJ | 01792 344244
Some 20 minutes north of Swansea, close to the M4, is Penllergare Valley Woods, offering 7.5 miles of paths, steps and historic views that have been opened up by local volunteers so people can enjoy them. There's plenty of walks to choose from, some with disabled access. Try the lakeside stroll, the heritage trail, a wild woodland walk or a riverside ramble. The waterfall is a must-see. Maps and snacks are available in the community coffee shop. The area is slightly work-in-progress, but bound to become better with time.

Tony Ridler's Garden
tonyridlersgarden.co.uk
7 Saint Peter's Terrace, Cockett,
SA2 0FW | 01792 588217
Half a mile northwest of Swansea is this garden of meticulously manicured hedges and perfect symmetry – helped by plants being arranged in twos, fours and sixes. There's not a leaf out of place and there's great innovative topiary. Paths lead to hidden sculptures and other decorative features. It's been created over 18 years and deserves visitors. Kids will no doubt like the giant hedges shaped like lollipops.

▶ **Teifi Estuary** MAP REF 323 E1

The whole length of the River Teifi is recognised as an internationally important wildlife site, largely owing to its range of habitats as it passes through on its way to the sea. In particular, the estuary is known for its variety of birdlife and population of bottlenose dolphins and Atlantic grey seals. Reed beds shelter birds, such as Cetti's warblers and kingfishers, while the mudflats out in the bay support waders, including greenshanks, dunlins, sandpipers and curlews.

Where the water meets the sea, just downstream from the town of Cardigan on Wales' west coast, it's a stunning view – with the golden Poppit Beach, soaring cliffs, Cardigan Island in the distance and white bobbing sailing boats on the water. In 2009, a remarkable discovery was made in this area, just around the headland from Poppit Sands. Aerial photographs showed a vast V-shaped fish trap more than 820 feet long and probably at least 1,000 years old, now underwater. Designed to trap fish behind rock walls and direct them into nets when the tide went out, these kinds of structures were so successful at harvesting fish that they were banned from rivers in the 13th century (in the Magna Carta, no less), and were allowed only for use in coastal areas.

HIT THE BEACH
Choose from either the pebbly Gwbert or the glorious sandy Poppit (see page 292).

TAKE A BOAT TRIP
Bay To Remember
baytoremember.co.uk
Departure point: Gwbert, SA43 1PP, except during high tide | 01239 623558 | Opening times vary; call or check website for details
Great trips with the opportunity to spot dolphins and seals.

EAT AND DRINK
Webley Waterfront Inn and Hotel
webleyhotel.co.uk
Poppit Sands, SA43 3LN
01239 612085
The inn offers outstanding views across the River Teifi and Poppit Sands to Cardigan Bay, where the daily catch comes in. The Pembrokeshire Coast National Park Trail starts within a mile of its door.

▶ Tenby MAP REF 323 E5

People have been singing Tenby's praises enthusiastically since the ninth century, when an anonymous Welsh poet composed verses in honour of the fine fortress on the bright headland and the courage and generosity of its late lords. More recently, people have fallen in love with the beautiful old harbour, handsome Regency houses and narrow medieval streets, all hemmed in by the best-preserved town walls in south Wales.

Tenby grew up as a prosperous fishing and cargo port and was, at one time, a smuggling haven for brandy brought across from France. Early in the 19th century, Sir William Paxton, a wealthy banker, began to convert Tenby into a charming seaside resort. He built Laston House to accommodate the indoor seawater swimming baths, with a Greek inscription on the building meaning 'The sea washes away all mankind's ills'.

Tenby is a town of two distinct parts. There's the intact medieval part inside the town walls, where many of its ancient narrow streets have been recobbled to recreate their original form, but outside the walls, overlooking the South Beach, the Victorian influence is clear, with traditional seaside terraces. Castle Hill looks down on both the old and new towns, but little remains of the castle due to its destruction during the Civil War.

You can visit the Tenby Museum and Art Gallery, which explores the town's history from the Stone Age to present times and includes displays on the town's lifeboat and a collection of pictures by Welsh artists – notably Augustus John (born in Tenby in 1878). Also born in Tenby, in 1510, was Robert Recorde, the mathematician who invented the sign '=' for 'equals'. There is a memorial to him in St Mary's, claimed to be the largest parish church in Wales and a mark of Tenby's earlier prosperity. Another attraction is the Tudor Merchant's House, now owned by the National Trust, which has authentic furnishings and three walls with the remains of early frescoes.

TAKE IN SOME HISTORY
Tudor Merchant's House
nationaltrust.org.uk
Quay Hill, SA70 7BX
01834 842279 | Open daily but hours vary; call for details
Recalling Tenby's history as a thriving and prosperous port, the Tudor Merchant's House is a fine example of gabled 15th-century architecture and is the oldest house in the town. There is a good Flemish chimney and, on three walls, the remains of seccos (decorative paintings done on dry plaster) can be seen. A small herb garden has been created, which is open weather permitting. Kids can try on Tudor costumes and play with replica toys of the period.

VISIT THE MUSEUM
Tenby Museum and Art Gallery
tenbymuseum.org.uk
Castle Hill, SA70 7BP
01834 842809 | Open summer daily 10–5, winter Mon–Fri 10–5
This gem of a museum covers the heritage of the area from prehistory to the present in galleries devoted to geology, archaeology and maritime history, and concentrates on local work. There are child-friendly trails, art exhibitions that change monthly and a bilingual audio tour.

ENTERTAIN THE FAMILY
Dinosaur Park
thedinosaurpark.co.uk
Gumfreston, Tenby | 01834 845272
Open 23 Mar–30 Sep daily 10–5, 1 Oct–25 Oct Tue–Thu, Sat–Sun 10.30–4, 26 Oct–2 Nov daily 10.30–4
Take a walk on the wild side with this informative and fun park. Kids will love the mile-long walk full of prehistoric surprises, the rides and the indoor and outdoor adventure playgrounds. You can try your hand at 'dino' crossbow shooting or Frisbee golf. At the activity centre, you can uncover skeletons and search for fossils – a great activity for children, particularly on a rainy day.

HIT THE BEACH
Tenby is in the fortunate position of having four beaches to choose from. South Beach

▲ Tenby harbour

has more than a mile of golden sand, backed by sand dunes and overlooking Caldey Island. Castle Beach lies in a cove a short walk from town, and has a cafe, toilets and deck chair rentals. Harbour Beach is a small, pretty beach at the rear of the harbour, while North Beach is a golden stretch of sand, dotted with occasional rock pools when the tide is out.

GO FISHING
Tenby Fishing
tenbyfishing.co.uk
07974 623542
Trips on offer to the sheltered waters between Tenby and Caldey Island.

PLAY A ROUND
Tenby Golf Club
www.tenbygolf.co.uk
The Burrows, SA70 7NP
01834 844447 | Open daily all year
The oldest club in Wales, this fine seaside links, with sea views and natural hazards, provides good golf all the year round.

EAT AND DRINK
Carew Inn
carewinn.co.uk
Carew, SA70 8SL | 01646 651267
Opposite the Carew Celtic cross and Norman castle, this traditional stone-built country inn is a great place to finish the one-mile circular walk around the castle and millpond. The

owners have been here for 25 years and in that time have built a strong reputation for quality ales and home-cooked food. There's also a children's play area in the garden with regular barbecues in summer.

Hope and Anchor

Saint Julians Street, SA70 7AX
01834 842131

Head down towards the harbour and beach at Tenby and you can't miss the blue Hope and Anchor pub. Traditionally a fishing pub, it has remained popular with locals for years and years. It offers seven real ales that change throughout the week, while the menus and special boards feature lots of tempting fish dishes.

▶ PLACES NEARBY

Close to Tenby are two castles, Caldey Island and a family-fun activity centre.

Caldey Island

caldey-island.co.uk
01834 844453

Caldey Island lies only a mile offshore, but a boat trip here is like taking a journey back in time –quiet tracks wind their way through fields of nodding barley and overgrown footpaths meander along secluded cliff-ringed coves. In 1929, Cistercian monks re-established a monastery on Caldey. Today, they still farm the island's 600 acres and make perfume from the flowers and herbs. Walkers can explore the ruins of the old priory or climb to lofty vantage points to take in stunning views of the coast.

Carew Castle

pembrokeshirecoast.org.uk
Carew, SA70 8SL | 01646 651782
Open daily 10–5

Carew Castle has a history spanning 2,000 years. Set in a stunning location, it displays the development from a Norman fortification to an Elizabethan country house. Overlooking a 23-acre millpond, the site also incorporates an 11th-century Celtic cross, the only restored tidal mill in Wales, a medieval bridge and a picnic area, all linked by a delightful one-mile circular walk. There's plenty to see and do here, with an exciting summer-long activity programme.

Manorbier Castle

see page 224

Heatherton World of Activities

St Florence, SA70 8RJ
01646 652000 | Open Easter to mid-Sep daily 10–6; mid-Sep to 2 Nov 10–5; 3 Nov–Easter 10–4.30

With more than 25 activities on site, this is a mixture of family-fun, kids-adventure, adrenaline and relaxation. Hit the high ropes, lose yourself in a maze or try your hand at adult or junior karting. Adrenaline activities include paintballing and exploring the tree-top trails, or try fishing on the lake, or a game of indoor bowls. There's a Landrover experience, Water Wars and a giant puzzle zone. Dogs are welcome.

▶ Usk MAP REF 327 E3

Usk is a small up-and-coming town set in some supremely
pretty countryside in the Monmouthshire border country. It's
basically one strip of shops and pubs. It's low-key and friendly
– dogs are allowed in most of the pubs and there's a relaxed,
rural vibe. The High Street has some clothes shops and an
antiques shop so jam-packed you can hardly get through the
front door.

The town itself lies virtually on top of the River Usk (yes,
flooding does happen here) and you'll need to cross a large
arched stone bridge to access the town from the west side. The
castle above the town overlooks the ancient crossing point and
also has a prison, which is still in use. Historically, Usk
developed as a small market town and remains so to this day.
It's also big on flowers, frequently being a top competitor or
winner of the annual Britain in Bloom competition.

▼ Usk's ruined Norman castle

TAKE IN SOME HISTORY
Usk Castle
Castle House, NP15 1SD
01291 672563 | Open all year daily dawn to dusk

You can't help but admire these enchanting, romantic ruins overlooking Usk and the wide river valley beyond. Once a medieval castle, it fell into disuse around 500 years ago and is slowly being reclaimed by nature. The setting is incredibly natural and peaceful, the ancient walls covered with creepers. The old stone towers invite exploration. The inner ward of the castle is a grassy level area, perfectly suited to modern celebrations. In summer it often hosts marquee events, open-air parties, picnics, plays and concerts. At night the ancient walls and paths are illuminated, There are modern 'green' toilets and there's ample parking space in the paddock.

EAT AND DRINK
The Nags Head Inn
Twyn Square, NP15 1BH
01291 672820

Fronting the old town square, midway between the castle and fine priory church, parts of this inn date from the 15th century. The same family has held sway for 46 years, lovingly caring for the highly traditional interior – all beams and polished tables, rural artefacts and horse brasses. The tempting menu draws on the wealth of prduce from the fertile Vale of Gwent. Seasonal game dishes are a speciality, and there is a good vegetarian selection.

The Three Salmons Hotel ◉◉
threesalmons.co.uk
Bridge Street, NP15 1RY
01291 672133

This old black-and-white coaching inn has served the community and weary travellers for more than 300 years. While the Grade II-listed building presents a traditional face to the world, inside, the restaurant combines the character of the old building with contemporary fixtures and fittings. There is also the less formal bar. The menu shows passion for the produce of the area, some of which is grown in the hotel's garden, and the rest is sourced just as discerningly for brasserie cooking that highlights its quality.

The White Hart Village Inn ◉◉
thewhitehartvillageinn.com
Old Usk Road, Llangybi, NP15 1NP
01633 450258

Situated in a pretty village in the beautiful Usk Valley, this picturesque historic inn offers a warm welcome, where no less than 11 fireplaces can be found. The building was part of Jane Seymour's wedding dowry on her marriage to King Henry VIII, and Oliver Cromwell based himself here during local Civil War campaigns. Add a priest hole, exposed beams, Tudor plasterwork and a mention in TS Eliot's poem *Usk* and you've a destination to savour. Regional produce is at the heart of the imaginative menus and daily-changing blackboards, plus a six-course tasting menu. The chefs are confident exponents of the modern British style, turning out accurately cooked ideas with punchy, well-balanced flavours In summer, head outside to the extensive seating area.

▶ **PLACES NEARBY**

Close to Usk is the market town of Abergavenny (see page 66), a new watersports visitor centre and a couple of pubs.

Llandegfedd Reservoir

llandegfedd.co.uk

Llandegfedd Reservoir, Coed y Paen, Pontypool, NP4 0SS | 01633 373401 or 01633 373408 for watersports enquiries

A few miles outside Usk is Llandegfedd Reservoir, which has just seen the opening of a brand new £2.5 million watersports and visitor centre. The lake offers water-based activities including windsurfing, dinghy sailing, stand-up paddle boarding, canoeing, kayaking, raft building, angling and sailing for all ages, as well as six miles of scenic footpaths. All equipment is available to hire. The protection of the rich local wildlife has taken centre stage, and the entire site is designated a Site of Special Scientific Interest. Following an afternoon on the lake, visitors can retire to the stylish restaurant which offers a variety of home-cooked meals and snacks.

Newbridge on Usk ◉

newbridgeonusk.co.uk

Tredunnock, NP15 1LY

01633 451000

This charming inn is in an exceptionally tranquil spot on a bend in the River Usk. It's an ideal location if you want to explore the countryside or enjoy a spot of fishing. The two-tiered, beamed dining room makes the most of its location – with window tables overlooking the river and bridge – while the menu of updated country inn fare offers plenty that will appeal.

The Raglan Arms

theraglanarms.co.uk

Llandenny, NP15 1DL

01291 690800

This flint-built pub traded up from a local boozer to lure in diners with a winning combination of great locally sourced food and a relaxing, informal ambience. It is set in a peaceful Monmouthshire village tucked between Tintern Forest and the rich agricultural lands of the Usk Valley. If you're into the pubby side of things, there's a cosy feel to the flagstoned bar serving well-kept real ales. The pub continues to receive praise for its varied and frequently changing menu. The head chef and his small team use high-quality ingredients for the imaginative menu. The pub is keen to reduce food miles and most suppliers are within a nine-mile radius, though their excellent fish is delivered from Cornwall each day.

▶ **Welshpool**   MAP REF 335 E4

Set amid Montgomeryshire's rolling verdant hills and the wide valley of the River Severn, Welshpool is a prosperous and bustling market town, known locally as 'Pool'. Trade initially grew around the River Severn, enhanced by the building of the Montgomery Canal in 1797. Today, you can stroll along the High Street, marvelling at the fine Georgian architecture, such as the Royal Oak Hotel. Note the cockpit on New Street, which would have been the popular venue for cockfights until their ban in 1849.

A visit to the town, however, isn't complete without a trip to Powis Castle, built for the princes of Powys in around 1200. You can access it through the estate's fine parklands of mature oaks and grazing deer. Today the old fortress has become more of a mansion, with castellated ramparts, tall chimneys, rows of fine leaded windows and 17th-century terraces overlooking manicured lawns and clipped yews. Lead statues of a shepherd and shepherdess survive and keep watch over the many shrubs and perennial borders. The town's also a great place from which to explore the nearby Montgomeryshire Hills.

TAKE A TRAIN RIDE
Welshpool and Llanfair Light Railway
wllr.org.uk
SY21 0SF | 01938 810441
Open Easter–Oct Sat–Sun (some extra days during Jun–Jul and Sep); daily during holiday periods; call or check website for a timetable and details of special events
The Welshpool and Llanfair Light Railway opened in 1906 and is now part of the Great Little Trains of Wales initiative. Built to carry livestock, coal, timber and merchandise between the farms and market towns, W&L was absorbed into the Great Western Railway in 1922, becoming part of the nationalised BR network in 1948. Nowadays, an awayday from Welshpool involves a 16-mile round trip through glorious scenery and up some very steep gradients.The line is home to a collection of engines and coaches from all round the world.

PLAY A ROUND
Welshpool Golf Club
welshpoolgolfclub.co.uk
Golfa Hill, SY21 9AQ
01938 850249 | Open daily all year
Nominated Welsh Golf Club of the Year in 2012, this hilly course, with a testing second hole, is known for its breathtaking views of the Snowdonia mountain range.

EAT AND DRINK
The Tuck Box Cafe
10 Hall Street, SY21 7RY
01938 554445

▶ Powis Castle

This friendly, family-run cafe offers hearty well-prepared traditional food, all in big portions. Visiting dogs may even be offered free sausages.

▸ **PLACES NEARBY**

Powis Castle and a gallery lie close to Welshpool.

Powis Castle

nationaltrust.org.uk
Welshpool, Powys, SY21 8RF
01938 551944 | Castle open Apr–Oct Thu–Mon 1–5, Mar Thu–Mon 1–4; garden open Apr–Oct Thu–Mon 11–5.30, Mar Thu–Mon 11–4.30, Nov Sat–Sun 11–3.30

This medieval castle is one of the most striking in Wales, its colouring derived from the red sandstone used to build it. It rises dramatically above a celebrated garden, a mile from Welshpool. Originally built around 1200, it began life as a medieval fortress, but is now more like a stately home, influenced and embellished through the centuries. Generations of the Herbert family, who acquired it in 1584, have added magnificent collections of paintings, sculpture, furniture and tapestries, as well as an Elizabethan long gallery and 17th-century state bedroom. As impressive as the building is, it's the grounds that really steal the show. During the 18th century, the architect William Winde landscaped the terraced gardens, planted with huge clipped yew hedges and many rare and tender plants. Laid out in the Italian and French styles, the garden retains its original lead statues, an orangery and an aviary on the terraces. There are wonderful views across the Severn Valley. There's also a superb collection of treasures from India.

Andrew Logan Museum of Sculpture

andrewloganmuseum.org
Berriew, SY21 8PJ | 01686 640689
Check website for opening times

This Museum of Sculpture is the only museum in Europe dedicated to a living artist. Opened by Logan in 1991 to share his unique approach to life and art with the world, it's a vibrant space displaying examples of his work from across the decades. On display are pieces of sculpture, mirrored portraits, jewellery, watercolours and photos from the mid-1960s to the present day. There are also personal items created by the artist for the late actor Divine, late painter Luciana Martinez de la Rosa and Joan Simon Menkes, editor of the *Beverly Hills Art Magazine 95201*, which have been left to the museum by their estates. There's Andrew's series of *Birds of a Feather*, created in the late 1970s during his 'mad' period, and also pieces such as *The Cosmic Egg*, *The Living Taj Mahal* and *Egypt Revisited*, inspired by his fantastic journeys.

▶ White Castle

see **Grosmont, Skenfrith & White Castle**, page 173

▶ Wrexham MAP REF 339 E4

Although the collieries and steelworks on which Wrexham prospered are largely things of the past, this bustling town is still the largest in north Wales. The church of St Giles is the chief architectural attraction, with its elegant 135-foot steeple dating from the 14th century.

A copy of the church tower was built on the campus of Yale University in the 1920s in memory of Elihu Yale, the pilgrim father who is buried in the churchyard here, and who gave his name to the distinguished American university. The town desperately wants to be a city and has applied for the status three times since the turn of the millennium. In 2012, it lost out again, this time to the community of St Asaph, which was already considered as a ceremonial city. A plan is now afoot to establish a 'city region' encompassing Wrexham, Deeside and Chester.

PLAY A ROUND

Wrexham Golf Club
www.wrexhamgolfclub.co.uk
Holt Road, LL13 9SB
01978 364268 | Open Mon–Fri except BHs

An inland, sandy course with easy walking.

▶ PLACES NEARBY

Not far from Wrexham is Erdigg (see page 164).

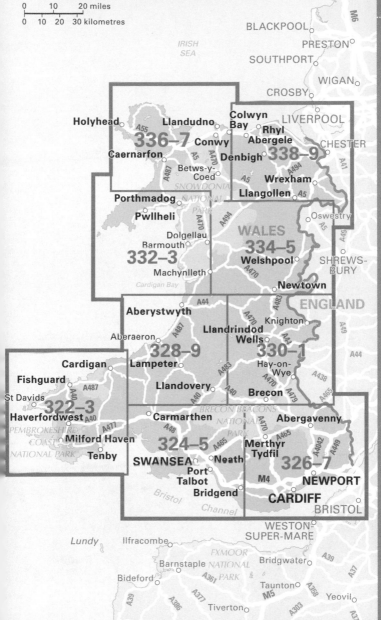

ATLAS

★ A-Z places listed

• Places Nearby

A **B** **C**

1

2

Dinas Head Heritage Coast

Strumble Head ★

Llanwnda ●

Goodwick ○

Carreg Sampson ●

Porthgain ●

A487

Crug Glâs
Country House ●

St Davids Head

Letterston ●

Western Cleddau

A40

3

Whitesands Bay ●

St Davids ★

Ramsey Island ●

Solva ★

Ramsey Sound

St Davids Peninsula Heritage Coast

P E M B R O K E S H I R E

Newgale ●

Roch ○

178
DUDWELL MT ▲

PEMBROKESHIRE

St Brides Bay Heritage Coast

Nolton Haven ●

COAST

A487

4

St Brides Bay ★

NATIONAL PARK
★

Haverfordwest

Broad Haven ●

Little Haven ●

Pembrokeshire Coast Path

Johnston ●

A4076

Grassholm Island ●

Marloes and Dale Heritage Coast

Wooltack Point

Marloes ○

Skomer Island ★

A411

Broad Sound

Marloes Sands ●

Milford Haven ★

5

Skokholm Island ★

Westdale Bay

Dale ○

Great Castle Head

Milford Haven

St Anns Head

Angle ○

Freshwater West ●

Castlema

PEMBROKESHIRE COAST

Linney Head

NATIONAL PARK
★

★
Stack Rocks and the Green Bridge of Wales

6

A **B** **C**

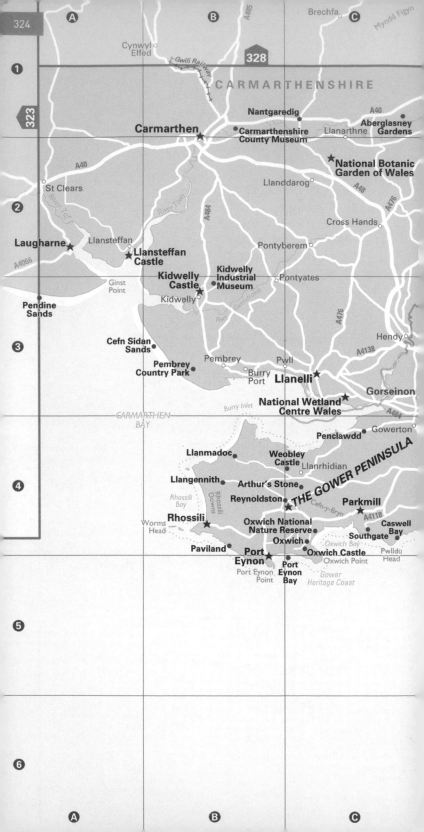

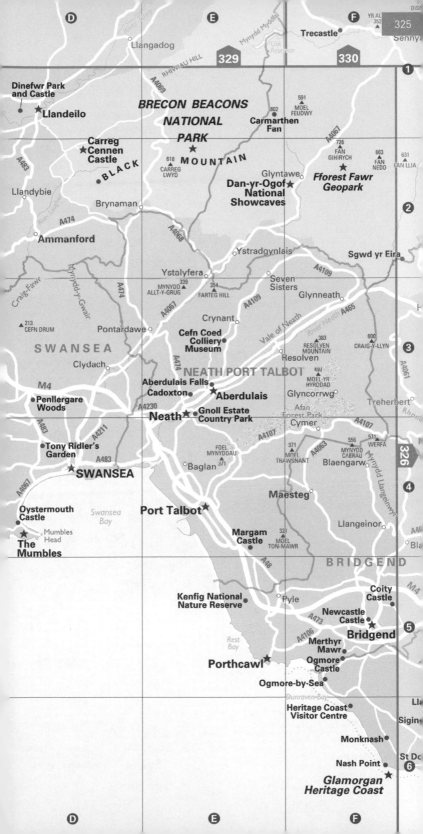

Ⓐ　Ⓑ　Ⓒ

①

752
Pumlumon Fawr

A44

546
Y FOEL

482
VAN HILL

Llandi...

Clywedog

River Severn

Llanidloes

564
BRYN
CEFN CROES ▲ LLYCHESE

573
▲

A470

Llangurig

Afon Rheidol

**Devil's Bridge
Falls**

P O W Y S

493
RED LION
HILL

l's
dge

Cwmystwyth

571
GEIFAS
▲

Pant-y-dwr

River Wye

②

Afon Elan

Craig-Goch
Reservoir

**Gilfach Nature
●Discovery Centre
and Reserve**

Pontrhydfendigaid

Pen-y-Garreg
Reservoir

Rhayader ★

A44

**Strata
Florida
Abbey** ★

530
DIBYN DU
▲

Claerwen
Reservoir

Elan Valley ★

Elan
Village

Caban Coch
Reservoir

River Wye

③

544
PEN-MAEN-
WERN
▲

A470

**Llandrindod
Wells** ★

27
CEFN CNWC
▲

645
DRYGARN
FAWR
▲

Newbridge-on-Wye ●

Howey ●

29

493
PEN
CARREG-DÂN
▲

500
CEFN COCH
▲

A483

CARNEDDAU

PEN-Y-
GURNOS
457
▲

CEFN
FANNOG
450
Forest
▲

462
CEFN
CRUG
▲

Beulah ○

A483

**Builth
Wells**

Tywi
Llyn
Brianne

487
CARCWM
▲

Garth ●

A470

④

517 MYNYDD
TRAWSNANT
▲

**Llangammarch
Wells**

472
BANC-Y-
CELYN
▲

**RSPB Nature Reserve
Gwenffrwd-Dinas** ●

**Llanwrtyd
Wells** ○

474
DRUM
DDU
▲

Rhandirmwyn ★

M Y N Y D D　E P P Y N T

463
BRYN DU
▲

384
CEFN CLAWOD
▲

River Brân

454
GWRHYD
▲

456
YSGWYDD
HWCH
▲

⑤

A483

411
NOETHGRUG
▲

Mynydd Bwlch-y-Groes

Llandovery ★

A40

417
TWYRN
DISGWYLFA
▲

River Usk

Mynydd Mydfai

YR ALLT
352
▲

Brecon ★

Usk
Reservoir

Trecastle ●

Sennybridge ○

A40

...adog

⑥

RHIWIAU HILL

**National Park
Visitor Centre** ●

A4068

A4215

B R E C O N

Cefn Cyff

**ECON BEACONS
NATIONAL**

Ⓐ

591
MOEL
FEUDWY
▲

Ⓑ

Ⓒ **Pen-y-Fan**

802
**Carmarthen
Fan**

873
▲
Carn Du BEACONS

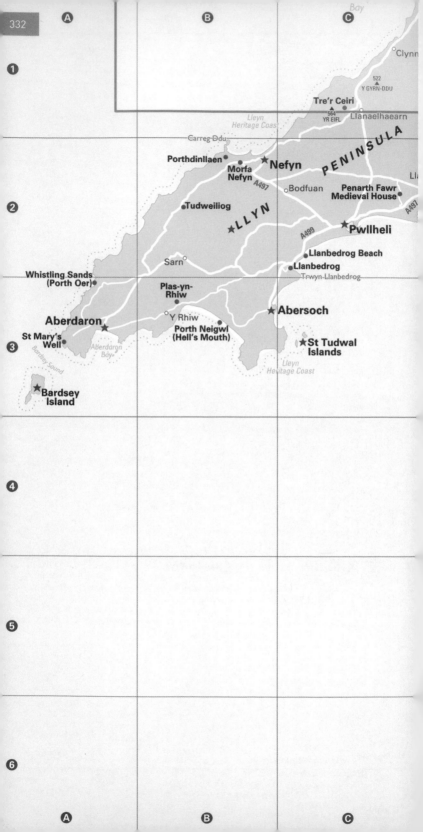

A   **B**   **C**

Bay

Clynn

1

522
Y GYRN-DDU

Tre'r Ceiri
Lleyn
Heritage Coas
564
YR EIFL
Llanaelhaearn

Carreg-Ddu

PENINSULA

Porthdinllaen
Morfa
Nefyn ★ **Nefyn**
A497
Bodfuan
Penarth Fawr
Medieval House

Ll

2

Tudweiliog
LLYN
A499

A497

★
Pwllheli ★ **Pwllheli**

Sarn
Llanbedrog Beach
Llanbedrog
Trwyn-Llanbedrog

Whistling Sands
(Porth Oer)
Plas-yn-
Rhiw

3

Aberdaron ★ **Abersoch**

St Mary's
Well
Y Rhiw
Porth Neigwl
(Hell's Mouth)

Aberdaron
Bay
Lleyn
Heritage Coast

★ St Tudwal
Islands

Bardsey Sound

★ **Bardsey
Island**

4

5

6

A   **B**   **C**

D   E   F

1

2

Great Orme Heritage Coast

GREAT ORMES HEAD

★ **Great Orme Country Park and Nature Reserve**

Puffin Island

Little Ormes Head

★ **Great Orme Bronze Age Copper Mines**

★ **Llandudno**

Red Wharf Bay ★

Black Point

Conwy Bay

Llangoed

Deganwy

Welsh Mountain Zoo ●

Rhôs-on-Sea

Conwy Sands ●

Castle Caer Lleion ★

Penmaenmawr ○

Conwy ★

Colwyn Bay ★

Lla

Beaumaris Gaol and Courthouse ●

Beaumaris ★

RSPB Nature Reserve Conwy ●

Llansanffraid Glan Conwy

3

○ Llanfairfechan

Bet

S t r a i t

610 ▲ TAL-Y-FAN

★

Bodnant Garden ★

Bangor

Penrhyn Castle ●

S N O W D O N I A

Tal-y-Cafn ●

Menai Bridge

A5

S

580 ▲ MOEL WNION

N A T I O N A L

Tal-y-Bont

Vale of Conwy

Langernyw ○

Greenwood Forest Park ★

Llanllechid ○

757 ▲ Y DROSGL

942 ▲ FOEL-FRAS

P A R K

Surf Snowdonia ●

A548

○ Bethesda

Llyn Eigiau

4

338

1062 ▲ CARNEDD LLEWELYN

Trefriw ●

Llanrug

1044 ▲ CARNEDD DAFYDD

Llyn Cowlyd

Llanberis Lake Railway

Llanrwst ★

Llanberis ★

National Slate Museum ●

Y TRYFAN 917 ▲

946 ▲ Y GARN

Llyn Crafnant

Gwydir Uchaf Chapel ●

Gwydir Castle ●

MOEL EILIO 726 ▲

Dolbadarn Castle ●

1001 ▲ GLYDER-FAWR

994 ▲ GLYDER-FACH

Capel Curig ●

Swallow Falls ●

467 ▲ MOEL SEISIOG

Snowdon Railway

Pass of Llanberis

A4086

Plas y Brenin (National Mountain Centre) ●

Gwydir Forest

Betws-y-Coed ★

Welsh Highland Railway

1085 ▲

Llyn Llydaw

872 ▲ MOEL-SIABOD

A470

Conwy Falls ●

Llyn Cwellyn

747 ▲ YR ARAN

Snowdon ●

Dolwyddelan Castle ★

Dolwyddelan ●

Pentrefoelas ○

5

Rhyd-Ddu ○

A498

Tŷ Mawr Wybrnant ●

Penmachno ●

River Conwy

Beddgelert ★

Sygun Copper Mine ●

Llechwedd Slate Caverns ●

669 ▲ CARNEDD Y-

782 ▲ MOEL HEBOG

MOELWYN MAWR 770 ▲

Zip World ★

333

Blaenau Ffestiniog ★

557 ▲ MOEL DDU

711 ▲ MOELWYN BACH

Ffestiniog Railway

Ffestiniog ○

690 ▲ ARENIG FACH

6

Prenteg ○

Maentwrog ●

Nation White W Centr

remadog ○

Porthmadog

Penrhyndeudraeth ●

334

853 ▲

orth-y-Gest ○

Minffordd ●

Portmeirion ●

Afon Trawsfynydd

D   Talsarnau ○   E   A4212   F

Traeth Bach

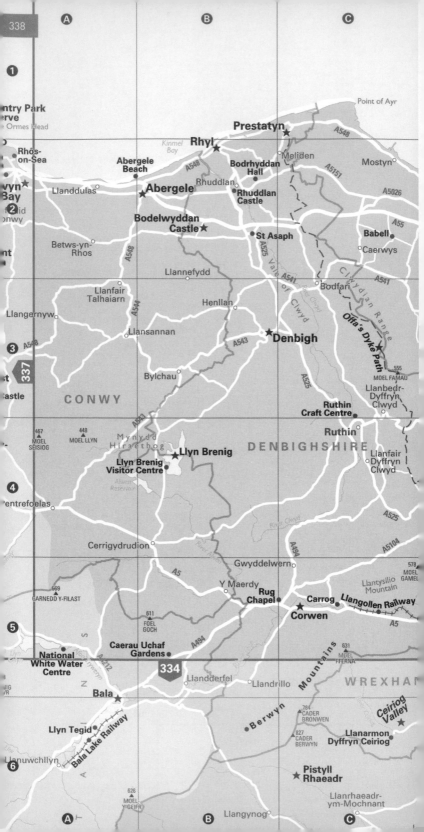

D   WALLASEY   E   LIVERPOOL   F

A553

A57

M57

1

West Kirby

A561

A562

WIDNES

A5300

Thurstaston   A41   A562   RUNCORN

WIRRAL   Bebington

Heswall

River Dee   M53   River Mersey

Greenfield   Childer   ELLESMERE   Frodsham

Basingwerk   Thornton   PORT   M56   2

Abbey   Neston   A5117   Helsby

Holywell   A41   A56

Bagillt   Burton

Flint   A540   A548   CHESHIRE

A548   Great Saughall   WEST

Connah's   A494   Queensferry   CHESTER   Tarvin

Quay   Ewloe   A51

Northop   Castle   A41   3

FLINTSHIRE   Hawarden

Cilcain   A55

Loggerheads   Mold

Country Park   Buckley   A483

Gwernymynydd   Pulford   Aldford

A494   Hope   Handley   4

A5104   Rossett

Llandegla   A525   Llay   Gresford

Coedpoeth   Hult   A534

Cyrn-y-brain   Wrexham   River Dee   A41

417   Erddig   Marchwiel

Horseshoe Pass   Rhosllanerchrugog   A528   Malpas   4

Valle Crucis   Ruabon   Bangor-is-y-coed

Abbey   Mountain   A539

Horseshoe   Ruabon   A525   Redbrook   5

Falls   A539   Pontcysyllte   Overton

Llangollen   Aqueduct   A539

Ty Mawr   A495

Glyn   Country Park

Ceiriog   Chirk

Castle   335

Llwynmawr   Chirk   A528

Offa's Dyke Path   Ellesmere   Welshampton

Pont-y-   Gobowen

Meibion   444

PEN-Y-   6

GWELY   Whittington

Oswestry   Wem

Rednal   A5

D   West   E   Burlton   F

Felton

Index, themed

Page numbers in **bold** refer to main entries

Index, places

Page numbers in **bold** refer to main entries; page numbers in *italics* refer to town plans